The Many Faces of Homosexuality

Anthropological Approaches to Homosexual Behavior

The Many Faces of Homosexuality
Anthropological Approaches to Homosexual Behavior

Edited by

Evelyn Blackwood

The Many Faces of Homosexuality: Anthropological Approaches to Homosexual Behavior was originally published in 1986 by The Haworth Press, Inc., under the title *Anthropology and Homosexual Behavior*. It has also been published as *Journal of Homosexuality*, Volume 11, Numbers 3/4, Summer 1985.

Harrington Park Press
New York • London

ISBN 0-918393-20-5

Published by

Harrington Park Press, Inc.   EUROSPAN/Harrington
28 East 22 Street   3 Henrietta Street
New York, New York 10010-6194   London WC2E 8LU England

Harrington Park Press, Inc., is a subsidiary of The Haworth Press, Inc., 28 East 22 Street, New York, New York 10010-6194.

The Many Faces of Homosexuality: Anthropological Approaches to Homosexual Behavior was originally published in 1986 by The Haworth Press, Inc., under the title *Anthropology and Homosexual Behavior*. It has also been published as *Journal of Homosexuality*, Volume 11, Numbers 3/4, Summer 1985.

Library of Congress Cataloging in Publication Data

The Many faces of Homosexuality.
    Anthropological Approaches to Homosexual Behavior.

    "Originally published in 1986 . . . under the title Anthropology and homosexuality; it has also been published as Journal of Homosexuality, volume 11, numbers 3/4, summer 1985."
    Includes bibliographies and index.
    1. Homosexuality—Cross-cultural studies. 2. Sex role—Cross-cultural studies. 3. Sex customs—Cross-cultural studies. I. Blackwood, Evelyn. II. Title.
GN484.35.A57 1986b   306.7'66   85-17757
ISBN 0-918393-20-5 (pbk.)

CONTENTS

The *Journal of Homosexuality* is devoted to theoretical, empirical, and historical research on homosexuality, heterosexuality, sexual identity, social sex roles, and the sexual relationships of both men and women. It was created to serve the allied disciplinary and professional groups represented by psychology, sociology, history, anthropology, biology, medicine, the humanities, and law. Its purposes are:

   a) to bring together, within one contemporary scholarly journal, theoretical empirical, and historical research on human sexuality, particularly sexual identity;
   b) to serve as a forum for scholarly research of heuristic value for the understanding of human sexuality, based not only in the more traditional social or biological sciences, but also in literature, history and philosophy;
   c) to explore the political, social, and moral implications of research on human sexuality for professionals, clinicians, social scientists, and scholars in a wide variety of disciplines and settings.

EDITOR

JOHN P. DE CECCO, PhD, *Professor of Psychology and Human Sexuality and Director, Center for Research and Education in Sexuality (CERES), and Director, Human Sexuality Studies, San Francisco State University*

ABSTRACTS AND BOOK REVIEW EDITOR

ANA VILLAVICENCIO-STOLLER, *Center for Research and Education in Sexuality, San Francisco State University*

COPYEDITOR

NORMAN C. HOPPER, *Center for Research and Education in Sexuality, San Francisco State University*

FOUNDING EDITOR

CHARLES C. SILVERSTEIN, PhD, *New York City*

KENT GERARD, PhD (cand.), *History and Anthropology, University of California, Berkeley*

BERNARD GOLDSTEIN, PhD, *Professor of Biology, San Francisco State University*

ERWIN HAEBERLE, PhD, EdD, *Director, Historical Research, Institute for the Advanced Study of Human Sexuality, San Francisco; Adjunct Professor of Human Sexuality status, San Francisco State University*

JOSEPH HARRY, PhD, *Associate Professor of Sociology, Northern Illinois University, DeKalb*

GILBERT HERDT, PhD, *Associate Professor, Human Development Committee, University of Chicago*

GREGORY M. HEREK, PhD, *Research Fellow, Psychology Department, Yale University*

RICHARD C. HOFFMAN, PhD, *Professor of History, San Francisco State University*

EVELYN HOOKER, PhD, *Retired Research Professor, Psychology Department, University of California, Los Angeles*

MONIKA KEHOE, PhD, *Research Associate, CERES, San Francisco State University*

HUBERT KENNEDY, PhD, *Providence College, Providence, RI*

FRITZ KLEIN, MD, *Clinical Institute for Human Relationships, San Diego*

MARY RIEGE LANER, PhD, *Associate Professor of Sociology, Arizona State University, Tempe*

RUDIGER LAUTMANN, Dr. phil., Dr. jur., *Professor, Abteilung fur Sociologie, Universitat Bremen*

A. P. MACDONALD, Jr., PhD, *Acting Director and Associate Professor, Center for the Family, University of Massachusetts, Amherst*

NORMA MCCOY, PhD, *Professor of Psychology, San Francisco State University*

WILLIAM F. OWEN, Jr., MD, *Founder, Bay Area Physicians for Human Rights, San Francisco*

JAY PAUL, PhD (cand.), *Clinical Psychology, University of California, Berkeley*

KENNETH PLUMMER, PhD, *Lecturer in Sociology, University of Essex, England*

DIANE RICHARDSON, MA, *Lecturer in Sociological Studies, University of Sheffield, England*

STEVEN J. RISCH, PhD, *Assistant Professor of Entomology, University of California, Berkeley*

MICHAEL ROSS, PhD, *Senior Demonstrator in Psychiatry, The Flinders University of South Australia, Bedford Park, South Australia*

RITCH SAVIN-WILLIAMS, PhD, *Associate Professor of Human Development and Family Studies, Cornell University*

GUNTHER SCHMIDT, PhD, *Professor, Abteilung fur Sexualforschung, Universitats-Krankenhaus, Universitat Hamburg*

FREDERICK SUPPE, PhD, *Professor, Committee on the History and Philosophy of Science, University of Maryland, College Park*

ROB TIELMAN, Dr. Phil., *Professor, Interfacultaire werkgroep homostudies, Riksuniversiteit Utrecht*

JEFFREY WEEKS, M. Phil., PhD, *Social Work Studies, University of Southhampton, England*

JACK WIENER, MA, *Retired, National Institute of Mental Health, Rockville, Maryland*

WAYNE S. WOODEN, PhD, *Associate Professor of Behavioral Science, California State Polytechnic University, Pomona*

Preface

In the current absence of anthropological studies of homosexuality and with the success of the Gay Liberation movement in achieving its psychological detoxification, the tide of research has shifted back to the search for a biological etiology. Several social scientists of homosexuality, including those formerly associated with the Kinsey Institute, appear to have surrendered a belief in its social causation for at least a wild flirtation with psychoendocrinal explanations. This swing back to the biological theories of the early twentieth century, I believe, reflects the paucity of knowledge we have about the rich and diverse manifestations of homosexuality in various historical periods and in non-western culture. It also reflects an almost total ignorance of the range of homosexual practice and relationships among women in any period or culture.

This volume may help stem the tide of biological reductionism by showing the many cultural faces of homosexuality. There are the astonishing forms of posturing, pluming, and puffing of male homosexuality and the intricate web of sexuality, nurturance, and affection in the homosexual relationships of women. In addition, there are the terribly graphic examples of males who assume the roles of not-men or established female roles and the women who take on male roles in the traditions of Native Americans.

Dr. Carrier, in the foreword that follows, describes the struggle within anthropology to overcome its professional reticence to conduct and publish studies of homosexuality. In the decade since 1974, the year in which the American Anthropological Association sponsored a historic symposium on homosexuality in Mexico City, much progress has been made. Within the Association there is now a well-organized group of anthropologists who meet to discuss research on the topic, sponsor papers and symposia, and publish a richly informative newsletter.

I wish to express my great appreciation to the guest editor, Evelyn Blackwood, who organized this prodigious effort, conducted an intercontinental correspondence, edited the papers of the contributors with a fitting blend of sensitivity and scholarly astuteness, and contributed a masterful introduction of her own. My gratitude also goes to Dr. Joseph Carrier and Dr. Clark Taylor who originally called my editorial attention to the lacuna in the anthropological knowledge of homosexuality and suggested a thematic issue. Finally my thanks go to the members of the *Journal* staff: Myrna Hughes, an anthropology student and the manuscript editor for this issue; Ana Villavicencio-Stoller, my administrative-assistant and the new abstracts editor; Corlyn Cognata, who assisted in entering the various editions of the manuscripts into the word-processor; and to my long-time, faithful editorial assistant, Mary Walsh, who unfortunately will leave the *Journal* staff now that graduation time has arrived.

John P. De Cecco, PhD
San Francisco, 1985

Foreword

Additional anthropological research on human sexual behavior is urgently needed in different culture areas of the world to expand social scientists' knowledge about this behavior and its meaning in different societies; and to counteract the myopia of many who continue to view it only through the screen of Western behavior, beliefs, and social and clinical labels. Much of the important data on human sexuality has been gathered by social scientists who have been heavily influenced by a Western heterosexual model of sexual activity that deems homosexual behavior both inappropriate and dysfunctional. As Read (1984) points out:

> Attitudes toward and the evaluation of male homosexual behaviors vary cross-culturally; but it is primarily the Western view (and Western inhibitions) that have colored the anthropological record, not only in those instances where homosexual practices have been mentioned but probably, too, in many in which one is led to believe (or to assume because of the absence of any references to them) that nothing of the kind exists. (p. 214)

This also holds true for female homosexual behaviors.

Few anthropologists to date have had the courage to study human sexual behavior in other cultures as a major focus of their research; even fewer have had the courage to study highly stigmatized homosexual behavior. This special collection presents the results of some of the best anthropological research on homosexuality that has been done during the past decade. It is the first collection of articles dealing with homosexual behavior in several different *culture areas* which is based on empirical data gathered by the authors in the field.

Compared to the other social sciences, the field of anthropology has been far behind in the study of human sexual behavior in general, and homosexual behavior in particular. The American Anthropological Association, for example, did not acknowledge the importance of sex research in anthropology until their annual meeting in 1961 ''. . . when a plenary session was devoted exclusively to human sexual behavior'' (Gebhard, 1971, p. xiii). Ten more years passed, however, before the Association specifically dealt with the topic of research on homosexual behavior by passing the following resolution (introduced by Clark Taylor) in 1970; ''Be it resolved that the American Anthropological Association recognizes the legitimacy and immediate importance of such research, and training, and urges the active development of both.'' Although passed overwhelmingly at the Association's business meeting, it barely passed on a mail ballot from the general membership.

The first symposium on homosexual behavior sponsored by the American Anthropological Association, "Homosexuality in Cross-cultural Perspective," was held at their annual meetings in Mexico City in 1974 in part as a result of that resolution. Professional resistance to the study of homosexuality as a legitimate topic of anthropological research, and to anthropologists who dare let it be known that their sexual orientation might be homosexual, continued, however.

A sad comment on our times is that many anthropologists have collected empirical data on homosexual behavior while doing fieldwork on other topics but have never published it partly because of the fear of being stigmatized and partly because anthropological journals have rarely accepted articles dealing with homosexuality. As Read (1984) notes: "Why, one is encouraged to ask, did Evans-Pritchard delay so long (almost thirty years) in reporting institutionalized male homosexuality among the Zande (Evans-Pritchard 1970)?" (p. 215).

Additionally, graduate students of anthropology may still be reluctant to study homosexuality as a dissertation topic because of the problems it often brings with members of their graduate committees and because they fear it may limit their future employability.

Hopefully, this special issue will encourage research anthropologists to write up their homosexual data, now hidden in the closet, and publish it; and will encourage more budding anthropologists to seriously consider the study of homosexual behavior in different cultures and subcultures around the world.

Although there is still a paucity of published anthropological data on homosexuality, it has been encouraging in recent years to see an increasing number of serious empirically based studies of homosexual behavior in different cultures and subcultures being done and put out in book form [for example, see Newton (1972), Wolf (1979) Read (1980), and Herdt (1981); and in the form of doctoral dissertations [for example, see Carrier (1972), Taylor (1978), and Gorman (1980)]. And recently Herdt (1984) was able to get a distinguished group of anthropologists to write up their data on institutionalized homosexuality in one culture area, Melanesia.

One hopes that many more anthropological studies are being done, will be done, and will be disseminated in one form or another; and that in the near future another collection of articles by anthropologists will appear in a special issue of the *Journal of Homosexuality*.

Joseph M. Carrier, PhD
University of California, Irvine

Inquiries should be addressed to Dr. Carrier, 17447 Castellammare, Pacific Palisades, CA.

REFERENCES

Carrier, J. (1972). *Urban Mexican male homosexual encounters: An analysis of participants and coping strategies*. PhD dissertation, University of California, Irvine.

Gebhard, P. (1971). Foreword. In D. Marshall & R. Suggs (Eds.), *Human sexual behavior: variations in the ethnographic spectrum* (pp. xi-xiv). New York: Basic Books.

Gorman, M. (1980). *A new light on Zion*. PhD dissertation, University of Chicago.

Herdt, G. (1981). *Guardians of the flutes: Idioms of masculinity*. New York: McGraw-Hill.

Herdt, G. (1984). *Ritualized homosexuality in Melanesia*. Berkeley: University of California Press.

Newton, E. (1972). *Mother camp: Female impersonators in America*. Englewood Cliffs, NJ: Prentice-Hall.

Read, K. (1980). *Other voices: The style of a male homosexual tavern*. Novato, California: Chandler & Sharp.

Read, K. (1984). The Nama cult recalled. In G. Herdt (Ed.), *Ritualized homosexuality in Melanesia* (pp. 211-247). Berkeley: University of California Press.

Taylor, C. (1978). *El ambiente: Male homosexual social life in Mexico City*. Ph.D. dissertation, University of California, Berkeley.

Wolf, D. (1979). *The lesbian community*. Berkeley: University of California Press.

Breaking the Mirror:
The Construction of Lesbianism
and the Anthropological Discourse
on Homosexuality

Evelyn Blackwood, PhD (cand.)
Stanford University

ABSTRACT. This essay reviews the anthropological discourse on homosexuality by examining the assumptions that have been used by anthropologists to explain homosexual behavior, and by identifying current theoretical approaches. The essay questions the emphasis on male homosexual behavior as the basis for theoretical analysis, and points to the importance of including female homosexual behavior in the study of homosexuality. Cross-cultural data on lesbian behavior are presented and the influence of gender divisions and social stratification on the development of patterns of lesbian behavior are broadly explored. The article outlines suggestions for examining the cultural context of lesbian behavior as well as the constraints exerted on women's sexual behavior in various cultures.

Recent years have seen a burgeoning of studies on homosexuality in the social sciences, much of it inspired by the feminist and Gay Rights movements of the 1970s. The focus of this new literature, particularly in sociology and history, concerns the historical and cultural influences on homosexual behavior. Plummer suggests that "specific ways of experiencing sexual attraction and gender behavior are bound up with specific historical and cultural milieux" (1981, p. 12). In a similar vein, historians looking at eroticism suggest that it is "subject to the forces of culture" (D'Emilio, 1983, p. 3), and thus accessible to historical analysis. The anthropological data on cross-cultural sexual variation provide much of the groundwork for such analyses; yet it has been one of the

The author received her MA in anthropology from San Francisco State University in 1984. She was a research associate with the Center for Education and Research in Sexuality from 1984-85.

Many thanks go to Professors Mina Caulfield and Gilbert Herdt for their helpful comments and suggestions on this article, and to Professor John De Cecco, who originally suggested this volume, and for his faith in me. I also appreciate the help of Professors Naomi Katz, Carolyn Clark, and Luis Kemnitzer in earlier phases of this work.

Inquiries can be sent to the author at the Department of Anthropology, Stanford University, Stanford, CA 94305.

1

failings of anthropology that the field itself has developed no adequate theory regarding the cultural construction of homosexual behavior.

To remedy this situation, the focus in this volume will be on homosexual behavior as it is organized both historically and culturally, with emphasis on the particular contexts in the cultures discussed that influence or shape homosexual behavior. The following essays show not only the wide variation in forms of female and male homosexuality, but also investigate the complex interaction of cultural and social factors affecting the expression of such behavior. The emphasis is on the cultural patterns or institutions rather than the individual who engages in same-sex behavior. In particular the articles diverge from the concept of homosexuality as a single cross-cultural institution. Instead they analyze homosexual behavior in terms of sexual patterns that are understandable only within the larger context of the culture that shapes it. Thus, it is hoped that this volume, by providing ethnographic and theoretical analyses of cross-cultural homosexual behavior, will advance the anthropological study of homosexuality and improve our understanding of the cultural construction of homosexual behavior.

This essay intends to place the following articles within the anthropological discourse on homosexuality by examining assumptions that have been used by anthropologists to explain homosexual behavior, and by identifying the current theoretical approaches. It also questions the continued emphasis on male homosexual behavior as a general model for theoretical analysis. It will bring women's sexual behavior within the purview of the current discussion on homosexuality by separating it from the historical construction of male homosexuality and by examining the particular cultural contexts of lesbian behavior. The terms *homosexuality* and *lesbianism*, as used in this essay, refer to sexual behavior between individuals of the same sex. Their use should not be construed as imposing the structure of western sexual ideology on cross-cultural practices; in western sexual systems, individuals who are identified by their sexual behavior form isolated subcultures. This pattern bears little resemblance to the integral nature of homosexual practices in many tribal societies.

CROSS-CULTURAL THEORIES AND STUDIES

The anthropological study of homosexuality has been limited by serious methodological and theoretical problems. As Langness has aptly stated, "it is fair to say that we have no anthropological *theory* of homosexuality . . ." (Foreword to Read, 1980, p. vii). The reasons for this absence are numerous and have been discussed in detail by several anthropologists (Carrier, 1980; Fitzgerald, 1977; Read, 1980; Sonenschein, 1966). In particular, most anthropologists have been affected by or accepted the prejudices of Western society toward homosexual behavior, and consequently have not considered the study of homosexuality to be a legitimate pursuit. The data they have gathered are limited to brief reports of homosexual practices. According to Carrier, these reports "(are) . . . complicated by the prejudice of many observers who consider the behavior unnatural, dysfunctional, or associated with mental illness. . ." (1980, p. 101). Discussion of the topic has, in general, been restricted to statements regarding the presence or absence of certain types of sexual acts. Such cataloguing has resulted in a considerable amount of information about sexual variation, but has provided little understanding of the cultural contexts within which these behaviors occur.[1]

Certain basic assumptions have colored the brief discussion of homosexuality in the anthropological literature. The theoretical models used in the past to analyze homosexual data derived directly from western psychological concepts of sexuality. Most anthropologists based their evaluation of homosexual practices in other cultures on the deviance model of psychology and sociology, assuming that heterosexuality represented the norm for sexual behavior, and, therefore, homosexuality was abnormal or deviant behavior. Such evaluations were often in direct contrast to the meaning or value attached to homosexual behavior in the culture studied, since many groups accepted homosexual practices within their social system. For example, Berndt labelled the male homosexual practices of Australian aborigines as "sexual abnormalities" and "perversions" (1963). Other anthropologists, however, have shown that the aboriginal practices were acceptable and institutionalized in the form of "brother-in-law" exchange among aborigines (Layard, 1959; Roheim, 1950; Spencer & Gillen, 1927). Hill (1935) described the Navajo *nadle* (hermaphrodites) as unhappy and maladjusted individuals despite the fact that the *nadle* were (or had been) highly revered and respected by the Navajo (see Greenberg, this issue, on ridiculing berdache). In a classic example of the contrast between emic and etic categories, Metraux declared that "*abnormal* sexual relationships between women (were) tolerated and *accepted*" on Easter Island (1940, p. 108, emphasis mine).

Implicit in this approach has been the belief that sexual behavior belonged to the domain of the individual (see Padgug, 1979). As a private act, it has not been considered relevant to the larger functioning of the social group. For psychological anthropologists who studied sexual behavior, such behavior served as an indicator of the individual's adjustment to society. These anthropologists considered the homosexual individual to be a person unable to adjust to the prescribed gender role. As evidence, they cited the males among the Plains Indians who were thought to lack the temperament for a warrior, and so turned to the berdache role (see Benedict, 1939; Mead, 1935).

Another assumption in the anthropological discourse on homosexuality has been the belief in a "homosexual nature" underlying all expressions of homosexuality. This assumption was the basis of Kroeber's "homosexual niche" theory, which he used to explain the Native American berdache. He maintained that American Indian culture *accommodated* individuals who were homosexual by creating the berdache institution (Kroeber, 1925, 1940). He believed that individuals took on the berdache role as the result of psychological or congenital problems, and that these individuals were found in most tribes. His ideas reflected what is currently being called "essentialism," the argument for a common trans-historical substrate of behavior or desire in all cultures.[2] In the study of homosexual behavior, this view is expressed in the perception that a certain percentage of homosexual individuals will take on the role in their culture which allows the expression of a homosexual nature, such as the Native American berdache, the Tahitian mahu, or Chukchee shaman role (see Callender & Kochems, this issue, for other male roles).

Although their views were to some extent within this essentialist frame-work, certain anthropologists foreshadowed a later historical-cultural construction of sexuality through application of a learning theory model. Both Mead (1935) and Benedict (1934) referred to the great arc of human potential from which cultures chose particular traits. Yet they found that this "essential" core was less and less relevant to the social design of human behavior. Benedict proposed that human behavior takes the forms that societal institutions prescribe, while Mead also argued for the malleability of humans in learning cultural forms. In considering "the homosexual," the emphasis in both their works, as noted above, was on the failure of the individual to adjust; nevertheless, it was argued that cultural factors shaped the homosexual response. Mead (1961) later pointed out that various individual personality cues combine with the cultural interpretation of sexuality to shape an individual's sex role. In contrast to the majority of anthropologists, both Mead and Benedict suggested that homosexual roles had certain valid cultural functions and were acceptable in some societies. Their suggestions opened the way for fuller analysis of the cultural context of homosexual behavior.

HISTORICAL-CULTURAL CONTEXT

Largely as a result of the feminist and gay movements of the late '60s and '70s, anthropologists began a new analysis of homosexual behavior. The feminist declaration that "the personal is political" underscored the realization, as Ross and Rapp point out, that "the seemingly most intimate details of private existence are actually structured by larger social relations" (1981, p. 51). Further prompted by the gay movement's rejection of the Western definition of homosexuality, anthropologists realized the need to understand sexuality from a perspective which took into account the importance of both the historical period and the cultural context. They joined other social scientists in the historical constructionist approach, or more appropriately for anthropology, the historical-cultural construction of sexuality.

Recent work on the historical-cultural construction of sexuality brings definition to the cultural factors which shape sexual behavior, and, in a sense, chips away at the essentialist core by establishing the importance of external, social factors. Ross and Rapp state that:

> Sexuality's biological base is always experienced culturally, through a translation. The bare biological facts of sexuality do not speak for themselves; they must be expressed socially. Sex feels individual, or at least private, but those feelings always incorporate the roles, definitions, symbols and meanings of the worlds in which they are constructed. (1981, p. 51)

Padgug has suggested the importance of the economic context in the construction of sexuality because "sexuality, class, and politics cannot easily be disengaged from one another" (1979, p. 5). Other areas that "condition, constrain and socially define" sexuality, as suggested by Ross and Rapp are: (1) kinship and family systems; (2) sexual regulations and definitions of communities; and (3) national and "world" systems (1981, p. 54). Patterns of homosexual behavior reflect the value system and social structure of the different societies in which they are found. The ideology regarding male and female roles, kinship and marriage regulations, and the sexual division of labor are all important in the construction of homosexual behavior. Thus, the historical-cultural factors affect and shape the expression of homosexuality.

Several recent works reflect this perspective to a greater or lesser degree. Levy (1971) suggested that the *mahu* of Tahiti, a traditional transvestite role for males (of which there was usually one in each village), functioned as a message to males regarding the non-male role which they should avoid. Others include Wolf's *The Lesbian Community* (1979), on the lesbian-feminist community in San Francisco, Read's *Other Voices* (1980), on the lifestyle in a male homosexual tavern in the U.S., Herdt's *Guardians of the Flutes* (1981) and *Ritualized Homosexuality in Melanesia* (1984), and Esther Newton's *Mother Camp: Female Impersonators in America* (1972). Carrier's (1980) cross-cultural survey established some basic correlations between socio-cultural context and the expression of homosexuality. He suggested that homosexual behavior correlated with the particular cultural ideology regarding sexuality and cross-gender behavior, as well as with the availability of sexual partners. Further, the articles in this volume examine the various cultural factors that shape the nature of homosexual behavior and, particularly for non-Western tribal societies, show how they are integrated within the social system.

Male vs. Female Homosexuality

Until now the historical-cultural construction of homosexuality has been based predominantly on the theories of male homosexuality which have been applied to both male and female homosexual behavior or, even more abstractly, to a "trans-gender" homosexuality. In looking back at her classic article on the homosexual role, Mary McIntosh stated that "the assumption always is that we can use the same theories and concepts for female homosexuality and that, for simplicity, we can just talk about men and assume that it applies to women" (1981, p. 45). Because men's and women's roles are structured differently in all cultures, however, the structure of female homosexuality must be examined as well. A one-sided discourse on homosexuality does not adequately comprehend the complex interplay of factors which shape homosexual behavior, male or female. Frequently, the construction of homosexual behavior occurs at the level of gender systems, for example, in the context of gender redefinition (cross-gender or gender mixing roles) or gender antagonism (ritualized male homosexuality). Because of the importance of gender roles in homosexual behavior, no analysis can be complete without adequately evaluating both female and male gender roles. As Lindenbaum states, "gender is the mutual production of men and women acting in concert, whether it be in the form of cooperation or of opposition" (1984, p. 338).

Further, the different constraints placed on women and men demand a separate analysis of lesbian behavior in order to identify the contexts of women's roles that uniquely shape its expression. Past research on homosexuality reflects the implicit assumption that lesbian behavior is the mirror-image of male homosexuality. Yet, the act of having sex with a member of one's own sex may be culturally defined in rather divergent ways for women and men. The basic difference derives from the gender division which is imposed in all cultures and based on the physical differences between the two sexes. As Mead stated,

> all known human societies recognize the anatomic and functional differences between males and females in intricate and complex ways; through insistence on small nuances of behavior in posture, stance, gait, through language, ornamentation and dress, division of labor, legal social status . . . (1961, p. 1451)

The different constraints imposed on men and women affect the construction of homosexual roles, behaviors, and meanings. Therefore, the factors that are significant in male homosexuality may not be significant to the construction of female homosexuality. For example, the ritual homosexuality of New Guinea men was a result of the need to separate boys from the contaminating power of their mothers and of the belief that boys did not develop strength or masculinity naturally. Adult men helped them grow through ritual insemination (see Gray, this issue; also Herdt, 1981, 1984). Girls, on the other hand, were believed to have an inherent femininity and reproductive competence, possessing the female essence from birth (Herdt, 1981). Since it was not necessary for women to ritually implant femaleness in young girls, no ritual homosexuality analogous to male behavior existed for women. On the other hand, patterns of homosexual behavior may be similar for men and women, such as the cross-gender role among Native Americans, although still differentially affected by their separate roles and statuses. Consequently, the discourse on homosexuality must be informed by an analysis of the construction of lesbianism, which this next section will attempt to provide.

APPROACHES TO LESBIANISM

Despite the fact that no anthropological study other than Wolf's (1979) has focused on lesbianism, anthropologists and other social scientists have attempted to compare female and male homosexuality. Although their conclusions are questionable because of the lack of attention to the subject, they suggest that female homosexuality is less institutionalized, less well-developed, less important or less visible than male homosexuality (Carrier, 1980; Ford & Beach, 1951). The reasons given for the lack of female homosexual patterns frequently rely on the notion of biological constraints. Mead, for example, despite the prevalence of a learning theory model in most of her work, reverts to an essentialist position in her analysis of female homosexuality. She suggested that "female anatomy dictates no choices as to activity, passivity, asymmetry, or complementariness and seems to lend itself much less to institutionalization as a counter-mores activity" (1961, p. 1471). Whitehead (1981), in considering the Native American female cross-gender role, is also inclined to place the onus on the greater constraints of female biology as compared to male biology. Such arguments do not sufficiently take into account the cultural constraints and influences on women's roles, but rather fall back on the notion of biological determinism to explain women's activities and roles. Carrier is more to the point when he suggests that the "higher status accorded men than women in most societies" may account for the lower incidence on female homosexuality (1980, p. 103). Rather than explaining the data of lesbianism in terms of the prerequisites of physiology, patterns of lesbian behavior can be more accurately explained by the type of gender system and the autonomy of women in particular cultures.

Anthropological Study of Women

In looking at the anthropological data on women and lesbianism, a majority of ethnographies contain little or no data on lesbian behavior. There are several factors, other than the absence of lesbianism, that have contributed to this lack of information. Traditional anthropologists were concerned with the normative female role, studying women in activities that reflected the western ideology of womanhood as supportive and nurturing of male concerns. Ethnographers focused on the role of women in domestic activities such as gathering, weaving, childrearing, and preparing food for their families, often to the exclusion of women's activities outside this domestic sphere. They typically assumed that within the normative female role women engaged exclusively in heterosexual behavior. Consequently, they were unable to identify non-heterosexual behavior, or if they did, they failed to understand that in many instances it was acceptable, desirable, or easily accessible to a large number of women in non-western cultures. For example, Firth concluded that Tikopia women did not engage in lesbianism because so many male partners were available to them (1936, p. 495). He was assuming a natural preference for heterosexuality over homosexuality.

To complicate the matter, anthropological fieldwork was done predominantly by males, talking to male informants about male activities. According to Reiter, the details of women's lives ''[come] from questions asked of men about their wives, daughters, and sisters, rather than the women themselves . . .'' (1975, p. 12). Male informants were frequently unqualified or unwilling to discuss women's business and their hesitance or lack of knowledge was particularly critical to the process of obtaining data on lesbian behavior. Evans-Pritchard (1970) reported that Azande women kept their lesbian relations as secret as possible even from their husbands. The data he gathered from his male informants on women's homosexual relations necessarily reflected male assumptions and feelings rather than the female experience.

On the other hand, though many ethnographies contain no reports of lesbian behavior, some anthropologists have had notable success eliciting such information from female informants. For instance Shostak's (1981) life-history of Nisa, a !Kung woman, reveals that homosexual relations among girls was an accepted adolescent phenomenon. Prior studies made no reference to lesbian behavior among the !Kung. Other data are muddled both by anthropologists' and informants' reticence on the subject. Mueller, who studied Lesotho ''mummy-baby'' relationships, did not obtain explicit information on the women's sexual activity because, as she admits, ''I was not able to ask such personal questions, largely because of my own embarrassment'' (1977, p. 167). Gay found that mummy-baby relationships are ''regarded as very personal and are only discussed reticently with a stranger whose disapproval they fear'' (this issue). In light of these discrepancies, references to the absence of homosexual behavior, whether female or male, may prove to be a poor basis for cross-cultural analysis.

Another problem with the anthropological data is that they have largely reflected the prevailing Western conception of lesbianism. From the late 1800s sexologists and social scientists identified masculine behavior in women as lesbianism; not surprisingly, women in "masculine" or cross-gender roles comprise nearly half of all the anthropological data on lesbianism (see Blackwood, 1984a). The remainder of the data simply reports the occurrence of sexual activity among adolescent girls or adult women. Anthropologists have ignored or overlooked other types of lesbian relations. Gay (this issue) candidly admitted that she was unaware of Lesotho girls' "mummy-baby" relationships, intimate girlfriend relationships, until a year after she had lived in her study area. She only then observed the relationship because her research assistant pointed it out. Thus, the anthropologist's knowledge or stereotype of Western lesbianism inhibits the collection of accurate data where relationships do not resemble the expected form.

The numerous problems with the data on lesbianism stem predominantly from the male biases and prejudices regarding lesbian behavior and women's roles. Although it is impossible to determine the universal prevalence of lesbianism, the small number of anthropological reports on the subject are more likely due to the limitation of the observers than to the condition of women's lives. Yet, even the perception that the amount of data is very small may be inaccurate. In Ford and Beach's (1951) cross-cultural survey of homosexual and lesbian behavior (the source most used in discussions of cross-cultural variation in homosexuality), 17 out of 76 cultures surveyed in the Human Relations Area File reported female homosexuality. By comparison, a recent survey of lesbian behavior (Blackwood, 1984a) found 95 cultures where lesbian and female cross-gender behavior occurred (plus several more that hinted at a possible lesbian role). Although one-third of these were Native North American tribes, the amount of data nevertheless indicates the limitations of previous studies as well as the misconceptions they have fostered regarding the prevalence of female homosexuality.

THE CONSTRUCTION OF LESBIANISM

Systems of gender, kinship and economy (as suggested by Adam, in this issue) affect the construction of both female and male homosexuality. Yet, the differential experiences of gender provide the basis for divergent lesbian and male homosexual patterns. In order to understand the cultural factors significant to the construction of lesbian behavior, the focus in this section will be on the female role and the contexts within which lesbian behavior appears. In particular it will outline the influence of differing gender systems and different levels of social stratification on the development of patterns of lesbian behavior.[3]

Putting aside cross-gender behavior for the moment, the construction of lesbianism, where it occurs, takes place within the sphere of female activities and networks. Women in all cultures are expected to marry and bear children; in many they are betrothed and wed before or soon after puberty. Consequently, for the most part lesbian behavior locates within the structure of marriage relations, but within that system a variety of sexual relations are possible.

The range of lesbian behavior that appears cross-culturally varies from formal to informal relations. These patterns may be described as follows. Informal relations among women are those which do not extend beyond the immediate social context. Examples of such would be adolescent sex play and affairs among women in harems or polygynous households. Formal lesbian relations are part of a network or social structure extending beyond the pair or immediate love relationship, and occur within such social relationships as bond friendship, sisterhoods, initiation schools, the cross-gender role, or woman-marriage. An examination of social stratification suggests that, in societies where women have control over their productive activities and status, both formal and informal relations may occur. Where women lack power, particularly in class societies, they maintain only informal lesbian ties or build institutions outside the dominant culture.

Non-Class Societies

In non-class societies, depending on the degree of economic autonomy of women, several patterns of formal and informal lesbian relations occur. These patterns can be found in both highly stratified states, such as those of the Azande and Dahomey in Africa, and the more egalitarian !Kung of southern Africa and the Australian aborigines. The patterns in each group result from cultural factors such as kinship regulations, the marriage system, trade rights, and sexual customs. Among the Azande the husband's kin arranged marriage by paying a brideprice to the wife's kin. The brideprice gave them the right to claim the offspring of the wife for their lineage. Wealthier men married several wives and built a dwelling in the compound for each wife. Wives were given a plot of land to cultivate, and they controlled the profits made from the produce through trade. Women married shortly after puberty, but as they fulfilled their duties as a wife, certain rights accrued to them. Consequently, despite the demands of the marriage system, some Azande women established formal lesbian relationships, often with their co-wives. According to Evans-

Pritchard (1970, p. 1429), "All Azande I have known well enough to discuss this matter have asserted . . . that female homosexuality . . . was practiced in polygamous homes in the past and still [1930] is sometimes."

Azande women usually kept the sexual nature of their friendships secret from their husbands, who felt threatened by such activities, yet could not forbid them. Such relationships may have been fairly common for adult women in certain other African groups where marriage was polygynous, as among the Nupe (Nadel, 1942), the Haussa (Karsch-Haack, 1975), and the Nyakyusa (Wilson, 1963). A relationship between two Azande women could be formalized through a ritual that created a permanent bond (Evans-Pritchard, 1970). This bond secured the emotional and economic support of the partner, and may have served to widen the trade network of the woman and possibly enhance her position in the community.[4] Thus, both formal and informal relationships occurred within the context of marriage among women who were in daily contact through their domestic and trade activities. It indicated that male control of female activities did not extend to interactions and concerns between females.

In other non-class societies lesbian relations occurred in sex-segregated childhood and adolescent groups. Among the highly stratified Dahomeyans, adolescent girls prepared for marriage responsibilities by attending initiation schools, where, among other activities, they performed exercises in each other's presence to thicken their genitalia. It has been noted that they engaged in sexual activities on these occasions (Herskovits, 1967). Such activity was congruent with their school training and served to heighten awareness of their erotic responses. Among the egalitarian !Kung, girls engaged in sexual play with other girls before they did so with boys (Shostak, 1981). In another egalitarian group, the Australian aborigines, adolescent sex play was an acknowledged and integral part of the social system. It conformed to the kinship regulations for marriage partners (Roheim, 1933), occurring among girls who were cross-cousins. Thus, an Australian girl formed lesbian relations with her female cross-cousin, whose family would later give her their son to marry, the girl-friends thereby becoming sisters-in-law.

In comparing the highly stratified social structure of Dahomey or the Azande to the more egalitarian Australian aborigines, the different constraints on lesbian behavior stand out. Herskovits (1932) stated that the adolescent period for Dahomeyan women was an acceptable time for lesbian activity. Some adult women also engaged in it, probably in the context of polygynous marriages, but this was secretly done. Azande women also maintained clandestine relationships. Roheim (1933) reported that married Australian women engaged in lesbian activities, one form of which was called *kityili-kityili*, tickling the clitoris with the finger. Although a woman's first marriage was controlled by her kin, she had the choice, following the death of her first husband, to engage in various marital and extramarital relations (Bell, 1980, 1981). While Dahomeyan women were forced to conceal their lesbian activities, the lesbian relationships of the Australian women were an acknowledged part of their sexual behavior and were included in ritual activities (Kaberry, 1939). Thus, different levels of social stratification and marriage systems shape different patterns of lesbian behavior in non-class societies.

Class Societies

The contrast in patterns of lesbian behavior is sharper between non-class and class societies. In those with rigid hierarchical gender systems women's sexual activities are strictly confined. Formal lesbian patterns do not exist unless they maintain a status marginal to the dominant culture. In such societies, with control of women's productive and reproductive rights vested in male kin, not only were women confined to heterosexual marriage, but also their sexual activities were restricted by law or custom to their marital partner. Islamic law called for imprisonment for homosexuality and death or divorce for a wife caught in adultery (Minai, 1981). In this context, lesbian behavior, if it occurred at all, was informal and private. Clandestine relationships developed among Near Eastern women in harems and within the Muslim institution of purdah. Wives of ruling class men rarely saw their husbands and therefore sought alternative sources of relationships. Some wealthy, educated Near Eastern women could choose to remain unmarried and found great satisfaction in lesbian relationships (Abbott, 1946; Bullough, 1976; Walther, 1981). Ultimately, the strict segregation of the sexes provided the only context for lesbian relations.

Conditions were similarly restrictive for Chinese women. The sisterhoods of Kwangtung province provide the only available evidence of lesbian relationships in China (Sankar, this issue). This institution of bond friendship necessarily arose outside the traditional marriage and kin structure. Although still guided by the cultural values of the dominant society, these women rejected the traditional gender role to form sisterhoods based on the traditions of girls' houses and celibacy vows. The availability of silk work in Kwangtung province gave them the economic independence to refuse marriage. Some women did not engage in heterosexual relationships because of cultural sanctions imposed on those who took non-marriage vows. Others formed lover relationships with a "sister" (Sankar, 1978). Thus, in the class societies of the Near East and China the construction of lesbian relations showed two opposing trends: First, an informal pattern resulting from the restrictions of male-dominant institutions and, second, a sisterhood existing outside the social relations of the dominant culture and dependent on the success of female bonding and the tolerance of the larger society. This second type applies as well to the lesbian subculture of western society in the last 80 years.

A formal pattern of age-graded lesbian relations appears in cultures with a dual economic system, such as black South Africa and Carriacou in the Caribbean. In both areas males participate in a capitalist wage-labor system through migration to industrial areas, while women work the land and direct the affairs of the household. On Carriacou husbands are separated from their wives for most of the year and at home are unable to command the exclusive attention of their wives. Older married women secure the affections and assistance of younger, often single women whom they support with income from the absentee husband (Smith, 1962). This relationship provides both economic and emotional support and is a viable alternative to the domestic isolation of the women. A similar pattern exists in South Africa, the mummy-baby game. It maintains the same functions of emotional and economic support as in Carriacou but the age range between women is smaller (Blacking, 1978; Gay, this issue; Mueller, 1977). Despite the imposition of a capitalist wage-labor system on these groups, its effects are mitigated through female bonding in mutually beneficial relationships. In South Africa these relationships may have derived from a traditional pattern of affective relations between older and younger women (Gay, this issue).

Cross-Gender Role

The cross-gender role for women constitutes another formal pattern of lesbian relations, which appears in certain classless societies and, in particular, in egalitarian societies. This role was institutionalized mainly among western Native American tribes and integrated into the social structure of the larger society. Five western tribes in which the cross-gender role has been observed at some length include the Mohave, Maricopa, Cocopa, Kaska, and Klamath (Blackwood, 1984b). Depending on their interest and ability, some women in these tribes took on the male gender role, usually at puberty, and performed the duties associated with men, such as hunting, trapping, and, for Cocopa *warrhameh*, fighting in battle. These women were not denied the right to marry and frequently took wives with whom they established a household and raised children. The significance of the female cross-gender role lay in the ability of women to take on a male role regardless of their biology. Further, it was possible for them to cross roles without threatening the definition of the male role because men and women had equal status and occupied complementary rather than antagonistic gender roles (Blackwood, 1984b).

In contrast to the flexibility of gender roles in egalitarian societies, class societies that have hierarchical gender systems define gender more rigidly. In such cultures the gender system is structured in a dichotomous fashion; neither sex participates in the behaviors nor activities of the other. In male-dominant cultures such as western Europe or the Near East, it is impossible for women to assume a cross-gender role because such behavior poses a threat to the gender system and the very definitions of maleness and femaleness. Those who did, such as the passing women of western Europe, risked grave repercussions; if discovered, they faced serious punishment or even death (Crompton, 1981; Faderman, 1981).

CONCLUSION

The construction of lesbianism shatters some basic assumptions about women which have been propounded in the discourse on homosexuality. The perception that men maintain universal hegemony over women's sexuality is contradicted by the data on alternative sexual relationships for women. Rubin (1975) theorized that women were forced, through marriage, to be heterosexual and that this condition prevailed in all cultures. Others have subscribed to the concept of "enforced heterosexuality"; for example, Adrienne Rich has suggested that lesbianism "comprises both the breaking of a taboo and the rejection of a compulsory way of life . . . a direct or indirect attack on male right of access to women" (1980, p. 649). In contrast to this analysis, the history of sexual relations is not one of total heterosexual dominance. The construction of sexuality in many non-class societies validated variant sexual behavior for women. Women's lives were not wholly constrained by the dictates of marriage and child-bearing, nor did they live in total submission to men. Other types of sexual relations existed both before and after marriage. As the Azande example shows, various formal and informal lesbian relations co-existed with marriage, giving women several options and avenues for control of their lives and sexual activities. In many tribal societies lesbian relations were not considered deviant nor were the women "breaking taboos"; on the contrary, lesbian bonds were institutionalized and integrated into kinship and other social structures.

Social stratification and gender ideology may place serious restrictions on women's sexuality. The constraints of marriage and lack of property rights imposed on women in many societies apparently limits the development of non-marital homosexual behavior and institutions. These constraints, however, should not be construed to be the result of the "limitations" of the female's biological sex. Enforced heterosexuality is tied to women's lack of economic power and the restriction of female activity to the domestic sphere. Further, the embeddedness of sexuality with gender roles in western societies proscribes homosexual activity and defines women as male sex objects.

The barriers to female power and sexuality in modern society reside in the male-dominant ideologies of gender and sexuality. Nevertheless, as the Chinese sisterhoods exemplify, even within strongly patriarchal societies women are capable of forming alternative institutions that circumvent male control. Similarly, lesbians in the United States are now building their own institutions and kin structures as well as creating sexual ideologies in opposition to the dominant society (Lockard, this issue).

Patterns of lesbian behavior develop from the particular conditions of the female gender role and the types of constraints which arise from the subordinate status women occupy in many societies. These constraints establish patterns which in many cases diverge from those for male homosexual behavior and yet are not less critical to a general understanding of homosexuality. Hopefully, future research will provide a more balanced approach to the study of the construction of both female and male homosexual behavior.

NOTES

1. Major works by non-anthropologists which make use of cross-cultural data are: Bullough, 1976; Burton, 1956; Ellis & Symonds, 1897/1975; Ford & Beach, 1951; Karsch-Haack, 1975; West, 1977; Westermarck, 1956; also Katz's (1976) chapter on Native Americans. The first anthropological cross-cultural survey by Opler (1965) strongly reflected western biases on homosexuality.

2. For further discussion of this theory see Weeks, 1981, pp. 2-3; Whitehead, 1984; Rubin, 1984; De Cecco & Shively, 1983/1984; and Richardson, 1983/1984.

3. Gender systems can be drawn to roughly parallel levels of social stratification, i.e., increased stratification, increased inequality of the sexes, though any particular society will need much greater analysis than can be provided here. The analysis here is suggestive rather than definitive.

4. Similar to men's blood-brotherhood, as described by Evans-Pritchard (1933).

REFERENCES

Abbott, N. (1946). *Two Queens of Bagdad*. Chicago: University of Chicago Press.
Adam, B. D. (1985). Age, structure, and sexuality: Reflections on the anthropological evidence on homosexual relations. *Journal of Homosexuality, 11*(3/4), 19-33.
Bell, D. (1980). Desert politics: Choices in the "marriage market." In M. Etienne & E. Leacock (Eds.), *Women and colonization* (pp. 239-269). New York: J. J. Bergin.
Bell, D. (1981). Women's business is hard work: Central Australian aboriginal women's love rituals. *Signs: Journal of Women in Culture and Society, 7,* 314-337.
Benedict, R. (1934). *Patterns of culture*. New York: Houghton Mifflin.
Benedict, R. (1939). Sex in primitive society. *American Journal of Orthopsychiatry, 9,* 570-573.
Berndt, R. M. & Berndt, C. H. (1963). *Sexual behavior in western Arnhem Land*. New York: Johnson Reprint.
Blacking, J. (1978). Uses of the kinship idiom in friendships at some Venda and Zulu schools. In J. Argyle & E. Preston-Whyte (Eds.), *Social system and tradition in southern Africa* (pp. 101-117). Cape Town: Oxford University Press.
Blackwood, E. (1984a). *Cross-cultural dimensions of lesbian relations*. Unpublished master's thesis. Department of Anthropology, San Francisco State University.
Blackwood, E. (1984b). Sexuality and gender in certain Native American tribes: The case of cross-gender females. *Signs: Journal of Women in Culture and Society, 10,* 27-42.

Bullough, V. L. (1976). *Sexual variance in society and history.* New York: John Wiley and Sons.

Burton, R. F. (1956). Terminal essay. In D. W. Cory (Ed.), *Homosexuality, a cross-cultural approach* (pp. 207-224). New York: Julian Press (originally published 1886).

Callender, C. & Kochems, L. (1985). Men and not-men: Male gender mixing statuses and homosexuality. *Journal of Homosexuality, 11*(3/4), 165-178.

Carrier, J. M. (1980). Homosexual behavior in cross-cultural perspective. In J. Marmor (Ed.), *Homosexual behavior: A modern reappraisal* (pp. 100-122). New York: Basic Books.

Crompton, L. (1981). The myth of lesbian impunity: Capital laws from 1270 to 1791. *Journal of Homosexuality 6*(1/2), 11-25.

De Cecco, J. P. & Shively, M. G. (1984). From sexual identities to sexual relationships: A contextual shift. *Journal of Homosexuality, 9*(2/3), 1-26.

D'Emilio, J. (1983). *Sexual politics, sexual communities: The making of a homosexual minority in the U.S., 1940-1970.* Chicago: University of Chicago Press.

Ellis, H. & Symonds, J. A. (1975). *Sexual inversion.* New York: Arno Press (reprint of Studies in the Psychology of Sex, Vol. I, 1897).

Evans-Pritchard, E. E. (1933). Zande blood-brotherhood. *Africa, 6,* 369-401.

Evans-Pritchard, E. E. (1970). Sexual inversion among the Azande. *American Anthropologist, 72,* 1428-1434.

Faderman, L. (1981). *Surpassing the love of men: Romantic friendship and love between women from the Renaissance to the present.* New York: William Morrow.

Firth, R. (1936). *We, the Tikopia.* New York: American Books.

Fitzgerald, T. K. (1977). A critique of anthropological research on homosexuality. *Journal of Homosexuality, 2,* 385-397.

Ford, C. S. & Beach, F. A. (1951). *Patterns of sexual behavior.* New York: Harper and Brothers.

Gay, J. (1985). "Mummies and babies" and friends and lovers in Lesotho. *Journal of Homosexuality, 11*(3/4), 97-116.

Gray, J. P. (1985). Growing yams and men: An interpretation of Kimam male ritualized homosexual behavior. *Journal of Homosexuality, 11*(3/4), 55-68.

Herdt, G. H. (1981). *Guardians of the flutes: Idioms of masculinity.* New York: McGraw-Hill.

Herdt, G. H. (1984). *Ritualized homosexuality in Melanesia.* Berkeley: University of California Press.

Herskovits, M. J. (1932). Some aspects of Dahomeyan ethnology. *Africa, 5,* 266-296.

Hershkovits, M. J. (1967). *Dahomey: An ancient West African kingdom* (2 vols.). Evanston: Northwestern University Press.

Hill, W. W. (1935). The status of the hermaphrodite and transvestite in Navaho culture. *American Anthropologist, 37,* 273-279.

Kaberry, P. M. (1939). *Aboriginal woman, sacred and profane.* London: George Routledge and Sons.

Karsch-Haack, F. (1975). *Das gleichgeschlechtliche leben der naturvolker.* [The homosexual life of primitive peoples.] New York: Arno Press (1st ed. Reinhardt 1911).

Katz, J. (1976). *Gay American history: Lesbians and gay men in the U.S.A.* New York: Thomas Y. Crowell.

Kroeber, A. L. (1925). *Handbook of the Indians of California.* United States Bureau of American Ethnology. (Bulletin 78).

Kroeber, A. L. (1940). Psychosis or social sanction. *Character and Personality, 8,* 204-215.

Layard, J. (1959). Homo-eroticism in a primitive society as a function of the self. *Journal of Analytical Psychology, 4,* 101-115.

Levy, R. I. (1971). The community function of Tahitian male transvestitism: A hypothesis. *Anthropological Quarterly, 44,* 12-21.

Lindenbaum, S. (1984). Variations on a sociosexual theme in Melanesia. In G. H. Herdt (Ed.), *Ritualized homosexuality in Melanesia* (pp. 337-361). Berkeley: University of California Press.

Lockard, D. (1985). The lesbian community: An anthropological approach. *Journal of Homosexuality, 11*(3/4), 83-95.

McIntosh, M. (1981). The homosexual role, with postscript: The homosexual role revisited. In K. Plummer (Ed.), *The making of the modern homosexual* (pp. 30-49). Totowa, N.J.: Barnes and Noble.

Mead, M. (1935). *Sex and temperament in three primitive societies* (3rd ed.). New York: William Morrow and Co.

Mead, M. (1961). Cultural determinants of sexual behavior. In W. C. Young, (Ed.), *Sex and internal secretions* (2 vols.) (pp. 1433-1479). Baltimore: Williams and Williams.

Metraux, A. (1940). *Ethnology of Easter Island*. Honolulu: Bernice P. Bishop Museum.

Minai, N. (1981). *Women in Islam*. New York: Seaview Books.

Mueller, M. B. (1977). *Women and men in rural Lesotho: The periphery of the periphery*. Unpublished doctoral dissertation, Brandeis University.

Nadel, S. F. (1942). *A black Byzantium: The kingdom of Nupe in Nigeria*. London: Oxford University Press.

Newton, E. (1972). *Mother camp: Female impersonators in America*. Englewood Cliffs, NJ: Prentice-Hall.

Opler, M. (1965). Anthropological and cross-cultural aspects of homosexuality. In J. Marmor (Ed.), *Sexual inversion: The multiple roots of homosexuality* (pp. 108-123). New York: Basic Books.

Padgug, R. A. (1979). Sexual matters: On conceptualizing sexuality in history. *Radical History Review, 20,* 3-23.

Plummer, K. (1981). *The making of the modern homosexual*. Totowa, NJ: Barnes and Noble.

Read, K. E. (1980). *Other voices: The style of a male homosexual tavern*. Novato, CA: Chandler and Sharp.

Reiter, R. R. (1975). *Towards an anthropology of women*. New York: Monthly Review Press.

Rich, A. (1980). Compulsory heterosexuality and lesbian existence. *Signs: Journal of Women in Culture and Society, 5,* 631-660.

Richardson, D. (1984). The dilemma of essentiality in homosexual theory. *Journal of Homosexuality, 9*(2/3), 79-90.

Roheim, G. (1933). Women and their life in central Australia. *Journal of the Royal Anthropological Institute of Great Britain and Ireland, 63,* 207-265.

Roheim, G. (1950). *Psychoanalysis and anthropology*. New York: International Universities Press.

Ross, E. & Rapp, R. (1981). Sex and society: A research note from social history and anthropology. *Comparative Studies in Society and History, 23,* 51-72.

Rubin, G. (1975). The traffic in women: Notes on the "political economy" of sex. In R. R. Reiter (Ed.), *Towards an anthropology of women* (pp. 157-210). New York: Monthly Review Press.

Rubin, G. (1984). Thinking sex: Notes for a radical theory of the politics of sexuality. In C. Vance (Ed.), *Pleasure and danger: Exploring female sexuality* (pp. 267-319). Boston: Routledge and Kegan Paul.

Sankar, A. P. (1978). *The evolution of the spinsterhood in traditional Chinese society: From village girls' houses to chai t'angs in Hong Kong*. Unpublished doctoral dissertation, University of Michigan.

Sankar, A. P. (1985). Sisters and brothers, lovers and enemies: Marriage resistance in southern Kwangtung. *Journal of Homosexuality, 11*(3/4), 69-81.

Shostak, M. (1981). *Nisa, the life and words of a !Kung Woman*. Cambridge: Harvard University Press.

Smith, M. G. (1962). *Kinship and community in Carriacou*. New Haven: Yale University Press.

Sonenschein, D. (1966). Homosexuality as a subject of anthropological inquiry. *Anthropological Quarterly, 39*(2), 73-82.

Spencer, B. Sir & Gillen, E. J. (1927). *The Arunta* (2 vols.). London: Macmillan and Co.

Walther, W. (1981). *Women in Islam*. C. S. V. Salt, transl. Montclair, N.J.: Abner Schram.

Weeks, J. (1981). *Sex, politics, and society: The regulation of sexuality since 1800*. London: Longman.

West, D. J. (1977). *Homosexuality re-examined*. Minneapolis: University of Minnesota Press.

Westermarck, E. (1956). Homosexual love. In D. W. Cory (Ed.), *Homosexuality, a cross-cultural approach* (pp. 101-136). New York: Julian Press.

Whitehead, H. (1981). The bow and the burden strap: A new look at institutionalized homosexuality in native North America. In S. B. Ortner & H. Whitehead (Eds.), *Sexual meanings: The cultural construction of gender and sexuality* (pp. 80-115). Cambridge: Cambridge University Press.

Whitehead, H. (1984). *Discussion of gender-crossing*. Paper presented at the 83rd Annual Meetings of the American Anthropological Association, Denver.

Wilson, M. (1963). *Good company: A study of Nyakyusa age-villages*. Boston: Beacon Press.

Wolf, D. G. (1979). *The lesbian community*. Berkeley: University of California Press.

Age, Structure, and Sexuality: Reflections on the Anthropological Evidence on Homosexual Relations

Barry D. Adam, PhD
University of Windsor

ABSTRACT. The paper compares selected examples of age-structured homosexuality to understand same-sex eroticism as a "predictable" outcome of particular combinations of age, gender, and kinship. Unlike traditional models of homosexuality which view it as exceptional or abnormal, cross-cultural evidence demonstrates that homosexuality is an inextricable component of the structural codes of the societies in which it appears.

The traditional preoccupation with homosexuality as a separate and unusual entity hindered investigation into the structural forms which make homosexuality possible and likely. The dominant theoretical legacy in sexuality is a biological model which equates heterosexuality with reproduction and subsumes reproduction within the scope of kin and family. The naturalistic and unproblematic core of this analytic paradigm pushes other forms of sexuality into residual categories of the deviant and pathological. Yet the very intransigence of human sexuality in the face of the social coding processes which would confine it to heterosexuality and the family offers an unrealized potential for reflecting upon sexuality itself. The social geography of homosexuality should reveal clues to the problem of why sexual desire arises at certain structural points and how it is ordered and made meaningful.

Recent cross-cultural work on the status of women challenges the naturalistic model and seeks to understand the structural foundations of gender. It is remarkable how the spell of naturalism and our own cultural presumptions have so long excluded homosexual relations from the basic tools of anthropological analysis.

Recent work, such as Dover's (1978) *Greek Homosexuality* and

---

Dr. Adam is Associate Professor of Sociology, University of Windsor, Windsor, Ontario, Canada N9B 3P4. Helpful comments were provided by Gilbert Herdt, Evelyn Blackwood, and Steven Murray. An earlier version of this paper was presented at the 81st Annual Meeting of the American Anthropological Association, Washington, D.C., 1982.

Herdt's (1984) *Ritualized Homosexuality in Melanesia*, represents a new order of analysis that explains sexuality as a set of social relationships constructed from a complex repertoire of indigenous signifiers. Here same-sex eroticism and bonding is not deviant in any sense but a "predictable" outcome of a particular combination of fundamental categories of age, gender, and kinship. The ethnographic literature reveals that same-sex bonds typically conform to the same kinship codes that arrange other aspects of life. Homosexual relationships illustrate Levi-Strauss's (1963) claim that "kinship does not consist in the objective ties of descent or consanguinity between individuals. It exists only in human consciousness; it is an arbitrary system of representations" (p. 51). When homosexual desire is routinized, it attains a place and meaning consistent with overall kinship logic. Similarly, different kinship structures create their own fields of eroticism and thus particular sets of occasions for sexualized relations between people, whether of different or the same sexes.

Of course, any single set of cultural institutions never completely contains the full range of human experience and innovation. Social coding practices may be uneven, incomplete, or in transition. Even where sexuality has a culturally specific complex of meanings, there remains a larger universe of experience, maladjustments, and emigrations from prescribed interpretive frameworks. The dominant sexual codes of one place take on subterranean aspects elsewhere as a "little tradition" or folk culture.

AGE

Linkages occur between age, kinship, and gender, on the one hand, and institutional forms of sexuality and bonding between same-sex partners on the other. This paper will be confined to a comparison of selected types of age-structured homosexuality in order to work toward an understanding of *intra*-gender sexuality, a predominantly male form of same-sex bonding. The conclusion makes some cursory comparisons between this form and *trans*-gender homosexuality, a type whose exposition falls outside the scope of this paper.

Ethnographic evidence, drawn from all continents except North America, suggests a special propensity for homosexual relations among unmarried male youths. It is among males between boyhood and marriage that homosexuality is most often permissible and sometimes obligatory. The category of "bachelorhood" contrasts with "adult" status wherein older men use women's productive and reproductive power for their own use. Bachelorhood is an interim status during which young men are frequently denied these rights and privileges. Youthful homosexuality no doubt is tolerated, if not accepted, by older males who seek to improve their own wealth and power through polygyny and to keep younger contenders in abeyance.

The Nyakyusa of the Lake Nyasa region of eastern Africa offer a clear example of this dynamic. Adult men are polygynous and, as Wilson (1951) notes, "plural marriages breed wealth, for the polygynist is likely to command the labor of many sons as well as several wives, and in due course, he expects to receive marriage cattle of many daughters" (p. 15). She explicitly links the Nyakyusa age system to the older men's desire to increase their holdings in women and cattle. The transition from boyhood to bachelorhood occurs when young men stop herding cattle for their fathers and form all-male adolescent societies based on hoe agriculture. Each new age cohort separates from its families to form peer groups which, by the age of 10 or 11, found entirely new villages for themselves. It is generally accepted that these youths engage in reciprocal homosexual relations, including sleeping and dancing together erotically (Wilson, 1951). Later, around the age of 25 when young men begin to marry, homosexuality is expected to cease. The privileges of adulthood, where wives and offspring provide the central source of personal wealth, help motivate the change to heterosexuality. In adulthood, then, homosexuality is thought to be so irrational as to be a sign of witchcraft (Wilson, 1951). Nevertheless, reports of occasional clandestine relationships between adult men and youths suggest that they do not always successfully make the expected transition.

The age structure of male homosexuality has few parallels among women. Whereas bachelorhood is a common stage for males, women are typically married soon after menarche. Wilson (1951, p. 14) remarks, "Girls are betrothed very young and finally join their husbands at puberty." Male and female genders then are not simply parallel or mirror images of each other but have significantly asymmetrical contents. For Nyakyusa women, reports of homosexual relations among co-wives exist, along with a number of other sketchy ethnographic reports of so-called "harem" lesbianism in other polygynous societies.

More common than the peer-oriented, youthful sexuality of the Nyakyusa are sexual relations between older and younger males. These relationships fall into two major categories. In the "ancient model," an older male takes a youth in a role-structured sexual relationship. In the "Melanesian model," older bachelors enter role-defined relationships with younger males, though some Melanesian societies also show evidence of the ancient form.

The core of this interpersonal dynamic is a pedagogic relationship between the "inspirer" and the "inspired," a terminology shared by the Greeks and the Etoro of New Guinea (Dover, 1978; Kelly, 1976). The younger man enters an erotic apprenticeship that immerses him in male culture and gender functions transmitted as a collective lore to new "adherents.'' Consistent with the ''one-way'' socialization process is role differentiation: The younger male is a ''recipient'' and the older, the ''provider,'' a role contrast that generally structures anal and oral intercourse. Unlike the Nyakyusa, the ancient model is a fundamentally intergenerational sexual dynamic in which exclusively ''homosexual'' younger men become ''bisexual'' in adulthood by acquiring wives and youthful lovers.

The ancient model finds its highest development in the early imperial societies of Greece, China, Byzantium, and medieval Persia where social class complicates the inequality between adult and youth. In these societies, it might be argued, categories such as ''heterosexual'' and ''homosexual'' are scarcely relevant at all. Sexual structure, along with other political relationships, is deeply informed by the division between the free, adult male citizen and all others (see Adam, 1981). This fundamental social cleavage, characteristic of the ancient mode of production, overrides gender as a sexual signifier. Sexuality is merely one of many rights exercised by the free male over women, youths, and slaves.

In Melanesia, gender ideology plays the pre-eminent role in determining sexuality among males. Sexual relationships are one among many ways in which men reproduce themselves in opposition to women. Boys, who have been deeply compromised by the feminine influence of their mothers, must be appropriated from them and transformed into men. The transmission of semen, along with special masculine rites and knowledge, assures the reproduction of the male group.

THE ANCIENT MODEL

In the ancient model, homosexuality is a medium for the transmission of folklore contained by the masculine gender and is a second stage of parenting that succeeds the mother-child relationship. The *Symposium* offers the analogy of the '''procreation' of rational knowledge'' in a younger male by an elder with ''the literal begetting of progeny by heterosexual intercourse'' (Dover, 1978, p. 164). The allegory of the ''double'' in the *Symposium* holds that lovers seek to unite themselves with their lost ''halves.'' While some men seek their ''other halves'' in women, the more masculine men

> pursue the masculine, and so long as their boyhood lasts show themselves to be slices of the male by making friends with men and delighting to lie with them and to be clasped in men's embraces. . . . So when they come to man's estate they are boy-lovers, and have no natural interest in wiving and getting children but only do these things under stress of custom; they are quite contented to live together unwedded all their days. (pp. 191-192)

Understood as the social reproduction of male culture, it is not surprising to find intermale sexuality most salient in masculine tasks. In more complex societies with more highly developed divisions of labor, homosexuality may be specialized in a military sector while heterosexuality dominates elsewhere. Even among the Greeks, the military function of inter-generational lovers appears in classic texts filled with stories of male lovers who were famous for slaying tyrants or resisting foreign invaders (see Ungaretti, 1978). In the Greek army military duties fell upon all men, but among societies with professional military classes, inter-generational male sexuality survived in such diverse instances as among the Azande and Mossi of the Sudan, the samurai of feudal Japan, and in Siwa in the Libyan desert.

At the height of the Azande imperial system (crushed by British forces in 1905), elements of the ancient model are discernible. The dominant Avongara clan functioned as an aristocracy with sexual rights over the women and youths of the Azande empire. At the pinnacle of Azande society were the largest and wealthiest households, which included hundreds of wives and some boys extracted as tribute. Page boys further increased the wealth and prestige of aristocratic households. They acted as messengers, confidantes, and sexual playthings of the patriarch. E. E. Evans-Pritchard (1971) reports that when page boys grew up, the patriarch gave them bridewealth, as they gave their own sons, in order to marry, and replaced them with younger youths.

Accompanying the bisexual polygyny of the aristocracy was a warrior class attached to aristocratic households among whom exclusive, inter-generational homosexuality was common. As members of aristocratic households, the "best" and most "trustworthy" warriors were those who posed no threat to the royal monopoly over women. Azande military homosexuality finds its place in a kinship system extended by incipient class differentiation.

> Many of the young warriors married boys and a commander might have more than one boy wife. When a warrior married a boy, he paid spears, though only a few, to the boy's parents as he would have done had he married their daughter. (Evans-Pritchard, 1971, p. 199)

The warrior fulfilled other kin obligations to his boy-wife's parents and addressed them with the appropriate terms for "father-in-law" and "mother-in-law." Evans-Pritchard (1970, p. 1430) continues,

> He gave the boy pretty ornaments; and he and the boy addressed one another as *badiare*, "my love" and "my lover." The boy fetched water for his husband, collected firewood and kindled his fire, bore

his shield when traveling and also a small bag containing wawa leaves.

At maturity the boy-wife himself became a warrior and acquired a boy-wife of his own.

It is noteworthy that female homosexual behavior did not parallel the male form but occurred among co-wives as with the Nyakyusa. Whereas warrior homosexuality was institutionalized as a structure complementary to aristocratic interests, lesbianism could not confirm aristocratic power and was thought "to cause the death of any man who witnesses [it]" (Evans-Pritchard, 1937, p. 57). Male anxiety about women's sexuality further expressed itself in this belief:

> Once a woman has started homosexual intercourse, she is likely to continue it because she is then her own master and may have gratification when she pleases and not just when a man cares to give it to her. (Evans-Pritchard, 1970, p. 1432)

Again, the different structure of women's social position results in a sexual organization with its own characteristics.

The ancient model of adult free men holding both wives and youthful male lovers, as well as the development of homosexual relations in a military context, appeared in the ancient civilization of the Siwa oasis. Though Siwa was known to Herodotus, modern ethnographic accounts largely reflect the period between the two World Wars (though Robin Maughan (n.d.) suggests that Siwan society continued as late as 1950 much as before). Despite the Siwans' ostensibly strict adherence to Islam, much of the ceremonial tradition and language of the oasis show roots in ancient Berber culture. The first British colonial governor of Siwa found it inward-looking and "ultra-conservative," resisting both Egyptian and European domination (Belgrave, 1923). The ethnographic accounts indicate (with varying degrees of explicitness) that the ancient model of sexuality was widespread. Youths entered sexual relationships with men and eventually grew up to acquire wives and young male lovers of their own ('Abd Allah, 1917). Oric Bates ('Abd Allah, p. 20) remarks, "arrangements between men and boys were openly made by go-betweens who followed much the same tactics as does the Egyptian matchmaker in promoting marriages. The boy received an initial present of 5 or 6 [Egyptian] pounds, a fee which contrasts strongly with the brideprice of 1 to 2 pounds." Men and boys entered into alliances then, with family approval and these alliances had many of the traits of formal marriage.

In addition, Belgrave (1923) and Cline (1936) state that in the 19th century, bachelors were excluded from the fortified town and formed military camps at its perimeters to defend it against desert marauders. In the

20th century, this military function faded, but the bachelor society retained its traditional structure now founded on agricultural labor. The *zaggalah* or bachelor society maintained clubhouses noted for their sybaritic style, with music, dancing, and drinking figuring prominently in local celebrations. Unlike the typical ancient model, however, Cline (1936) states that sexual practices between men and youths were not confined to special roles but tended toward the orgiastic.

Finally, evidence from feudal Japan shows many of the traits of the ancient model with its miliary specialization (Ihara, 1972; Shively, 1970).

Monastic age-structured homosexuality reported in Japan, China, Tibet, and medieval Europe may be likened to military forms in the sense that religion, like war, is a singularly masculine activity in these societies. Where hierarchical, all-male professions appear in imperial societies, sexual specialization may become possible and exclusive homosexuality emerges. Whereas adult bisexuality is prescribed for virtually all men in a simple-division of labor, social differentiation has its effects upon intimate relations as on relations of production.

THE MELANESIAN MODEL

Recent work by Gilbert Herdt (1984) has synthesized a "thick" description of a Melanesian model. For purposes of structural comparison, some of the logical strands that organize homosexual relations can be contrasted with ancient and transgenderist forms. In comparison with societies where homosexuality is associated with gender mixing, ancient and Melanesian societies show a high degree of gender differentiation. In particular, Melanesia relations between the sexes are uneasy and hedged in by strict avoidance rules. Most of the personal world is gender-charged; men and women have separate residences, pathways, crops, foods, and rites (Allen, 1967). Male attitudes toward women share a deep ambivalence, in that men believe women are threatening and polluting yet valuable and necessary. This anxiety influences heterosexuality itself, turning it into a "necessary evil" which drains men of their life-force and hastens their decline into old age and death. Male contact with female excrescences, such as menstrual blood, is thought to result in stunted growth and premature aging, and to render male tools useless. Men typically practice purgative rites to rid themselves of female contamination and ingest male-identified foods, herbs, blood, or semen to maintain themselves as men.

The strong collective identity of men restructures the problems of reproduction and socialization. The male unit becomes a collectivity which appropriates itself from its female bearers and so develops a complex and extended system of magical practices to "rescue" boys from impure contact with their mothers and convert them into men. This conversion is not easy and typically involves the seclusion of youths during which time they are fed and "grown" by older men. Native informants explain this practice as a method by which boys can catch up with the fast growth of their female peers. That such rites are secret and show envy of women's procreative powers has not been lost on theorists. A number of these societies have myths which reveal a belief that much of men's power and ability were once known or even invented by women and then stolen by men and held secret. It is as if men feel it necessary to develop a countermagic to the mysterious but natural power of women to give birth.

Secret envy aside, the initiation and maintenance ceremonies of the male unit show a highly developed sense of male lineage, the essence of which is embodied in blood or semen. The outcome is a highly consolidated fighting unit, not unlike the cases adduced above. It is in this cultural semiology that homosexuality finds a place. Homosexuality is one rite among many by which the male group affirms and reproduces itself. Homosexual relations are almost always age-graded so that older males contribute their semen to the young.

The ritualized homosexuality found in southern New Guinea and some of the northeastern island societies of Melanesia expresses, not surprisingly, an extraordinarily high valuation of semen as the vehicle of life. Herdt (1984, p. xiv) remarks, "sperm not only conceives babies, it is believed to magically build the embryo's body, to be transformed into breast milk, to produce postnatal physical strength, and to precipitate puberty and biological reproductive competence, that is, adult personhood." Among the Marind, men believed semen helped heal wounds, stimulated the libido when eaten, and improved plant growth (Baal, 1966). They put it on the end of spears to assure their aim and dabbed it over eyes to improve vision. As a necessary component of growth, insemination is then obligatory and universal for all boys, who receive it throughout the initiation period. Semen is the continuous link which binds the male line, the spiritual emanation of ancestral ghosts. Just as people are conceived as the result of the expenditure of semen, they are the vehicles by which the male line and essence continues itself.

Work by Raymond Kelly (1976) and Donald Tuzin (1980) reveals a world of male rites structurally opposed to the social obligations of the "traffic in women." Homosexuality, as an element of male culture, can thereby become infused with the promise of a timeless, carefree utopia free of the fundamental social exchanges which apparently make life burdensome, historical, and finite. This Melanesian semiology meshes with Luce Irigaray's (1981) use of Levi-Strauss to understand lesbianism as the "revolt of the trade goods," a conceptualization which construct homosexual relations in opposition to heterosexual "duty."

To help sort through the variations of the Melanesian model, a pair of contrasting types will be examined, starting with the Big Nambas of Malekula, a group whose practice most closely resembles the ancient model, and following with the Sambia of New Guinea. A. Bernard Deacon (1934) states that among the Big Nambas, fathers seek out guardians or *dubut* to guide their sons through the transition to manhood. The pairing between *dubut* and novice complies strictly with the exogamy rules that govern heterosexual marriage (Layard, 1942). The novice calls the guardian *nilagh sen*, the same word as for sister's husband, while the guardian calls the boy *mugh vel* (novice). The novice assumes many of the traits and responsibilities of female wives. ''The boy accompanies his 'husband' everywhere; works in his garden (it is for this reason a chief has many boy-lovers) and if one or other of the two should die the survivor will mourn him deeply'' (Deacon, 1934, p. 261; see Harrisson, 1937). Besides assuming a similar place to wives in the division of labor, the novice also must be sexually faithful. In return, the guardian ''mothers and tends him [the novice] as a mother would tend her child and feeds him royally'' (Layard, 1958, p. 110). The relationship comes to an end when the novice is circumcised and then marries, at which time he may acquire a *mugh vel* of his own. The Big Nambas show the familiar traits of youthful sexual subordination to a bisexual adult in a society with at least incipient class divisions.

In the New Guinea societies, on the other hand, ''shifting subsistence horticulture exists side by side with hunting and gathering in some areas'' (Herdt, 1984, p. 56). The opposite extreme from the Big Nambas is the Sambia, an Anga group of the Eastern Highlands of New Guinea. Founded in ''rampant misogyny,'' the Sambia socialize boys during an extended ten to fifteen year seclusion away from women in forest lodges. The boys pass through a series of rites designed to accomplish the transition from feminine origins to adult manhood. Herdt sums up the essentials of male initiation rites as: (1) tanning of the skin to remove female contamination; (2) nose-bleeding for internal purification; (3) ingestion of male-identified plants and ointments; and (4) fellatio practiced as regularly as eating with as many partners as possible (1981, p. 22). From the age of 7 to 10 and continuing until 14 or 16, boys fellate older youths of 14 to as old as 25. Fellatio, like other forms of sexuality, observes the incest taboo. Herdt (1981, p. 238) states ''Ideally all male kin including cross cousins are taboo. . . . Fellatio is prohibited among friends and permissible among potential enemies.'' At the end of the initiation period, males are expected to marry and to end homosexual relations; homosexual interests among adult married men are thought to be peculiar. Thereafter, strict moderation is thought advisable in marital sex to minimize the risk of pollution, while a monthly nose-bleeding ritual counteracts the contamination of heterosexuality.

Other societies show some mix of these contrasting forms. Baal (1966) describes an extended relationship between adult married men and un-married youths among the Marind of Irian Jaya, along with age-graded relationships among secluded bachelors.

> At puberty, youths live during the daytime in forest lodges. At night, they sleep with the older men [binahor-evai] in the men's house. The relationship between the boy and his mentor is a homo-sexual one, the binahor-evai having the right to use him. The boy assists his binahor in gardening and hunting and renders him and his wife small services. The two in turn help him make his first garden, give him food, and assist him in making his ornaments. (pp. 117-118)

Herdt (1984, p. 70) remarks, "that sister exchange and moiety exogamy, as among the Marind . . . are frequently correlated in societies [with ritual homosexuality]; both are present in Irian Jaya, the Trans-Fly area, and Eastern Melanesia." Sexual connections structured by this kinship code virtually leap over gender to obey moiety and age rules. At its core the older males of one moiety inseminate the younger bachelors of the other moiety as well as the bachelors' *sisters*. Among the Marind, the *binahor-evai* is typically the mother's brother of the youth. During their approximately six-year seclusion in the forest lodge, boys are also in-seminated by the older bachelors of the other moiety who will eventually marry their sisters.

Raymond Kelly (1976, p. 52) states of the Etoro, "the ideal insemi-nator . . . is a boy's true sister's husband or her betrothed; brother and sister will then receive semen from the same man (ideally a FMBS [father's mother's brother's son]) and be in a sense co-spouses to him." Upon marriage, the Etoro male will switch over from being inseminated by his sister's husband to inseminate his wife's brother, a relationship which ends around age 40 when his wife's brother, in turn, makes the same switchover. Following this transition, he "can continue to serve as an inseminator in the context of initiation ceremonies" (Kelly, 1976, p. 52).

For the Keraki, cross-moiety sexuality focuses on the relationship be-tween older and younger bachelors in seclusion (Rubel and Rosman, 1978). Williams (1936, p. 189) states, "While the older men are not de-barred from indulging and actually do so at the bullroarer ceremony, sodomy is virtually restricted as a habit to the [bachelors]." This situation moves back towards the Sambian model where older males are more quickly eased out of homosexual relations.

In Melanesia, then, sexual contact between older and younger bache-lors in seclusion appears to be typically plural, collective, and strictly "sexual," while relationships between youths and older men more closely approximate the ancient model of personal, exclusive, and educative relations. Most societies seem to endorse some combination of the two models. The absence of the latter model among the Sambians likely results from their propensity for sex with "potential enemies" (Herdt, 1981).

Finally, it should be noted that almost nothing is known of lesbianism among these societies. If Melanesian lesbianism is as "secret" as its male counterpart, it may go undetected particularly when the ethnographers are men. Tom Harrisson (1937, p. 395) states in passing that, "the women have developed a parallel pleasure system of their own, less elaborate than the male" among the Big Nambas. Raymond Kelly (1976) found that Etoro men think that women engage in some form of homosexual activities and transmit the seed of witchcraft in this way. These casual comments leave the social organization of lesbianism largely unknown.

KINSHIP

Most remarkable in the Melanesian examples is the way in which the kinship code functions successfully to create categories of the attractive and the erotic. These structures do work, such that sexual arousal occurs and is consummated repeatedly for most participants. In contrast to earlier cross-cultural work that attempted to preserve homosexuality as an aberration or pathology, it is clear that homosexuality, like heterosexuality, can be rule-bound and predictable. Sexual interest does arise at the prescribed structural locations and prescribed categories of people, regardless of gender, are eroticized. The structural code allows sexual and, indeed, homosexual interests to come about for virtually all men in some societies.

Scattered turn-of-the-century Australian references suggest a sex structure consistent with the above observations. Carl Strehlow (1913, p. 98; [see also Levi-Strauss, 1969]) argues that the Aranda eight-class moiety system, combined with the polygyny of the older men, made it particularly difficult for a young adult man to find a suitable mate. Mathews (1900) and Purcell (1893) noted that bachelors in the Kimberley district of Western Australia would take boys as wives pending the maturation of the boys' sisters as subsequent wives. Both Mathews and Purcell argue that the subincision, which marked passage into adulthood, served also to facilitate homosexuality by offering a unique way to juxtapose penes. Phyllis Kaberry, in *Aboriginal Woman*, adds:

> the youths of 17 or 18 who were still unmarried would take boys of 10 or 11 as lovers. The women had no hesitation in discussing the

> matter with me, did not regard it as shameful, gave the names of different boys, and seemed to regard the practice as a temporary substitute for marriage. (1939, p. 257)

This age-graded system conforms strictly to the exogamy requirements governing marriage; the moieties thought appropriate for wife selection also defined sexual partners among men (Layard, 1942). Given the cross-generational character of marriage categories, the older bachelor "grows" his boy-wife and later his boy-wife's younger sister, a process called *onkalji* (Roheim, 1950; see Layard, 1958).

In contrast to the mutual brother-in-law relationship among the Aranda, Roheim reports an alternative kin structure among the Nambutji of Central Australia:

> The future father-in-law goes about with his son-in-law after initiation and regularly has intercourse with him. They call the younger man the "boy-wife" of the elder one. As a sort of compensation for this intercourse, in which he is made to accept the passive role, he then receives the daughter of his "husband" as his wife. (1932, p. 51)

Herdt (1984) notes a parallel of this unusual system among the Jaquai of Irian Jaya. Alongside this variant, the "Nambutji also practice homosexuality with the brother-in-law" (Roheim, 1950, p. 119).

Furthermore, sexual relations between women were widespread in central Australia. Roheim (1933, p. 238; [see also Strehlow, 1913]) notes that the women are "usually cross-cousins (*ilchila*), for the cross-cousin is the proper person for all kinds of sexual intimacy." As well, in a stray sentence in another text, Roheim writes, "two women of Tauru (Fergusson Island), cross-cousins, ran away into the inland and lived there, mutually doing cunnilingus to each other" (1950, p. 174).

Finally, evidence from Amazonia supports the power of kinship structures to define intimate and erotic relations between same-sex persons. Stephen Hugh-Jones (1979, p. 110) observes a high level of intimacy among initiated Barasana bachelors: "A young man will often lie in a hammock with his 'brother-in-law', nuzzling him, fondling his penis, and talking quietly often about sexual exploits with women." Hugh-Jones is uncertain if this behavior leads to "sexual satisfaction." Among the Nambikwara, Levi-Strauss found

> The brother-in-law is ally, collaborator, and friend. . . . In the same band, the potential brother-in-law, that is, the cross-cousin is the one with whom, as an adolescent, one indulges in homosexual

activities which will always leave their mark in the mutually affectionate behavior of the adults. (1969, pp. 483-484)

CONCLUSION

Age-structured homosexuality appears in one "slice" through the
ethnographic literature. Besides this clearly intra-gender form is the
trans-gender form best known in the Polynesian *mahu* and North
American *berdache* (Callender & Kochems, 1983; Jacobs, 1968; Katz,
1976, ch. 4). Juxtaposition of these "macro" structures shows that
homosexuality is a relationship with extraordinarily protean content. For
participants in age-graded forms, for example, homosexual relations
masculinize youths, while for trans-gender forms, they are part of the
feminization of male participants. One might suggest that Melanesians
think dialectically, using the insemination of youths as a solution to the
supposed femininity of boys, while societies with trans-gender forms
think positivistically, seeing homosexuality as one element among many
confirming the trans-gender nature of one participant in a homosexual
relationship. Herdt (1981) points out that the contrary-to-orthodox meaning occurred to at least one Sambian youth who wondered if fellatio might
"really" feminize him. Thus, whereas the age-structured form is more
often universal but transitory, the trans-gender form applies to only a few
men and women, but more often as a long-term "career."

With the inextricable relationship between gender meanings and the
division of labor by sex, we are left to ponder how intimacy, within and
across genders, is infused by the particulars of those tasks. In gender-
polarized societies, homosexual relations are prominent within gender-
segregated sectors such as the military, monasteries, or the domestic
realm of co-wives. With low gender differentiation, homosexual relations
are often socially recognized between gender-consistent and gender-
mixed persons in an analogy to the heterosexual division of labor.

More complex divisions of labor may stimulate sexual specialization,
allowing for the development of exclusive homosexuality (though still
gender-age-kin structured) in certain sectors. The association of trans-
gender forms with shamans and itinerant entertainers, especially in Asia,
Indonesia, and the Middle East, may be the structural counterpart to the
intra-gender military and monastic forms of ancient and imperial societies. Finally, the current structure of the lesbian and gay worlds shows
radical breaks with both the intra- and trans-genderist forms and merits
analysis of its own to determine how intimacy is expressed within a
capitalist context (see Adam, 1986).

The anthropological evidence challenges the deeply held western characterization of homosexuality as entirely alien to gender, kinship, and economy, revealing homosexual relations as inextricably involved in the larger articulation of social relationships. Indeed, it clarifies the uniqueness and particularity of the modern structuring of homosexuality into a gay world when compared to precapitalist forms.

REFERENCES

'Abd Allah, M. M. (1917). Siwan customs. *Harvard African Studies, 1*, 7.

Adam, B. D. (1981, August). *Christianity, social tolerance and homosexuality: A symposium.* Paper presented to the Society for the Study of Social Problems, Toronto, Canada.

Adam, B. D. (1986). *The rise of a gay and lesbian movement.* Boston: GK Hall/Twayne.

Allen, M. R. (1967). *Male cults and secret initiations in Melanesia.* Melbourne: Melbourne University Press.

Baal, J. van (1966). *Dema.* Hague: Martinus Nijhoff.

Belgrave, C. (1923). *Siwa.* London: John Lane, The Bodley Head.

Callender, C., & Kochems, L. (1983). The North American berdache. *Current Anthropology, 23*(4), 443.

Cline, W. (1936). Notes on the people of Siwah and El Garah in the Libyan desert. *General Series in Anthropology, 4.* Menasha, WI: George Banta.

Deacon, A. (1934). *Malekula.* London: George Routledge & Sons.

Dover, K. J. (1978). *Greek homosexuality.* New York: Vintage Books.

Evans-Pritchard, E. E. (1937). *Witchcraft, oracles and magic among the Azande.* Oxford: Clarendon.

Evans-Pritchard, E. E. (1970). Sexual inversion among the Azande. *American Anthropologist, 72*, 1430.

Evans-Pritchard, E. E. (1971). *The Azande.* Oxford: Clarendon.

Harrisson, T. (1937). *Savage civilization.* London: Victor Gallancz.

Herdt, G. (1981). *Guardians of the flutes.* New York: McGraw-Hill.

Herdt, G. (1984). *Ritualized homosexuality in Melanesia.* Berkeley: University of California Press.

Hugh-Jones, S. (1979). *The palm and the Pleiades.* New York: Cambridge University Press.

Ihara, S. (1972). *Comrade loves of the Samurai.* Rutland, VT: Charles E. Tuttle.

Irigaray, L. (1981). When the goods get together. In E. Marks & I. de Courtivron (Eds.), *New French feminisms.* New York: Schocken.

Jacobs, S. (1968). Berdache. *Colorado Anthropologist, 1*(1), 25.

Kaberry, P. (1939). *Aboriginal woman.* London: Routledge & Kegan Paul.

Katz, S. (1976). *Gay American history.* New York: Crowell.

Kelly, R. (1976). Witchcraft and sexual relations. In P. Brown & G. Buchbinder (Eds.), *Man and woman in the New Guinea highlands.* Washington: American Anthropological Association.

Layard, J. (1942). *Stone men of Malekula.* London: Chatto & Windus.

Layard, J. (1958). Homo-eroticism in primitive society as a function of the self. *Journal of Analytical Psychology, 3*, 110.

Levi-Strauss, C. (1963). *Structural anthropology.* New York: Basic Books.

Levi-Strauss, C. (1969). *The elementary structures of kinship.* Boston: Beacon Press.

Mathews, R. H. (1900). Native tribes of Western Australia. *Proceedings of the American Philosophical Society, 39*(161), 125.

Maugham, (n.d.) *Journey to Siwa.* New York: Harcourt Brace.

Purcell, H. (1893). Rites and customs of Australian aborigines. *Verhandlungen der Berliner Gesellschaft fur Anthropologie, Ethnologie und Urgeschichte, 287.*

Roheim, G. (1932). Psycho-analysis of primitive cultural types. *International Journal of Psycho-Analysis, 13*, 51.

Roheim, G. (1933). Women and their life in Central Australia. *Journal of the Royal Anthropological Institute of Great Britain and Ireland, 63*, 238.

Roheim, G. (1950). *Psychoanalysis and anthropology.* New York: International Universities Press.

Rubel, P., & Rosman, A. (1978). *Your own pigs you may not eat.* Chicago: University of Chicago Press.

Shively, D. (1970). Tokugawa Tsunayoshi, the Genroku Shogun. In A. Craig & D. Shively (Eds.), *Personality in Japanese history.* Berkeley: University of California.

Strehlow, C. (1913). *Das soziale Leben der Aranda und Loritje.* [Translation] New Haven, CT: Human Relations Area Files.

Tuzin, D. (1980). *The voice of the Tambaran.* Berkeley: University of California Press.

Ungaretti, J. (1978). Pederasty, heroism, and the family in Classical Greece. *Journal of Homosexuality, 3,* 291-300.

Williams, F. E. (1936). *Papuans of the trans-fly.* London: Oxford University Press.

Wilson, M. (1951). *Good company.* Boston: Beacon Press.

The Hijras of India: Cultural and Individual Dimensions of an Institutionalized Third Gender Role

Serena Nanda, PhD
John Jay College of Criminal Justice (CUNY)

ABSTRACT. The hijra (eunuch/transvestite) is an institutionalized third gender role in India. Hijra are neither male nor female, but contain elements of both. As devotees of the Mother Goddess Bahuchara Mata, their sacred powers are contingent upon their asexuality. In reality, however, many hijras are prostitutes. This sexual activity undermines their culturally valued sacred role. This paper discusses religious meanings of the hijra role, as well as the ways in which individuals and the community deal with the conflicts engendered by their sexual activity.

The hijra, an institutionalized third gender role in India, is "neither male nor female," containing elements of both. The hijra are commonly believed by the larger society to be intersexed, impotent men, who undergo emasculation in which all or part of the genitals are removed. They adopt female dress and some other aspects of female behavior. Hijras traditionally earn their living by collecting alms and receiving payment for performances at weddings, births and festivals. The central feature of their culture is their devotion to Bahuchara Mata, one of the many Mother Goddesses worshipped all over India, for whom emasculation is carried out. This identification with the Mother Goddess is the source both of the hijras' claim for their special place in Indian society and the traditional belief in their power to curse or confer blessings on male infants.

The census of India does not enumerate hijras separately so their exact

Serena Nanda, PhD, is Professor of Anthropology at John Jay College of Criminal Justice (CUNY), 445 West 59th Street, New York, New York 10019.

For their assistance is developing the ideas in this paper, grateful acknowledgement is made to Joseph Carrier, David Greenberg, A.M. Shah, Rajni Chopra, Evelyn Blackwood, John Money, the participants of the Columbia University Seminar on the Indian Self, and most especially, Owen Lynch and Alan Roland. I am also grateful to Mrs. Banu Vasudevan, Bharati Gowda, and Shiv Ram Apte, as well as my friends among the hijras, without whom this paper could not have been written.

numbers are unknown. Estimates quoted in the press range from 50,000 (*India Today*, 1982) to 500,000 (*Tribune*, 1983). Hijras live predominantly in the cities of North India, where they find the greatest opportunity to perform their traditional roles, but small groups of hijras are found all over India, in the south as well as the north. Seven "houses," or subgroups, comprise the hijra community; each of these has a guru or leader, all of whom live in Bombay. The houses have equal status, but one, Laskarwallah, has the special function of mediating disputes which arise among the others. Each house has its own history, as well as rules particular to it. For example, members of a particular house are not allowed to wear certain colors. Hijra houses appear to be patterned after the *gharanas* (literally, houses), or family lineages among classical musicians, each of which is identified with its own particular musical style. Though the culturally distinct features of the hijra houses have almost vanished, the structural feature remains.[1]

The most significant relationship in the hijra community is that of the *guru* (master, teacher) and *chela* (disciple). When an individual decides to (formally) join the hijra community, he is taken to Bombay to visit one of the seven major gurus, usually the guru of the person who has brought him there. At the initiation ritual, the guru gives the novice a new, female name. The novice vows to obey the guru and the rules of the community. The guru then presents the new chela with some gifts.

The chela, or more likely, someone on her behalf, pays an initiation fee and the guru writes the chela's name in her record book. This guru-chela relationship is a lifelong bond of reciprocity in which the guru is obligated to help the chela and the chela is obligated to be loyal and obedient to the guru.[2] Hijras live together in communes generally of about 5 to 15 members, and the heads of these local groups are also called guru. Hijras make no distinctions within their community based on caste origin or religion, although in some parts of India, Gujerat, for example, Muslim and Hindu hijras reportedly live apart (Salunkhe, 1976). In Bombay, Delhi, Chandigarh and Bangalore, hijras of Muslim, Christian, and Hindu origin live in the same houses.

In addition to the hierarchical guru-chela relationship, there is fictive kinship by which hijras relate to each other. Rituals exist for "taking a daughter" and the "daughters" of one "mother" consider themselves "sisters" and relate on a reciprocal, affectionate basis. Other fictive kinship relations, such as "grandmother" or "mother's sister" (aunt) are the basis of warm and reciprocal regard. Fictive kin exchange small amounts of money, clothing, jewelry and sweets to formalize their relationship. Such relationships connect hijras all over India, and there is a constant movement of individuals who visit their gurus and fictive kin in different cities. Various annual gatherings, both religious and secular, attract thousands of hijras from all over India.[3]

The extant literature on the hijras is scant, confusing, misleading, contradictory, and judgmental. With few exceptions (Salunkhe, 1976; Sinha, 1967) it lacks a basis in fieldwork or intensive interviewing. A major dispute in that literature has been whether or not the hijra role encompasses homosexuality.

In my view, the essential cultural aspect of the hijra role is its asexual nature. Yet, empirical evidence also indicates that many hijras do engage in homosexual activity. This difference between the cultural ideal and the real behavior causes a certain amount of conflict within the community. The present paper, based on a year's fieldwork among hijra communes in various parts of India, examines both the cultural ideal of asexuality and the behavioral dimension of homosexuality, and how the conflict is experienced and handled within the community.

CULTURAL DIMENSIONS OF THE HIJRA ROLE

Hijras as Neither Man nor Woman

A commonly told story among hijras, which conceptualizes them as a separate, third gender, connects them to the Hindu epic, the *Ramayana:*

> In the time of the Ramayana, Ram . . . had to leave Ayodhya (his native city) and go into the forest for 14 years. As he was going, the whole city followed him because they loved him so. As Ram came to . . . the edge of the forest, he turned to the people and said, "Ladies and gents, please wipe your tears and go away." But these people who were not men and not women did not know what to do. So they stayed there because Ram did not ask them to go. They remained there 14 years and snake hills grew around them. When Ram returned from Lanka, he found many snake hills. Not knowing why they were there he removed them and found so many people with long beards and long nails, all meditating. And so they were blessed by Ram. And that is why we hijras are so respected in Ayodhya.

Individual hijras also speak of themselves as being "separate," being "neither man nor woman," being "born as men, but not men," or being "not perfect men." Hijras are most clearly "not men" in relation to their claimed inability and lack of desire to engage in the sexual act as men with women, a consequence of their claimed biological intersexuality and their subsequent castration. Thus, hijras are unable to reproduce children, especially sons, an essential element in the Hindu concept of the normal, masculine role for males.

But if hijras are "not men," neither are they women, in spite of several aspects of feminine behavior associated with the role. These behaviors include dressing as women, wearing their hair long, plucking (rather than shaving) their facial hair, adopting feminine mannerisms, taking on women's names, and using female kinship terms and a special, feminized vocabulary. Hijras also identify with a female goddess or as wives of certain male deities in ritual contexts. They claim seating reserved for "ladies only" in public conveyances. On one occasion, they demanded to be counted as women in the census.[4]

Although their role requires hijras to dress like women, few make any real attempt to imitate or to "pass" as women. Their female dress and mannerisms are exaggerated to the point of caricature, expressing sexual overtones that would be considered inappropriate for ordinary women in their roles as daughters, wives, and mothers. Hijra performances are burlesques of female behavior. Much of the comedy of their behavior derives from the incongruities between their behavior and that of traditional women. They use coarse and abusive speech and gestures in opposition to the Hindu ideal of demure and restrained femininity. Further, it is not at all uncommon to see hijras in female clothing sporting several days growth of beard, or exposing hairy, muscular arms. The ultimate sanction of hijras to an abusive or unresponsive public is to lift their skirts and expose the mutilated genitals. The implicit threat of this shameless, and thoroughly unfeminine, behavior is enough to make most people give them a few cents so they will go away. Most centrally, as hijras themselves acknowledge, they are not born as women, and cannot reproduce. Their impotence and barrenness, due to a deficient or absent male organ, ultimately precludes their being considered fully male; yet their lack of female reproductive organs or female sexual organs precludes their being considered fully female.

Indian belief and the hijra's own claims commonly attribute the impotence of the hijra as male to a hermaphroditic morphology and physiology. Many informants insisted "I was born this way," implying hermaphroditism; such a condition is the standard reason given for joining the community. Only one of 30 informants, however, was probably born intersexed. Her words clearly indicate how central this status is to the hijra role, and make explicit that hijras are not males because they have no male reproductive organ:

> From my childhood I am like this. From birth my organ was very small. My mother tried taking me to doctors and all but the doctors said, "No, it won't grow, your child is not a man and not a woman, this is God's gift and all . . ." From that time my mother would dress me in girl's clothes. But then she saw it was no use, so she sent me to live with the hijras. I am a real hijra, not like those others who

are converts; they are men and can have children, so they have the (emasculation) operation, but I was born this way. (Field notes, 1981-2)

Hijra Impotence and Creative Asceticism

If, in Indian reality, the impotent male is considered useless as a man because he is unable to procreate, in Indian mythology, impotence can be transformed into generativity through the ideal of *tapasya*, or the practice of asceticism. *Tapas*, the power that results from ascetic practices and sexual abstinence, becomes an essential feature in the process of creation. Ascetics appear throughout Hindu mythology in procreative roles. In one version of the Hindu creation myth, Siva carries out an extreme, but legitimate form of tapasya, that of self-castration. Because the act of creation he was about to undertake had already been accomplished by Brahma, Siva breaks off his linga (phallus), saying, "there is no use for this linga . . ." and throws it into the earth. His act results in the fertility cult of linga-worship, which expresses the paradoxical theme of creative asceticism (O'Flaherty, 1973). This theme provides one explanation of the positive role given the hijras in Indian society. Born intersexed and impotent, unable themselves to reproduce, hijras can, through the emasculation operation, transform their liability into a source of creative power which enables them to confer blessings of fertility on others.

The link between the Hindu theme of creative asceticism and the role and power of the hijras is explicitly articulated in the myths connecting them to their major point of religious identification—their worship of Bahuchara Mata, and her requirement that they undergo emasculation. Bahuchara was a pretty, young maiden in a party of travelers passing through the forest in Gujerat. The party was attacked by thieves, and, fearing they would outrage her modesty, Bahuchara drew her dagger and cut off her breast, offering it to the outlaws in place of her body. This act, and her ensuing death, led to Bahuchara's deification and the practice of self-mutilation and sexual abstinence by her devotees to secure her favor.

Bahuchara has a special connection to the hijras because they are impotent men who undergo emasculation. This connection derives special significance from the story of King Baria of Gujerat. Baria was a devout follower of Bahucharaji, but was unhappy because he had no son. Through the goddess' favor a son, Jetho, was born to him. The son, however, was impotent. The King, out of respect to the goddess, set him apart for her service. Bahucharaji appeared to Jetho in a dream and told him to cut off his genitalia and dress himself as a woman, which he did. This practice has been followed by all who join the hijra cult (Mehta, 1946).

Emasculation is the *dharm* (caste duty) of the hijras, and the chief source of their uniqueness. The hijras carry it out in a ritual context, in which the client sits in front of a picture of the goddess Bahuchara and repeats her name while the operation is being performed. A person who survives the operation becomes one of Bahuchara Mata's favorites, serving as a vehicle of her power through their symbolic rebirth. While the most popular image of Bahuchara is that of the goddess riding on a cock, Shah (1961) suggests that her original form of worship was the *yantra*, a conventional symbol for the vulva. A relation between this representation of the goddess and emasculation may exist: emasculation certainly brings the hijra devotee into a closer identification with the female object of devotion.

Identification of the hijras with Bahuchara specifically and through her, with the creative powers of the Mother Goddess worshipped in many different forms in India, is clearly related to their major cultural function, that of performing at homes where a male child has been born. During these performances the hijras, using sexual innuendos, inspect the genitals of the infant whom they hold in their arms as they dance. The hijras confer fertility, prosperity, and health on the infant and family.

At both weddings and births, hijras hold the power to bless and to curse, and families regard them ambivalently. They have both auspicious functions and inauspicious potential. In regard to the latter, charms are used during pregnancy against eunuchs, both to protect against stillbirth, and a transformation of the embryo from male to female. Hiltebeitel (1980) suggests that the presence of eunuchs at birth and weddings:

> marks the ambiguity of those moments when the nondifferentiation of male and female is most filled with uncertainty and promise—in the mystery that surrounds the sexual identity of the still unborn child and on that [occasion] which anticipates the re-union of male and female in marital sex. (p. 168)

Thus, it is fitting that the eunuch-transvestites, themselves characterized by sexual ambiguity, have ritual functions at moments that involve sexual ambiguity.

The eunuch-transvestite role of the hijras links them not only to the Mother Goddess, but also to Siva, through their identification with Arjuna, the hero of the Mahabharata. One origin myth of the hijras is the story of Arjuna's exile. He lives incognito for one year as part of the price he must pay for losing a game of dice, and also for rejecting the advances of one of the celestial nymphs. Arjuna decides to hide himself in the guise of a eunuch-transvestite, wearing bangles made of white conch, braiding his hair like a woman, clothing himself in female attire, and serving the ladies of the King's court (Rajagopalchari, 1980). Some hijras say that whoever is born on Arjuna's day, no matter where in the world, will

become a hijra. Hiltebeitel (1980) makes a persuasive case for the identification of Arjuna with Siva, especially in his singer/dancer/eunuch/
transvestite role.

The theme of the eunuch state is elaborated in a number of ways in the
Mahabharata, and it is Arjuna who is the theme's central character. Arjuna, in the disguise of eunuch-transvestite, participates in weddings and
births, and thus provides a further legitimatization for the ritual contexts
in which the hijras perform. At one point, for example, Arjuna in this
disguise helps prepare the King's daughter for her marriage and her
future role as mother-to-be. In doing this, he refuses to marry the princess
himself, thus renouncing not only his sovereignty, but also the issue of an
heir. His feigned impotence paves the way for the birth of the princess'
child, just as the presence of the impotent hijras at the home of a male
child paves the way for the child's fertility and the continuation of the
family line.

This evidence suggests that intersexuality, impotence, emasculation
and transvestism are all variously believed to be part of the hijra role, accounting for their inability to reproduce and the lack of desire (or the
renunciation of the desire) to do so. In any event, sexual abstinence,
which Hindu mythology associates with the powers of the ascetic, is in
fact, the very source of the hijras' powers. The hijras themselves
recognize this connection: They frequently refer to themselves as *sannyasin*, the person who renounces his role in society for the life of a holy
wanderer and begger. This vocation requires renunciation of material
possessions, the duties of caste, the life of the householder and family
man, and, most particularly, the renunciation of sexual desire (*kama*). In
claiming this vocation, hijras point out how they have abandoned their
families, live in material poverty, live off the charity of others, and "do
not have sexual desires as other men do."

Hijras understand that their "other-worldliness" brings them respect
in society, and that if they do not live up to these ideals, they will damage
that respect. But just as Hindu mythology contains many stories of
ascetics who renounce desire but nevertheless are moved by desire to
engage in sexual acts, so, too, the hijra community experiences the tension between their religious, ascetic ideal and the reality of the individual
human's desire and sensuality.

INDIVIDUAL DIMENSIONS OF THE HIJRA ROLE

Hijras as Homosexuals

The remainder of this paper focuses on the sexual activities of hijras,
and the ways in which the community experiences the conflict between
the real and the ideal.

A widespread belief in India is that hijras are intersexed persons claimed or kidnapped by the hijra community as infants. No investigator has found evidence to support this belief. Given the large and complex society of India, the hijra community attracts different kinds of persons, most of whom join voluntarily as teenagers or adults. In appears to be a magnet for persons with a wide range of cross-gender characteristics arising from either a psychological or organic condition (Money & Wiedeking, 1980). The hijra role accommodates different personalities, sexual needs, and gender identities without completely losing its cultural meaning.

While the core of the positive meaning attached to the hijra role is linked to the negation of sexual desire, the reality is that many hijras do, in fact, engage in sexual activities. Because sexual behavior is contrary to the definition of the role such activity causes conflict for both the individuals and the community. Individual hijras deal with the conflict in different ways, while the community as a whole resorts to various mechanisms of social control.

Though it is clear from the literature that some hijras engage in homosexual activity, there has been controversy over the centrality of this activity in the institutionalization of the role in India.[5] In his psychoanalytical study of high castes in a village in Rajasthan, Carstairs (1957) asserted that the hijra role is primarily a form of institutionalized homosexuality that developed in response to tendencies toward latent homosexuality in the Indian national character. Morris Opler (1960) contested both Carstairs' evaluation of Indian character and his assertion that hijras are primarily conceptualized as homosexuals or that they engaged in any sexual activity.

Opler argued that the cultural definition of their role in Indian society was only one of performers. Sinha (1967), who worked in Lucknow in North India, acknowledged their performing role, but treated hijras primarily as homosexuals who join the community specifically to satisfy their sexual desires. Lynton and Rajan (1974), who interviewed hijras in Hyderabad, indicate that a period of homosexual activity, involving solicitation in public, sometimes precedes a decision to join the hijras. Their informants led them to believe, however, that sexual activity is prohibited by hijra rules and that these are strictly enforced by the community elders. Freeman (1979), who did fieldwork in Orissa at the southern edge of North Indian culture, discusses hijras as transvestite prostitutes and hardly mentions their ritual roles.

My own data (Nanda, 1984), gathered through fieldwork in Bangalore and Bombay, and in several North Indian cities, confirm beyond doubt that, however deviant it may be regarded within the hijra community, hijras in contemporary India extensively engage in sexual relations with men. This phenomenon is not entirely modern; 19th-century accounts

(Bhimbhai, 1901; Faridi, 1899) claim that hijras were known to kidnap small boys for the purposes of sodomy or prostitution. Such allegations still find their way into the contemporary popular press (*India Today*, 1982).

Although hijras attribute their increased prostitution to declining opportunities to earn a living in their traditional manner, eunuch-transvestites in Hindu classical literature also had the reputation of engaging in homosexual activity. The classic Hindu manual of love, the *Kamasutra*, specifically outlines sexual practices that were considered appropriate for eunuch-transvestites to perform with male partners (Burton, 1962).[6] Classical Hinduism taught that there was a "third sex," divided into various categories, two of which were castrated men, eunuchs, and hermaphrodites, who wore false breasts, and imitated the voice, gestures, dress and temperaments of women. These types shared the major function of providing alternative techniques of sexual gratification (Bullough, 1976). In contemporary India, concepts of eunuch, transvestite and male homosexual are not distinct, and the hijras are considered all of these at once (O'Flaherty, 1980).

The term hijra, however, which is of Urdu origin and the masculine gender, has the primary meaning of hermaphrodite. It is usually translated as eunuch, never as homosexual. Even Carstairs' informants, among whom the homosexuality of the hijras was well known, defined them as either drum players at the birth of male children, or eunuchs, whose duty was to undergo castration. In parts of North India, the term for effeminate males who play the passive role in homosexual relations is *zenanas* (women); by becoming a hijra, one removes oneself from this category (see also Lynton & Rajan, 1974). Furthermore, a covert homosexual subculture exists in some of the larger cities in North India (Anderson, 1977), but persons who participate in it are not called hijras. In fact, as in other cultures (Carrier, 1980; Wikan, 1977) men who play the insertor role in sexual activities between men have no linguistically or sociologically distinguished role. Unlike western cultures, in India sexual object choice alone does not define gender. In some South Indian regional languages, the names by which hijras are called, such as *kojja* in Telegu (Anderson, 1977) or *potee* in Tamil, are, unlike the term *hijra*, epithets used derogatorily to mean a cowardly or feminine male or homosexual. This linguistic difference, however, is consistent with the fact that in South India the hijras do not have the cultural role which they do in North India.

According to my research, homosexual activity is widespread among hijras, and teenage homosexual activity figures significantly in the lives of many individuals who join the community. As Sinha's interviews also indicate (1967), those hijras who engage in homosexual activity share particular life patterns before joining the community. Typically, such individuals liked during childhood to dress in feminine clothes, play with girls, do traditionally female work, and avoid the company of boys in rough play. In lower class families, the boy's effeminacy is both ridiculed and encouraged by his peers, who may persuade him to play the insertee role for them, possibly with some slight monetary consideration. At this stage the boy lives with his family, though in an increasingly tense atmosphere. He thinks of himself as a male and wears male clothing, at least in public. As his interest in homosexual activity increases, and his relations with his family become more strained, he may leave home. In most cases their families make serious attempts to inhibit their feminine activity with scoldings, surveillance, restrictions, and beatings, so that the boy finally has no choice but to leave.[7]

There are two modes of sexual relations among hijras. One is casual prostitution, the exchange of sexual favors with different men for a fixed sum of money, and the other is "having a husband." Hijras do not characterize their male sexual partners as homosexuals; they quite explicitly distinguish them as being different than homosexuals. One hijra, Shakuntala, characterizes the customers in the following way:

> these men . . . are married or unmarried, they may be the father of many children. Those who come to us, they have no desire to go to a man . . . they come to us for the sake of going to a girl. They prefer us to their wives . . . each one's tastes differ among people. . . . It is God's way; because we have to make a living, he made people like this so we can earn. (Field notes, 1981-2)

Shakuntala clearly expressed a feminine gender identity and was, in fact, the person who came closest to what would be called in the west a transsexual that is, experiencing himself as a "female trapped in a male body." She remembered having felt that she was a female since childhood, liking to dress in female clothing, doing woman's work inside the house and playing with girls rather than boys. She was introduced to homosexual activity in her teens, which she claims "spoiled" her for the normal, heterosexual male role. She has a very maternal, nurturing temperament, and emphasizes the maternal aspect of the guru role to her young chelas.[8] She is currently involved in a long-term, monogamous relationship with a young man who lives in her neighborhood and whom she hopes will "marry" her. She underwent the emasculation operation because she wanted "to become more beautiful, like a woman." She was the only hijra interviewed who was taking hormones "to develop a more feminine figure." She always dressed as a woman and was very convincing in a feminine role, not exhibiting the more flamboyant mannerisms and gestures of the typical hijra. Because of her strong attachment to her present boyfriend, she is sometimes criticized by her hijra friends as having "husband fever." As one of her friends says:

Those people, like Shakuntala, with husband fever, they are mad over their husbands, even to the point of suicide. If that fellow even talks to a[nother] girl, immediately they'll fight with him. If he is out at night, even if it is three o'clock in the morning, they'll go in search of him. They won't even sleep till he returns. (Field notes, 1981-2)

This devotion to one man is seen as typical of Shakuntala's extremely feminine identification.

Not all hijras who engage in sexual relations with other men express such complete feminine identification. One hijra, for example, explained the attraction of men to hijras on different grounds:

See, there is a proverb, "for a normal lady [prostitute] it is four annas and for a hijra it is twelve annas." These men, they come to us to have pleasure on their own terms. They may want to kiss us or do so many things. For instance, the customer will ask us to lift the legs (from a position lying on her back) so that they can do it through the anus. We allow them to do it by the back [anal intercourse], but not very often. (Field notes, 1981-2)

This statement suggests that the attraction of the hijras is that they will engage in forms of sexual behavior in which Indian women will normally not engage. Several of my non-hijra male informants confirmed this view.

Having a husband is the preferred alternative for those hijras who engage in sexual relations. Many of my informants have, or recently had, a relatively permanent attachment to one man whom they referred to as their husband. They maintain warm and affectionate, as well as sexually satisfying and economically reciprocal, relationships with these men, with whom they live, sometimes alone, or sometimes with several other hijras. Lalitha, a very feminine looking hijra in her middle thirties, has had the same husband for nine years. He used to come for prostitution to the hijra commune in which Lalitha lived and then they lived together in a small house until he got married. Now Lalitha has moved back with the hijras, where she cooks their meals in return for free food and lodging. But she still maintains her relationship with her "husband":

My husband is a Christian. He works in a cigarette factory and earns 1000 rupees a month. He is married to [another] woman and has got four children. I encouraged him to get married and even his wife and children are nice to me. His children call me *chitti* [mother's sister] and even his wife's parents know about me and don't say anything. He gives me saris and flowers and whenever I ask for money he never says no. When he needs money, I would give him also. (Field notes, 1981-2)

Hijras who have husbands do not break their ties with the hijra community, although sometimes their husbands urge them to do so. Sushila, an attractive, assertive, and ambitious hijra in her early thirties has a husband who is a driver for a national corporation headquarters and earns 600 rupees a month. She continues to be very active in the local hijra community, however, and even refuses to give up practicing prostitution in spite of her husband's objections:

> My husband tells me, "I earn enough money. Why do you go for prostitution?" I tell him, "You are here with me today. What surety is there you will be with me forever? I came to you from prostitution, and if you leave me, I'll have to go back to it. Then all those other hijras will say, 'Oh, she lived as a wife and now look at her fate, she has come back to prostitution.'" So I tell him, "don't put any restrictions on me; now they all think of me as someone nice, but when I go back to prostitution, they will put me to shame." If he gives me too much back talk, I give him good whacks. (Field notes, 1981-2)

Sushila is saving the money she makes from prostitution and from that her husband gives to her so that she can buy a business, probably a bathhouse for working class men. In Bangalore, bathhouses are commonly run by hijras.

Although many hijras complain that it is hard for them to save money, some have a good business sense and have invested in jewelry and property so that they can be relatively independent financially in their old age. For hijras who are not particularly talented singers and dancers, or who live in cities where their ritual performances are not in demand, prostitution provides an adequate way of earning a living. It is a demanding and even occasionally dangerous profession, however, because some customers turn out to be "rowdies." Although a hijra living in a commune has to pay 50% of her fees from prostitution to her household head, few of the younger hijra prostitutes can afford their own place; and living with others provides a certain amount of protection from rough customers and the police. In spite of the resentment and constant complaints by younger hijra prostitutes that they are exploited by their elders, they are extremely reluctant to live on their own.

Hijra Sexuality as a Source of Conflict

The attraction that the hijra role holds for some individuals is the opportunity to engage in sexual relations with men, while enjoying the

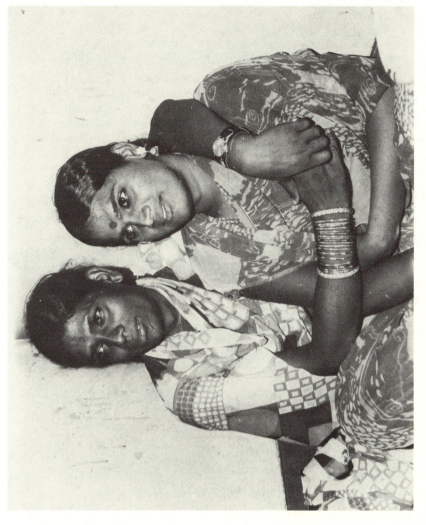

PHOTO 1. Shakuntala (left), who expresses a complete feminine identity, emphasizes the maternal aspect of her her chelas, one of whom she is pictured with here. Photo by Serena Nanda.

47

sociability and relative security of an organized community; these advantages are apparent in contrast to the insecurity and harassment experienced by the effeminate homosexual living on his own. But, whether with husbands or customers, sexual relations run counter to the cultural definitions of the hijra role, and are a source of conflict within the community. Hijra elders attempt to maintain control over those who would "spoil" the hijras' reputation by engaging in sexual activity.

Hijras are well aware that they have only a tenuous hold on respectability in Indian society, and that this respectability is compromised by even covertly engaging in sexual relations. Ascetics have always been regarded with skepticism and ambivalence in Indian society. While paying lip service to the ascetic, conventional Hinduism maintained a very real hostility to it. It classed the non-Vedic ascetic with the dregs of society, "such as incendiaries, poisoners, pimps, spies, adulterers, abortionists, atheists and drunkards"; these fringe members of society found their most respectable status among the Siva sects (O'Flaherty, 1973, p. 67). This ambivalence toward ascetics accurately describes the response of Indian society to the hijra as well, who are also, not coincidentally, worshippers of Siva. In addition, the notion of the false ascetic (those who pretend to be ascetics in order to satisfy their lust) abounds in Hindu mythology. This contradictory attitude, a high regard for asceticism coupled with disdain for those who practice it, characterizes contemporary as well as classical India. Even those families who allow the hijras to perform at births and weddings ridicule the notion that they have any real power.

Indian audiences express their ambivalence toward the hijras by challenging the authenticity of hijra performers. The hijras' emasculation distinguishes them from *zenanas*, or practicing effeminate homosexuals, who do not have the religious powers ascribed to the hijras, but who sometimes impersonate them in order to earn a living. Thus, hijras state that emasculation is necessary because, when they are performing or asking for alms, people may challenge them. If their genitals have not been removed, they will be reviled and driven away as imposters. Hijra elders themselves constantly deride those "men who are men and can have children" and join their community only to make a living from it, or to enjoy sexual relations with men. The parallel between such "fake" hijras and the false ascetics is clear.

Hijras consider sexual activity offensive to the hijra goddess, Bahuchara Mata. Upon initiation into the community, the novice vows to abstain from sexual relations or to marry. Hijra elders claim that all hijra houses lock their doors by nine o'clock at night, implying that no sexual activities occur there. In the cities where hijra culture is strongest, hijras who practice prostitution are not permitted to live with hijras who earn their living by traditional ritual performances. Those who live in these respectable or "family" houses are carefully watched to see that they do not have contact with men. In areas more peripheral to the core of hijra culture, including most of South India, prostitutes do live in houses with traditional hijra performers, and may, in fact, engage in such performances themselves whenever they have an opportunity to do so.

Sexually active hijras usually assert that all hijras join the community so that they can engage in sexual relations with men. As Sita, a particularly candid informant, said:

> Why else would we wear saris? Those who you see who are aged now, when they were young they were just like me. Now they say they haven't got the sexual feeling and they talk only of God and all, but I tell you, that is all nonsense. In their younger days, they also did this prostitution and it is only for the sexual feeling that we join. (Field notes, 1981-2)

The hijras who most vehemently denied having sexual relations with men were almost always over 40. It appears that as they get older, hijras give up sexual activity. Such change over the life cycle parallels that in India generally; in the Hindu cultural ideal, women whose sons are married are expected to give up sexual activity. In fact, not all women do so, but there is social pressure to do so. People ridicule and gossip about middle aged women who act in ways that suggest active sexual interest (Vatuk, 1985). The presentation of self as a non-sexual person that occurs with age also appears among the hijras. The elderly ones may wear male clothing in public, dress more conservatively, wearing white rather than boldly colored saris, act in a less sexually suggestive manner, and take on household domestic roles that keep them indoors.

Although hijra elders are most vocal in expressing disapproval of hijra sexual relations, even younger hijras who have husbands or practice prostitution admit that such behavior runs counter to hijra norms and lowers their status in the larger society. Hijra prostitutes say that prostitution is a necessary evil for them, the only way for them to earn a living. They attribute the frequency of hijra prostitution to the declining economic status of the hijras in India since the time of Independence. At that time the rajas and nawobs in the princely states, who were important patrons of hijra ritual performances, lost their offices. Hijras also argue that in modern India, declining family size and the spread of Western values, which undermine belief in their powers, also contributes to their lowered economic position, making prostitution necessary.

INDIA AS AN ACCOMMODATING SOCIETY

India is characteristically described as a sexually tolerant society (Bullough, 1976; Carrier, 1980). Indeed, the hijra role appears to be elastic enough to accommodate a wide variety of individual temperaments, identities, behaviors, and levels of commitment, and still function in a culturally accepted manner. This elasticity derives from the genius of Hinduism: although not every hijra lives up to the role at the highest level, the role nonetheless gives religious meaning to cross-gender behavior, that is despised, punished and pushed beyond the pale of the cultural system in other societies.

Several different aspects of Hindu thought explain both the ability of Indian society to absorb an institutionalized third gender role, as well as to provide several contexts within which to handle the tension between the ideal and real aspects of the role. Indian mythology contains numerous examples of androgynes (see O'Flaherty, 1980), impersonators of the opposite sex, and among both deities and humans individuals with sex changes. Myths are an important part of popular culture. Sivabhaktis (worshippers of Siva) give hijras special respect because one of the forms of Siva is Ardhanarisvara, ("the lord who is half woman"). Hijras also associate themselves with Vishnu, who transforms himself into Mohini, the most beautiful woman in the world, in order to take back the sacred nectar from the demons who have stolen it. Further, in the worship of Krishna, male devotees may imagine themselves to be female, and even dress in female clothing; direct identification with Krishna is forbidden, but the devotee may identify with him indirectly by identifying with Radha, that is, by taking a female form. Thousands of hijras identify themselves as Krishna's wives in a ritual performed in South India. These are only a few of the contexts within which the hijras link themselves to the Great Tradition of Hinduism and develop a positive definition for their feminine behavior.

In handling the conflict between the real and the ideal, hijras and other groups in the Indian population are confronted with the seemingly conflicting value which Hinduism places on both eroticism and procreation, on the one hand, and non-attachment and asceticism, on the other. Both Hinduism and Islam are what Bullough calls "sex-positive" religions (1976). Both allow for the tolerance of a wider range of sexual expression than exists in western culture with its restrictive Judeo-Christian, religious heritage. Hinduism explicitly recognizes that humans achieve their ultimate goals—salvation, bliss, knowledge and (sexual) pleasure—by following many different paths because humans differ in their special abilities and competencies. Thus, Hinduism allows a different ethic according to one's own nature and affords the individual temperament the widest latitude, from highly idealistic morality, through genial toleration, and, finally, to compulsive extremes (Lannoy, 1975).

Hindu thought attempts to reconcile the value conflict between sexuality and chastity through the concept of a life cycle with four stages. Each stage has its appropriate sexual behavior: In the first stage one should be a chaste student, in the second a married householder, in the third a forest

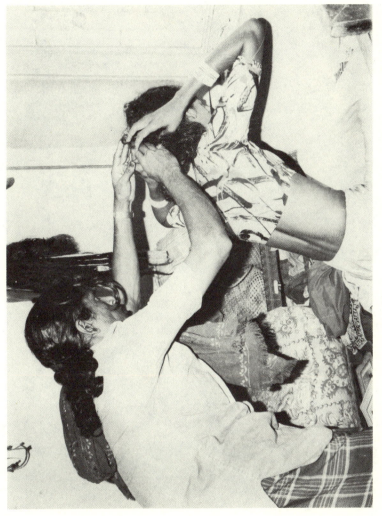

PHOTO 2. Ramachandra (left) is a hijra who was not yet fully adopted wearing women's clothing, as he works as a milkman, delivering milk on his bicycle. Here he is helping his chela, Kokila, get ready for a dance performance. Photo by Serena Nanda.

PHOTO 3. Kokila, a young hijra gets ready for a dance performance. Photo by Serena Nanda.

dweller preparing for withdrawal from society, and in the final stage, a sannyasin, the ascetic who has renounced everything. Thus, the Hindu ideal is a fully integrated life in which each aspect of human nature, including sexuality, has its time. Hijras implicitly recognize these stages in their social organization through a hierarchy in which one begins as a chela and moves into the position of guru as one gets older, taking on chelas and becoming less sexually active.

Hindu mythology also provides some contexts within which the contradictions between the ascetic ideal and the sexual activity are legitimate: Siva himself is both the great erotic and the great ascetic. In myths he alternates between the two forms. In some mythic episodes Siva is unable to reconcile his two roles as ascetic and householder, and in others he is a hypocritical ascetic because of his sexual involvement with Parvati, his consort (O'Flaherty, 1973). Indian goddesses as sexual figures also exist in abundance and in some stories a god will take on a female form specifically to have sexual relations with a male deity.

Where Western culture feels uncomfortable with contradictions and makes strenuous attempts to resolve them, Hinduism allows opposites to confront each other without a resolution, "celebrating the idea that the universe is boundlessly various, and . . . that all possibilities may exist without excluding each other" (O'Flaherty, 1973, p. 318). It is this characteristically Indian ability to tolerate, and even embrace, contradictions at social, cultural and personality levels, that provides a context for hijras. Hijras express in their very bodies the confrontation of femaleness and maleness as polar opposites. In Indian society they are not only tolerated but also valued.

NOTES

1. I would like to thank Veena Oldenburg for calling this to my attention. A similar pattern exists among the courtesans in North India (Oldenburg, 1984).

2. Alan Roland (1982) has insightfully examined some of the emotional and psychological aspects of hierarchy within the Hindu joint family, and many of his conclusions could well be applied to the hijra hierarchy.

3. Some of these religious occasions are participated in by non-hijras as well, while others celebrate events specific to the hijra community, such as the anniversary of the deaths of important gurus.

4. More recently, hijras have been issued ration cards for food in New Delhi, but must apply only under the male names.

5. A more detailed description of this literature is found in Nanda (1984) and Nanda (in press).

6. "Mouth Congress" is considered the appropriate sexual activity for eunuchs disguised as women, in the Kama Sutra. An Editor's note (Burton, 1962, p. 124) suggests that this practice is no longer common in India, and is perhaps being replaced by sodomy, which has been introduced since the Muslim period.

7. Social class factors are relevant here. Boys who are born with indeterminate sex organs (I came across three such cases by hearsay) to upper middle class families would not be likely to join the hijras. In two of these cases the men in question were adults; one had been sent abroad to develop

his career in science with the expectation that he would not marry, but at least would have the satisfaction of a successful and prestigious career. The other was married by his parents to a girl who, it was known, could not have children. The third is still a toddler and is being brought up as a boy. I also had the opportunity to interview a middle-aged, middle-class man who was desperately trying to find a doctor to perform the transsexual operation on him in a hospital. He chose not to join the hijras because of their "reputation" but envied them their group life and their ability to live openly as women.

8. Gurus are sometimes considered like mothers, sometimes like fathers, and sometimes like husbands. Their female aspect is related to the nurturing and care and concern they have for their chelas; the male aspect refers more to the authority they have over their chelas and the obedience and loyalty that is due them.

REFERENCES

Anderson, C. (1977). *Gay men in India*. Unpublished manuscript, University of Wisconsin.
Bhimbhai, K. Pavayas. (1901). Gujarat population, Hindus. In J. M. Campbell (Compiler), *Gazetteer of the Bombay Presidency, 4,* part 1. Bombay: Government Central Press.
Bradford, N. J. (1983). Transgenderism and the cult of Yellamma: Heat, sex, and sickness in South Indian ritual. *Journal of Anthropological Research, 39,* 307-322.
Bullough, V. L. (1976). *Sexual variance in society and history*. Chicago: University of Chicago Press.
Carrier, J. (1980). Homosexual behavior in cross cultural perspective. In J. Marmor (Ed.), *Homosexual behavior: A modern reappraisal* (pp. 100-122). New York: Basic Books.
Carstairs, G. M. (1957). *The twice born*. London: Hogarth Press.
Faridi, F. L. (1899). Hijras. In J. M. Campbell (Compiler), *Gazetteer of the Bombay Presidency, 9,* part 2. Bombay: Government Central Press.
Freeman, J. M. (1979). *Untouchable: An Indian life history*. Stanford, CA: Stanford University Press.
Hiltelbeitel, A. (1980). Siva, the goddess, and the disguises of the Pandavas and Draupadi. *History of Religions, 20*(1/2), 147-174.
India Today. Fear is the key. (1982, September 15), pp. 84-85.
The Kama Sutra of Vatsyayana. (1964). (R. F. Burton, Trans.). New York: E. P. Dutton.
Lannoy, R. (1975). *The speaking tree*. New York: Oxford University Press.
Lynton, H. S., & Rajan, M. (1974). *Days of the beloved*. Berkeley: University of California Press.
Mark, M. E. (1981). *Falkland Road: Prostitutes of Bombay*. New York: Knopf.
Mehta, S. (1945-1946). Eunuchs, pavaiyas and hijadas. *Gufarat ahitya Sabha*, Amdavad, Karyavahi, Part 2. Ahmedabad.
Money, J. & Wiedeking, C. (1980). *Handbook of human sexuality* (pp. 270-284). B. B. Wolman & J. Money (Eds.) Englewood Cliffs, N.J.: Prentice-Hall.
Nanda, S. (1984). The hijras of India: A preliminary report. *Medicine and Law, 3,* 59-75.
Nanda, S. (in press). Dancers only? In Murray (Ed.), *Cultural diversity and homosexualities*. New York: Longman.
O'Flaherty, W. (1973). *Asceticism and eroticism in the mythology of Siva*. London: Oxford University Press.
O'Flaherty, W. (1980). *Women, androgynes, and other mythical beasts*. Chicago: University of Chicago Press.
Oldenburg, V. (1984). *The making of colonial Lucknow*. Princeton: University Press.
Opler, M. (1960). The hijara (hermaphrodites) of India and Indian national character: A rejoinder. *American Anthropologist, 62,* 505-511.
Rajagopalachar, C. (1980). *Mahabharata*. Bombay: Bharatiya Vidya Bhavan.
Roland, A. (1982). Toward a psychoanalytical psychology of hierarchical relationships in Hindu India. *Ethos, 10*(3), 232-253.
Salunkhe, G. (1976, August 8). The cult of the hijaras. *Illustrated Weekly*, pp. 16-21.
Shah, A. M. (1961). A note on the hijaras of Gujerat. *American Anthropologist, 61,* 1325-1330.
Sinha, A. P. (1967). Procreation among the eunuchs. *Eastern Anthropologist, 20,* 168-176.
The Tribune. (1983, August 26). Five eunuchs in India, Pak. p. 2.
Vatuk, S. (1985). South Asian cultural conceptions of sexuality. In J.K. Brown & V. Kerns (Eds.), *In her prime: A new view of middle-aged women* (pp. 137-152).
Wikan, U. (1977). Man becomes woman: Transsexualism in Oman as a key to gender roles. *Man, 12,* 304-319.

Growing Yams and Men:
An Interpretation of
Kimam Male Ritualized
Homosexual Behavior

J. Patrick Gray, PhD
University of Wisconsin-Milwaukee

ABSTRACT. This paper explores the meaning of Kimam (Irian Jaya) male ritualized homosexual behavior by placing the behavior within a broad cultural context. It demonstrates that males claim to foster the growth of yams and to make men from boys by manipulating the processes of fertilization. One aspect of this manipulation involves the transfer of sperm from older males to boys. Exploration of Kimam ideas of death and burial rituals suggests that members of one village sector see their fertility as under attack by males of the opposite sector. At the conclusion of mortuary ceremonies, the two sectors engage in competitive feasts in which the successful control of fertility is symbolized by the presentation of finished products of male vitality: yams and children, especially boys. The analysis indicates that an understanding of homosexual behavior requires that attention not be restricted to the sexual behavior itself, but rather include various domains of meaning associated with it.

This paper analyzes one component in the symbolics of ritualized male homosexual behavior formerly practiced by the Kimam of Irian Jaya. The material illustrates a theme unique in the literature on ritualized homosexuality in New Guinea: competition between adult males in growing boys into men. Further, the analysis demonstrates the value of locating homosexual behavior within its total cultural context rather than viewing it as an isolated behavioral complex.

ETHNOGRAPHIC BACKGROUND

Kimam is the name given the inhabitants of Kolepom Island. Most of the island, which is just off the southern coast of Irian Jaya, is usually

J. Patrick Gray received a PhD in anthropology from the University of Colorado. His research interests include primate sociobiology, human sexual behavior, and holocultural research. He is currently an assistant professor in the Department of Anthropology, University of Wisconsin-Milwaukee, Milwaukee, Wisconsin 53201.

under water and cultivation involves creating hundreds of small garden islands built of mud and clay spread over batches of cut reeds and patches of drift grass. In 1959, villages on the island were fairly large, ranging in population from 100 to 700.

This paper utilizes the data on Bamol, the largest village in Kimam, which Laurent Serpenti studied for about 19 months between 1960 and 1962. For our purposes, Serpenti's (1965) study has three serious limitations. First, the government and the missions had suppressed the bachelor huts, where homosexual behavior had occurred, for over 15 years before his research. This forced him to rely on the recollection of middle-aged and older men. There can be no doubt that much detail is missing. Second, the study lacks data on headhunting rituals, cosmology, ethnopsychology, and other topics necessary to provide a complete contextualization of homosexual behavior. Third, and most important, the voices of females are largely absent from the study. Thus, it is impossible to provide a complete analysis of ritualized male homosexual behavior for there is little information on how females understand, interpret, or evaluate this behavior. In spite of these problems, Serpenti's material does allow glimpses of the underlying logic of ritualized homosexual behavior in Kimam culture.

The Kimam are characterized by a pervasive dualism which can be illustrated by a discussion of the social structure. Descent is bilateral, but residential practices strongly influence social behavior and create a patrilineal bias. Serpenti identifies four major levels of territorial units. The *patha* is a dwelling-island usually containing a small number of nuclear families. The patha often consists of the families of a father and his sons, or the families of a set of brothers. Within the patha generalized reciprocity is more or less the rule. *Kwanda* (village-wards) are units composed of two or more patha. The wards are comprised of an original dwelling-island and subsequent fissions. Several wards, conceptualized as being linked by now forgotten kinship ties, combine to create the most important unit in Kimam ceremonial life, the *paburu* (village sector). Finally, the *pa* (village) is composed of two ceremonially opposed paburu. The presentation below refers to the idealized situation of a village having only two paburu.

Marriage ideally involves sister exchange between males belonging to different kwanda of the same paburu. Villagers believe incest is disgusting and dangerous, and do not permit first cousins to marry. Upon marriage the wife usually resides with her husband's kinsmen (patri-virilocal residence). Inter-paburu and even inter-village marriages do occur, but are responses to shortages of marriage partners and not ideal. The nuclear family is the residential unit, and married men sleep in the same hut with their wives and children.

Two features of the Kimam male initiation rites are pertinent to the study of ritualized homosexuality. The first is that the feasts marking transitions within the initiation sequence can only be held during the final mortuary ceremonies for deceased members of the paburu. Secondly, the sperm utilized to grow a boy is not donated by males in the opposite paburu, but must come from males within the boy's village sector. Given the New Guinea pattern of opposed groups initiating one another's sons (Herdt, 1982b; Williams, 1936), this practice appears unusual. These two features of male homosexual behavior become meaningful, however, when placed in their cultural context—the domains of yam growing, rites of passage for children, and burial rituals.

GROWING YAMS

In common with many Melanesian societies (Sillitoe, 1981) food serves as a gender marker in Kimam. Women collect food and males cultivate it. Root crops are the major responsibility of males and entail a division of labor based on age, planting skill, and ability to control fertility through magic. Younger males, who lack skills and magic, grow nonceremonial crops such as sweet potatoes and cassava.[1] These, together with sago palms and flour made from a fern collected by women, comprise the bulk of the everyday diet. Older men grow the ceremonial crops of yams and taro which are displayed and presented to opponents at competitive ceremonial feasts. Yams are the major ceremonial crop, with taro an acceptable substitute when conditions demand. The origin myth of the yam concerns a woman who gave birth to a child with one arm and one leg. The child had requested upright burial and when the grave was opened later, the child had become a yam. Outer layers of the original yam were taken by various villages until only the innermost part remained to be claimed by the village of Wanggambi. This village is the place where the dead start their journey to the underground. It provides one of many associations between yams and death. Although a woman was responsible for the first yam, males assert that there is now an antipathy between women and yams. Sexual intercourse is banned when yam magic is in effect, and women rarely eat yams because they might be harmed by the strong magic used to grow them.

The Kimam see yams as children magically grown by men with the aid of female spirits, who are also controlled by masculine magic. The most important feature of this magic is that it can be strengthened, weakened, or even lost. Further, a major theme of Kimam ceremonial life is the demonstration of the continued strength of the paburu's masculine magic.

All men may become yam sorcerers, but Serpenti notes that only a few in each paburu will have the strength to complete the training at the hands of older sorcerers and win acceptance by the spirits. Therefore, a yam sorcerer usually has a following of men who get their magic from him and plant it in their gardens. This theme is encountered in other areas of Kimam life: Older men who control magic pass on their fertility-creating magic on to young, magically weaker, males. However, a man cannot receive yam magic from a sorcerer in a different paburu. Since the main competitive feasts are between paburu, these feasts implicitly compare the strength of the fertility controlled by the men in each unit.

The planting of the yams does not involve a major ritual. The yam sorcerer simply prepares medicine and sprays saliva over the plant mounds in the gardens to make the yams grow quickly. Serpenti argues that the planting of a yam is equivalent to the burial of a human, an event also not marked by a major ritual. However, there is a key difference: when yams are planted, the only people present are the males of the paburu, while males of the opposite paburu conduct the burial of a human.

The first major ritual occurs when the shoot separates from the "mother" tuber. At this time a taboo is placed on sexual intercourse within the paburu. In one of the songs performed during this ritual the yam requests that its "mother" not approach her human grower too closely, lest the yam be overwhelmed by the father's magic and die. After the yam is "born" the yam beds are placed off limits to ordinary members of the paburu. Women and children stay away from the beds as protection against the strong magic there. Men are not to approach each others' gardens even if they are followers of the same yam sorcerer.

The yam birth occasions the most important fertility ritual, since it is only by male magic that yams (and humans) leave the influence of their mothers and grow big and strong. While singing, the yam sorcerer and his followers mix various ingredients. In the songs the new yam tells its mother that it is not yet out of the earth but that its friends will soon come to measure it and see how big it is. The men intersperse these songs with others calling on female spirits and containing words glossed as "belly" and "pregnant." Serpenti suggests that the Kimam believe that these spirits give birth to the adult yam.

The yam sorcerer shapes the mixture into a plant mount, places it over a previously dug hole, and refers to it by the word translated as "pregnant." A man waves bundled red leaves over this mound while others sing songs referring to how large the yam will grow. Later in the ceremony songs refer to young female dancers, pregnancy, and sexual intercourse. At the end of the day the sorcerer adds more saliva to the mixture. He fashions a long rod-shaped projection on top of the mound over which he places the leaves. The leaves are then covered with coconut shells. Later he reopens the hole and cuts the mound into pieces which are given to his followers. These pieces are to be planted in their gardens so that the scent of the mixture will enter each yam and cause it to grow. Care must be taken that not too much magic is introduced into the garden, or the yams will die.

The same ritual is repeated when the top of the tuber protrudes from the mound. The sorcerer blows saliva over the yam and smears it with medicine. The next ritual occurs when the leaves wither and the largest yams are measured. The sorcerer loosens the earth around the yams and measures their length and width with the rib of a sago leaf. At the final ritual the coconut shells used in the magic are thrown away. Because the yam is now strong enough not to be harmed, sexual intercourse may resume in the paburu. A few days later the yams are harvested at the direction of the sorcerer, who smears medicine on them and covers them with mud and grass in order to keep their size a secret from opponents in competitive feasts.

The Kimam believe that a man who eats his own yams is disgusting and runs the risk of illness or accidents. Their attitude toward incest is similar. Since they explicitly equate eating with sexual intercourse, a man eating his own yams would be committing incest. Thus, a man should present his yams at a competitive feast to a non-relative in the opposite paburu. The tubers are so filled with magic that the recipient must have the grower symbolically cut them before they are fit for consumption. Even then, women may not eat them, and will usually give them to their older children.

This brief review of yam ritual indicates that males see themselves as growing weak yam children into strong yam adults without the help of human females. Males make the same claim with regard to men.

GROWING MEN

Unfortunately, Serpenti does not discuss Kimam ideas of male and female essences, the process of conception, or the nourishing of the fetus. There is enough material, however, to indicate the outlines of the metaphorical relation between children, especially boys, and yams and between yam medicines and semen.

Kimam males believe an antagonism exists between the fetus and yams. A man whose wife is pregnant avoids both planting ceremonial crops and associating with those who have planted them. The power of the magically grown crops would be too strong for the frail fetus. Kimam exhibit both a post-partum sex taboo and a couvade, in which male activity is restricted after the birth of an infant. Among other restrictions, the father must continue to avoid yams. Further, he must not view the newborn child until its navel string has dropped off. To do so would cause the infant to grow too quickly. Both the post-partum sex taboo and the fear of too rapid growth induced by contact with strong maculine magic are found in the yam rituals.

The growth of children is marked by a number of rites of passage such as hair cutting, piercing the ear, piercing the nasal septum, etc., which contain certain common features. First, these rites occur only when a paburu celebrates the competitive feast marking the last mortuary ritual for a member of the unit. Second, in the pre-initiation rites the individual who pierces the child's body is a close relative of the father residing in the opposite paburu. Finally, the rituals occur upon what may be called a food pile. The father arranges a heap of yams and other food and places a pig on top. While seated on the pig the child's hair or blood, depending upon the rite, falls on the food. The food is distributed to the opposite paburu. In these rites the food pile and the child's growth are statements about the strength of the father's, and by extension, the paburu's, magic.

These rituals are conducted for both male and female children. Unfortunately, Serpenti's monograph does not contain enough information on the transition from girlhood to womanhood to permit an exploration of its symbolism. Therefore, the remainder of the discussion will focus on the men's claim to the ability to grow boys into adult men.

The most important ceremonial sequence in growing men involves the rituals of the bachelors' hut. The huts are larger versions of the ordinary dwelling house and each paburu has one or more. Women cannot enter the huts, and it is forbidden for a member of one paburu to enter a hut of the other. Because the entry ceremony can only be held in conjunction with a final mortuary ceremony, the age of boys at entry varies; Serpenti notes that it is usually from 10 to 14 years.

The entry ceremony is a burial rite. The boy's older relatives paint his face with the same paint and designs used for a corpse. They construct a raft similar to that used to transport the dead to the gravesite. On this raft they prepare a food pile upon which the boy sits. Women mourn the boy's death, jerking his hands and legs as they do with a corpse. Members of the opposite paburu row the boy to the dancing ground. When he arrives, a member of the opposite paburu presents him to the group and throws a mourning hood over his head, stopping all dancing and drumming (drums and dancing are taboo within a paburu during the mourning rites of a member). The men of the boy's paburu take him immediately to the bachelors' hut and the men of the opposite paburu go home.

When the boy enters the hut he becomes a *munaka*, a first stage novice. A "mentor" who is a *tjutjine*, a second stage initiate, takes charge of the boy. The mentor is said to adopt the boy and acts as a father. Serpenti states that the mentor is often a cross-cousin or the boy's mother's younger brother. He should never be the boy's actual brother, although Serpenti cites a case where this happened and was permitted since no sexual contact occurred.

A complex symbolism is embodied in bachelors' hut rituals. Men smear the novice with coconut oil and charcoal and tell him that he cannot enter water while he is a munaka. They instruct him to wear his mourning hood when he leaves the hut and to avoid being seen by women. For the first time he receives the hair-appendages worn by young males. His hair is plaited and tied with areca or sago leaves. These appendages hang down to his ears. On the first day the mentor makes incisions on the novice's upper arms, upper legs, and abdomen. These cuts will be rubbed with sperm from older men many times during the initiation sequence.

The form of indirect homosexual behavior that takes place here can be understood by exploring Kimam ideas of sperm. According to Serpenti, the Kimam hold that sperm contains "great powers." He notes that it is regarded as an excellent medicine. For example, a sorcerer's sperm is consumed by the victim when the sorcerer undoes his spell. When an epidemic occurred, villagers smeared sperm on bamboo poles and sago leaf ribs and placed these at the village entrance for protection. The people of the village were rubbed with the remaining sperm. In the context of sexual activity, there are indications that the Kimam, in common with many Melanesian societies (Brown & Buchbinder, 1976; Herdt, 1981; Meggitt, 1964), believe sperm lost through intercourse drains a man's vitality. Kimam ban sexual intercourse prior to any activity which demands an expenditure of male energy (e.g., wrestling, hunting) and will accuse an unsuccessful wrestler or hunter of breaking this taboo. Further, sexual activity by an unmarried youth is seen as undoing the growth effect of the sperm.

The Kimam practice of indirect homosexuality (sperm rubbing) and direct homosexual behavior can be explained by their notions that the fertility of powerful older males is too strong for weaker males. The yam sorcerer and head-takers of the paburu provide the sperm smeared upon the first stage novice by his mentor. It is collected when a group of these powerful men engage in intercourse with the betrothed of the novice's mentor. The novice is betrothed before entering the bachelors' hut, but his future wife is not yet sexually mature and therefore the mentor's betrothed is substituted. Serpenti writes that in repayment the mentor has sexual contact with the novice. He also suggests that, as with the Keraki (Williams, 1936) and the Marind-amin (Baal, 1966), the transfer of sperm through homosexual intercourse serves to make the novice grow big and strong.[2] Thus, the young boy is grown into an adult through two processes. Rather than men directly infusing sperm into him, women provide the mediation for the very strong sperm of the sorcerers and head-takers which the mentor smears on the novice. Because the fertility of the mentor is believed to be less potent, he can directly transmit his sperm to the novice.

Sperm smearing continues throughout the initiation sequence, which lasts for a number of years, but direct sexual contact apparently involves only the first two grades. When the novice reaches the second stage he will cease being inseminated and, instead, start inseminating his first stage "sons."

A second feast occurs about a year after entry into the bachelors' hut and consists of sperm smearing and a renewal of the novice's hair-appendages, which are now made to reach half-way down his back. A third feast marks the transition from munaka to tjutjine. A reed replaces the areca or sago leaves of the hair-appendages, which now reach to the boy's waist. The boy receives his first pubic covering, a large shell, and the upper-half of his body is painted red and the lower-half black. In the evening he is taken to the dancing place and formally presented. Since this occurs during a mortuary ritual, members of the opposite paburu are probably present. The men presenting the boy hold torches near his face so that people can identify him. The boy is allowed to dance, but near dawn he must cover up with the mourning hood and return to the bachelors' hut.

The next feast, which moves the boy to the third grade (mabureede), marks the last time he is smeared with sperm, and apparently ends his involvement with homosexual behavior (although this is not stated explicitly in Serpenti's monograph). He now discards his mourning hood and moves about freely, although he cannot enter his father's house and continues to live in the bachelors' hut. He may be seen by women, but not have sexual intercourse with them. His hair-appendages are renewed for the last time, and in this case they only reach to his elbows. The men smear the boy's entire body with red clay, and the small penis cap worn by adult males replaces the shell pubic covering.

After a boy has been a mabureede for several years he is eligible for marriage. At a final feast his mentor places a woven belt with a tail of rushes on the boy as he lies on the ground. The drawing of the narrow belt over the buttocks to the waist endangers the genitals which the boy's former mentor protects during the rite. The rushes on the belt hang down to the boy's ankles. The belt is so tight that the boy can hardly eat. After a few days the mentor removes the belt and replaces the long rushes with the short ones worn by adults.

This description of the male initiation sequences shows that the Kimam view the growing of men as a process similar to that for growing of yams. Several of the rites in the initiation sequence closely resemble rites in the yam growing. In both sequences pregnancy is not a major focus of ritual. Rather, the child is separated from the mother so that male control can begin. The ceremony marking the transition from munaka to tjutjine closely resembles the mound building ceremony of the yam sequence. In both cases phallic elements are focal. In the yam ritual the magic prepared by the sorcerer is taken to his followers' gardens to strengthen their yams, while in the initiation sequence the boy moves from being a recipient of sperm to being both a donor and recipient. The ritual marking entry into the third grade corresponds in many ways to the harvest of the yam and the final application of medicine by the sorcerer. Finally, the narrow belt forced on the boy in the final ceremony serves to measure his width and length (the rushes) in a manner similar to the way yams are measured at competitive feasts.

The analysis of the yam rituals and male initiation suggests that the Kimam conceptualize males as controlling the growth of both yams and men. The successful growth of these entities requires that the males of the paburu unit be strong and virile. Further, the evidence suggests that the Kimam equate the medicines utilized in the yam rituals with the use of sperm in creating and growing human males. From this perspective both sperm smearing and infusion are nothing more than the use of medicine to create growth.

The equation of sperm smearing and homosexual intercourse with male growth is a common one in Melanesia. As mentioned earlier, the unexpected element in this system is the Kimam insistence that male fertility must be kept within the paburu. For this reason, males of one paburu do not inseminate the boys of the other, as is commonly found in cases of ritualized homosexuality in Melanesia. Yet, it is clear that men of the opposite paburu do play important roles in this system. For example, during the entrance ceremony at the bachelor hut they symbolically bury the novice. Further, the members of one paburu are the ideal audience before which men in the other present the products of male magic—yams and men.

DEATH AND THE TRIUMPH OF THE PABURU

Except those of children and old people, the Kimam hold that all deaths are caused by sorcery from outside the paburu. They are usually suspicious of members of the opposite paburu as well as members of different villages. Significantly, sorcerers who kill outsiders are often the same men who control the yam magic of their paburu (Serpenti, 1965).

The rich mortuary ceremonies reveal important relationships. First, members of the opposite paburu bury the corpse. They do so because the Kimam believe that if members of the deceased's paburu conducted the burial the ghost might assume that they desired its death. The burial organizers place the corpse in a grave of white clay covered with black earth. The paburu of the dead person gives food to the burial party as a reward for burying the corpse, and for all the services they perform during the mortuary sequence. Following the burial, the burial party must stay away from its own yam beds until they conduct rituals to remove any negative influences resulting from handling the corpse of a member of the opposite paburu.

A relationship exists between the burial of a human and the planting of yams. The relationship between burial and the entry into the bachelors' hut is much clearer, since in both cases the opposite paburu participates, while this is not the case in yam planting. The charcoal mixture smeared on the novices when they are initiated into the bachelors' hut is analogous to the black earth placed over the grave. Further, the fate of the various spiritual aspects of the deceased also relates to both the initiation sequence and yam growing. One spiritual aspect undertakes a journey to the village of Wanggambi, where it enters a hole and goes underground to the land of the dead. The lengthening of the hair-appendages of the novice symbolizes this journey; the transition from first to second grade occurs when the novice symbolically reaches the land of the dead. The painting of the novice half-red and half-black also marks this transitional phase. It identifies him with an individual in the land of the dead (black), but the color red represents his "rebirth" and potential fertility, which corresponds to the use of red leaves in yam rituals.

There is also a horizontal component to the dead person's fate. The essence of the person leaves his body and begins to diffuse into the land around the island where he is buried. As the body continues to decompose this essence spreads to all the gardens of the paburu. The essence is a fertilizing principle, and, as it diffuses, more and more gardens in the paburu are barred from ordinary use. The produce of these gardens is utilized in paying burial debts to members of the opposite paburu and for the competitive feast marking the final mortuary ceremony. At the first planting season following the death of an individual, the other men in the paburu replant his yam beds, which they had destroyed at his death. These yams will also be utilized in the competitive feast.

Members of the opposite paburu reopen the grave in a ceremony which Serpenti links to the opening of the yam mounds. These men clean the skull and other bones, and, in some villages, smear the bones with coconut oil and red paint. The lower jaw is tied to the skull with rattan fiber and the remains are reburied. This ritual corresponds to the transition from the second to the third grades in the male initiation sequence. In all three cases there is a completed product: a mature yam, an adult human male, and a dead individual whose fertility has completely diffused throughout the paburu's gardens. All that remains in each case is to measure the product and present it to members of the opposite paburu. This action is accomplished at the competitive feast marking the last mortuary ritual.

These competitive feasts represent assertions by the males of the dead person's paburu of their vitality and fertility in the face of attempts by enemies to steal or destroy these attributes (graves must be protected from outside sorcerers seeking fluids from the cadaver). The paburu's men bring out their yams from under their cover of mud and medicine and exhibit them to members of the opposite paburu. This audience contains sorcerers who might be responsible for the death of the paburu member who is being commemorated. The yams presented are the result of the combination of yam magic controlled by the host paburu and the essence of the dead individual diffusing throughout its gardens. The men carefully measure the length and width of the yams and challenge members of the opposite paburu to match them for size and quality.[3] During these ceremonies the men assemble the children undergoing various rites of passage, place them on food piles, and exhibit them to the opposite paburu. They invite the men of the opposing paburu to symbolically kill these children, but this presentation of children at all stages of growth symbolizes the continued fertility of the host paburu in the face of constant external attacks.

The equation of yams and children is illustrated in Serpenti's description of a competitive feast held between Bamol and Kalwa. Both sides danced competitively, almost until dawn, when the yam sorcerers and great cultivators from Bamol went to the spot where the largest yams had been stored and lifted the yams to their shoulders:

> In a long procession they walked towards the dancing site, where only those of Kalwa were still dancing. Slowly and solemnly the men walked around the dancers, singing: "See how big this man, see how big this woman, see how big this yam." In front of the men walked the children for whom various feasts were being given in combination with this ndambu. During the singing they were sprinkled with sago. When the procession had circled the dancing-site a few times and the guests had plenty of time to admire the yams, a halt was made and the men placed their yams in a row before the guests, sprinkling them with sago. (Serpenti, 1965, pp. 249-250)

Demonstration of continued male fertility requires exhibition of children, who remain in the paburu, and yams, which leave it. However, no all elements of the yam complex can leave the unit. Before display, the men remove the medicine covering the yams and hide it to prevent opponents from learning the secret of growing large yams. Further, one of the yams is held out of the distribution and replanted in the paburu's garden. Serpenti writes that giving away all the yams would give away all the magical fertility that allows men to grow large yams. The desire not to give children in marriage to the opposite paburu has a similar logic. The less desirable inter-paburu marriages still feature patrivirilocal residence, so that the males who grow men and yams always remain in the community and their fertility is not lost to the paburu.

CONCLUSION

In this analysis the place of ritualized homosexual behavior in Kimam culture can be seen. The paburu is an entity whose health depends upon male control of certain types of fertility. Men demonstrate their control in the growth of yams and male children. They believe that one paburu attacks the fertility of the other by killing adults through sorcery and symbolically killing children in rites of passage. Both living and dead males, however, cooperate to make possible the competitive feasts demonstrating the ability of the paburu to withstand such attacks.

Homosexual behavior is the mechanism whereby boys are grown into men who will be strong enough to maintain the fertility of the paburu. Homosexual relationships are not the result of individual choice, but rather they develop from the concept that the fertility of the more powerful males is too strong to be accepted directly by weaker males. Initiation is a process of gaining the strength to accept such power and then utilizing it for the good of the paburu.

As in many instances of ritualized homosexuality in Melanesia, the Kimam case raises important questions regarding the development and interrelationship of sexual behavior, sexual orientation, and gender role. Some Kimam males probably find the homosexual activity in the bachelors' hut to be more gratifying than the heterosexual even though they marry as adults. In Kimam, compared with other societies, there is no evidence of a higher percentage of homosexuals, i.e., individuals desiring sexual activity exclusively with partners of their own biological sex (see Money, 1980). Serpenti does not mention non-ritualized homosexual behavior between males outside of the bachelors' hut and it is impossible to know whether or not it occurs. One can conjecture that the Kimam males are heterosexuals who engage in homosexual behavior only as part of a symbolic process of masculinization (Herdt, 1981).

In Herdt's (1981) discussion of ritualized homosexual behavior among the Sambia of Papua New Guinea, he notes that, even if the individuals engaging in ritualized homosexual behavior have a heterosexual orientation, it is still necessary for them to eroticize the body parts involved in homosexual activity. Unfortunately, the suppression of the bachelors' hut in Kimam precludes investigation of this question.

Ritualized homosexual behavior in Kimam fits in with many of the other Melanesian societies exhibiting such behavior.[4] Features such as small population size, horticulture, male-female antagonism, a sharp division between adult males and boys, agnatic ideology, initiation rites, frequent warfare, and long post-partum sexual taboo are common in these societies. The contextualization of homosexual behavior as an aspect of male concern over fertility and growth, however, greatly expands the number of societies which must be included in a complete analysis of ritualized homosexual behavior in Melanesia. Themes of a male essence that is transmitted from one generation to another and male claims of control over certain forms of fertility are found in many societies that do not exhibit ritualized homosexual behavior (for Melanesia see essays in Herdt, 1982b; Tuzin, 1972).[5] The reasons some societies use homosexual behavior to communicate these ideas while others resort to different idioms (e.g., the letting, smearing, and/or drinking of blood) will not be clear until there are more data on the distribution of ritualized homosexuality in Melanesia. However, the topic of interest to general anthropology is how these ideas of male control over fertility relate to other social and cultural patterns. In this investigation the relevant distinction may not be between societies with ritualized homosexual behavior and those without, but rather between societies in which males assert ritual claims of fertility that exclude females and in which they demand that boys undergo harsh rituals to achieve adult status, and those societies with contrasting structures of relationships for males and females and for older and younger men.[6]

NOTES

1. For scientific identificaton of these plants see Serpenti (1965).

2. Serpenti (1965) does not describe the form of homosexual behavior between the novice and his mentor. Societies in Melanesia seem to limit ritual homosexual behavior to either oral or anal intercourse, but not both. Anal intercourse is most frequently reported in the area of the Kimam.

3. Other foods are also given at competitive feasts, but yams play the central role in competition. It should also be noted that competitive feasting occurs on many occasions not linked with mortuary ceremonies. Serpenti discusses these occasions in more detail (1965).

4. Societies on the island of New Guinea where ritualized homosexual behavior has been reported include the Kimam, Kiwai (Landtman, 1927), Keraki (Williams, 1936), Marind-anim (Baal, 1966), Baruya (Godelier, 1976), Kaluli (Schieffelin, 1976, 1982), Etoro (Kelly, 1976, 1977), Gebusi (Knauft & Cantrell, 1983), and Sambia (Herdt, 1981, 1982a). To date, such behavior has not been reported in the better described groups in the highlands or the Sepik River area. Davenport (1965) reports on non-ritualized homosexual behavior in East Bay. Male ritualized homosexual behavior has been described for the Big Nambas and Small Islands of Vanuatu (Deacon, 1934; Layard, 1942, 1959). Allen (1981) describes the role of dances exhibiting symbolic homosexual behavior in the secret society rites of West Aoba, Vanuata. Evidence for homosexual behavior in Australian societies is discussed by Layard (1959). Herdt's (1984) volume on ritualized homosexuality in Melanesia adds to this list.

5. At present there is no clear evidence on why some New Guinea societies exhibit ritualized homosexual behavior and others do not. Many of the societies not exhibiting the behavior are characterized by the same features as those exhibiting it (male-female antagonism, warfare, agnatic ideology, concern with male creativity, harsh initiation rites, etc.). Lowland South American groups should be compared with New Guinea. The elements of sexual antagonism, warfare, male initiation rites, and male control of fertility are found in some South American groups (e.g., the Mundurucu, see Murphy, 1959, Murphy & Murphy, 1974; Nadelson, 1981; see also Bamberger, 1974), yet ritualized homosexual behavior has not, to my knowledge, been reported in these cases.

6. Serpenti (Herdt, ed., 1984) analyzes the relationship of ritualized homosexuality and the headhunting cult. The article became available after the completion of this paper.

REFERENCES

Allen, M. (1981). Innovation, inversion, and revolution as political tactics in West Aoba. In M. Allen (Ed.), *Vanuatu: Politics, economics, and ritual in Island Melanesia* (pp. 105-134). New York: Academic Press.

Bamberger, J. (1974). The myth of matriarchy: Why men rule in primitive society. In M. M. Rosaldo & L. Lamphere (Eds.), *Woman, culture, and society*. Stanford: Stanford University Press.

Baal, J. van. (1966). *Dema*. The Hague: Martinous Nijhoff.

Brown, P., & Buchbinder, G. (Eds.). (1976). *Man and women in the New Guinea Highlands*. Washington, D.C.: American Anthropological Association.

Davenport, W. (1965). Sexual patterns and their regulation in a society of the southwest Pacific. In F. Beach (Ed.), *Sex and behavior* (pp. 164-207). New York: John Wiley.

Deacon, A. (1934). *Malekula*. London: Routledge and Kegan Paul.

Godelier, M. (1976). Le sexe comme fondement ultime de l'ordre social et cosmique chez les Baruya de Nouvelle-Guinée. (Sex as the ultimate foundation of the social and cosmic order of the New Guinea Baruya). In A. Verdiglione (Ed.), *Sexualité et pouvoir* (pp. 268-306). Paris: Traces Payot.

Herdt, G. (1981). *Guardians of the flutes: Idioms of masculinity*. New York: McGraw-Hill.

Herdt, G. (1982a). Fetish and fantasy in Sambia initiation. In G. Herdt (Ed.), *Rituals of manhood* (pp. 44-98). Berkeley: University of California Press.

Herdt, G. (1982b). (Ed.). *Rituals of manhood*. Berkeley: University of California Press.

Herdt, G. (Ed.). (1984). *Ritualized homosexuality in Melanesia*. Berkeley: University of California Press.

Kelly, R. (1976). Witchcraft and sexual relations: An exploration in the social and semantic implications of the structure of belief. In P. Brown & G. Buchbinder (Eds.), *Men and women in the New Guinea Highlands* (pp. 36-53). Washington, D.C.: American Anthropological Association.

Kelly, R. (1977). *Etoro social structure*. Ann Arbor: University of Michigan Press.

Knauft, B., & Cantrell, E. (1983). *Ritual form and permutation in the Strickland-Bosavi area*. Paper presented at the annual meeting of the American Anthropological Association.

Landtman, G. (1927). *The Kiwai Papuans of British New Guinea*. London: Macmillan.

Layland, J. (1942). *Stone men of Malekula*. London: Chatto and Windus.

Layand, J. (1959). Homo-eroticism in primitive society as a function of the self. *Journal of Analytical Psychology, 4*, 101-115.

Meggitt, M. (1964). Male-female relationships in the highlands of Australian New Guinea. In J. Watson (Ed.), *New Guinea: The Central Highlands. American Anthropologist, 66*, pt. 2, 204-284.

Money, J. (1980). *Love and love sickness*. Baltimore: The John Hopkins University Press.

Murphy, R. (1959). Social structure and sex antagonism. *Southwestern Journal of Anthropology, 15*, 89-98.

Murphy, Y., & Murphy, R. (1974). *Women of the forest*. New York: Columbia University Press.

Nadelson, L. (1981). Pigs, women, and the men's house in Amazonia: An analysis of six Mundurucu myths. In S. Ortner and H. Whitehead (Eds.), *Sexual meanings* (pp. 240-272). Cambridge: Cambridge University Press.

Schieffelin, E. (1976). *The sorrow of the lonely and the burning of the dancers*. New York: St. Martin's Press.

Schieffelin, E. (1982). The bau a ceremonial hunting lodge: An alternative to initiation. In G. Herdt (Ed.), *Rituals of Manhood* (pp. 115-200). Berkeley: University of California Press.

Serpenti, L. (1965). *Cultivators in the Swamps*. Assen: Van Gorcum.

Sillitoe, P. (1984). The gender of crops in the Papua New Guinea Islands. *Ethnology, 20*, 1-14.

Tuzin, D. (1972). Yam symbolism in the Sepik: An interpretive account. *Southwestern Journal of Anthropology, 28*, 230-254.

Williams, F. (1936). *Papuans of the Trans-Fly*. Oxford University Press.

Sisters and Brothers, Lovers and Enemies: Marriage Resistance in Southern Kwangtung

Andrea Sankar, PhD
University of Michigan

ABSTRACT. This article examines the structure and content of relation-ships among members of a sisterhood in Hong Kong. These women, who at the time of the research were members of a Buddhist vegetarian hall, had been participants in what can be termed a marriage resistance move-ment, that took place in the Pearl River Delta surrounding Canton from approximately 1865 through 1935.

From approximately 1865 through 1935 in three districts of the Pearl River Delta, there arose a singular social phenomenon which Marjorie Topley (1975) has called the "marriage resistance movement." Women who chose *not* to marry were called *sou hei*, "self-combers," referring to the fact that they combed their own hair in the fashion of married women rather than having it done for them in a marriage ceremony. Most sou hei formed sisterhoods which, if successful, served as a substitute for the family throughout their lives. The movement was spontaneous and un-organized, spurred by the economic leverage which some women gained through the wages earned in the production of silk, and popularized through song and story. At its height, in the early twentieth century, the movement may have included up to 100,000 women. There is very little known about the origin of marriage resistance. Most of the women in-volved were illiterate or semi-literate. Little official notice was taken of the movement, because of the political upheavals of the time, and because the movement concerned only women. Yet many members in the last cohort to resist marriage are still alive and living in the cities of Southeast Asia and Hong Kong and in the People's Republic of China. It is through them that we come to know of the movement.

Andrea Sankar is a visiting lecturer in the School of Public Health, University of Michigan, Ann Arbor, MI 48109. She pursues her interest in Chinese women through research in health policy and aging in the PRC.

69

In the late 1920s the silk industry in which most sou hei were employed began to collapse as part of the world-wide depression. It finally ceased in 1935 with the Japanese invasion. Sou hei women still working in silk production were thrown out of work and migrated to cities in search of employment as servants. Many, however, had already left in search of servant jobs because of the grueling conditions in the silk factories. In the cities those who already had jobs helped their sisters find work. Many of these women who migrated to Hong Kong and other cities in Southeast Asia joined Taoist vegetarian halls, or *jaai tong*. The sect promoting the halls had been popular in the marriage resistance areas and some women had previously been members. Many women who joined these Taoist halls did so for reasons of social security. Taoist halls offered single women social legitimacy which supported their distinctive lifestyles.

In the marriage resistance areas a women who made the vow to remain unwed and performed the sou hei ceremony, moved out of her parents' home, like a bride, and built a spinster house, usually with other women like herself. This house was primarily used for her retirement and old age. Many women stayed in close contact with their families, contributing their wages to their brothers' families. These women remained at home and their nieces and nephews cared for them through old age. They built spinster houses because they believed no unmarried woman could die in her natal home without causing spiritual danger for her family. Although many women had built spinster houses in the People's Republic to which they had planned to retire, the victory of the Chinese Communists dissuaded them from returning. Frightened by rumors that cadres had forced elderly spinsters to marry bachelors or widowers in order to care for them, the women decided to remain permanently in Hong Kong or other Southeast Asian cities. Some of these women established secular spinster houses much as they had known in China; others joined or established the vegetarian halls.

The bond among these women was expressed in the formation of sisterhoods. These sisterhoods first came into being in the girls' houses of the marriage resistance area. There it was the custom upon reaching puberty to sleep in girls' houses rather than in their parent's houses. Sometimes these houses were large, formal associations located in buildings constructed by the lineage. More often they were informal, a few girls sleeping at the home of a widow or an elderly couple. Strong friendship bonds formed among the girls in the houses. Women who followed the popular custom of *mh lohk ga*, not residing with the husband after marriage and not consummating the marriage, often returned to sleep in the girls' houses until they became pregnant, sometimes up to five or even ten years later. Women who chose to resist marriage completely often turned to their sisters for security, companionship, and affection.

Most sou hei women lived their adult lives in the company of their sisters. Usually sisterhoods had five to six members, although they were frequently called seven-sisters associations, after the seven sisters in the Pleiades constellation. Sometimes two or three women would form especially strong attachments and become sworn sisters. In the cities to which the women migrated, several sisterhoods would join together to form larger associations of up to 40 members. These associations performed many useful purposes from recreational to labor union roles. These larger associations did not have the strong commitment characteristic of the smaller groups.

THE ETHNOGRAPHY

As in any ethnographic encounter, it is initially difficult, if not impossible, to understand the meaning behind the various forms of relationship with which the outsider is presented. This was certainly my experience with the sisterhoods. Before embarking upon the fieldwork, I had not been able to ascertain whether any former members of marriage-resistance were still alive and living in the vegetarian halls, or jaai tong. Lacking this assurance, I had designed a research project focusing on the structure and function of the halls, hoping to obtain from this archeology some understanding of their former occupants, should none have survived. Not until my first encounter with the residents of a Buddhist vegetarian hall four months later, did I realize that the spinsters still existed, and, in fact, whole sisterhoods remained intact.[1]

Understanding the subtleties and obvious differences incorporated in the term "sisterhood" or *jimui*, would still have been an elusive goal had I not been present at a key event which served to distinguish these relationships.

The Fight

During the initial part of the fieldwork I had discovered a great deal about the women's reasons for resisting marriage. I did not, however, understand the complex relationships denoted by the term "sisters." This lack of understanding became apparent when different women privately informed me that a member of the jaai tong whom I had not yet met was not actually a "sister" but had been married, had a child and seven grandchildren, and had deserted her marriage. The incident which led me to understand the complicated relationships among my informants was a fight which took place between two sisters three months after I had arrived.

One weekend several of the part-time members arrived to visit the *Louh Yahn Yuen*, or old people's association, a death-benefit association which held yearly health festivals. They also came to escape the heat of the city and to air their stored belongings in the hot sun. Yaan, Baat, Guh, and Au Suk were expected. Sifu, Ming Guh, Ah Puk and Luhk Guh were already there. Yan Fei, a Buddhist nun who lived at the next-door monastery, was also staying at the jaai tong. Her residence at the jaai tong was unusual and caused some contention among the members. She had not purchased a membership in the hall. The room she occupied had previously belonged to her friend, the natural sister of the founder of the hall. This friend had died a few years ago. Although the room had not been bequeathed to Yan Fei, because such an act was impossible according to membership rules, Yan Fei had appropriated the room as her own. She was able to do this because she was a sister to many of the members. During the war she had been a member of a large sisterhood to which most of the members had belonged. All members claimed to have been members in this key group but this was not true (Sankar, 1978).

Yan Fei had introduced the women who had actually founded the jaai tong to Ah Sam, the sister who was the leader of the hall. Because Yan Fei was a contemporary of the founder of the hall, and they both lived in the monastery together, and had taken their religious vows together; they were religious brothers. (In Buddhism all religious kinship terminology is male.) Yan Fei drew on both her fictive ties as an "uncle" to the members and on the affectionate ties of sisterhood to secure for herself a room where she could sleep when she wished to escape the noise of the monastery. She was careful not to eat there, because she had made no financial contribution, unless she was invited to do so for a special occasion. Yan Fei had also assisted Ah Sam in finding members for the hall, one of whom was her natural sister, Yaan. This weekend, as for much of the summer, Yan Fei was sleeping at the hall.

Members arrived on Friday. They came early in the day and after an initial greeting, lunch was served. Sifu, a nun and the manager of the hall, prepared a huge pot of noodles with condiments. Everyone helped themselves to a bowl and took it to the porch to eat and catch the breeze. Yan Fei appeared from the monastery and was invited to lunch. People eagerly began exchanging news from town with her and gave her the provisions she had requested them to purchase. She took a bowl of noodles and sat down. Suddenly, she spat out the food and began haranguing Ah Puk, "This is too bitter to eat; it is your fault. I saw you put the wok cover on the floor while you were cleaning this morning. I told you to pick it up and wash it, but you didn't. Now you have poisoned the noodles with your slovenly ways." Ah Puk was not a sister; she was a peasant woman who had lost most of her family in the wars. Her daughter had found her a place in the monastery as a servant in exchange for board and room. Because the monastery already had several servants, Yan Fei arranged for Ah Puk to stay at the jaai tong.

Yan Fei refused to finish the dish. Her sister Yaan picked it up and ate it saying, "good food shouldn't be wasted." As Yan Fei continued to complain that Ah Puk had poisoned her, Yaan responded that, because she herself had eaten more of the noodles, they both would suffer the same fate. She tried to cajole Yan Fei out of her bad mood and restore the light-hearted atmosphere which Yan Fei had completely dispelled. Yan Fei stopped her tirade and turned her attention toward the others. She tried to pay them for the provisions they had brought, but the women insisted they were gifts. The conversation returned to its peaceful course and the gossip was resumed. Sifu, the most recent member of the hall and the sisterhood, did not know most of those about whom they gossiped, so she sat quietly listening.

The next morning Yan Fei returned to the hall after early morning prayer and breakfast at the monastery. It was another extremely hot day and everyone was at work early trying to finish chores before the sun was fully risen. Au Suk was sweeping the floors and muttering to herself, something she often did, when Yan Fei walked in. Yan Fei seemed cheerful and, assuming Ah Suk's comments were directed against Ah Puk, as indeed they often were, she quickly joined in. "Yes, these ignorant, uneducated peasants are good for nothing. They can't even keep a floor clean," she commented, sitting down in the area Ah Suk had just finished sweeping and taking out a cigarette. She, Yan Fei, had tried to teach Ah Puk some standards appropriate for a Buddhist hall but Ah Puk was too stupid to learn. In an angry whisper, loud enough for everyone in the area to hear, Ah Suk said she was not talking about Ah Puk. Yan Fei was startled and glared at Ah Suk, who continued her sweeping. Then she quickly sought out her old friend Ming Guh upstairs. In a loud voice she complained of the unfairness of the attack; after all she only visited there and never ate their food unless invited. Ming Guh calmed her down and urged her to ignore the insult. Yan Fei left after this talk.

Nothing more was said until a short time later when the nun who lived alone in a small hall nearby came to use the phone. Ping Ngon was greatly respected at the monastery, where she was one of the few nuns ever chosen to act as manager of the whole monastery. Everyone looked forward to her visits and enjoyed them. When she had gone inside to use the phone, Ah Suk commented that it was such a pity that Ping Ngon would not live with them because Yan Fei's domination drove her away.

That evening Yaan offered to relieve Sifu of cooking, for Sifu had been extremely busy all day. Yaan spent some time and effort making Singapore noodles. As the meal began, tension again became apparent. Ah Suk politely but firmly refused the noodles, saying they were too hot for her stomach. She then prepared her own meal. Others tasted some of Yaan's food but soon followed Ah Suk's example. Yan Fei and Yaan sat together and discussed the matter. Yan Fei offered the explanation that the others did this because Yaan was her sister. The other members remarked to me that it was not personal; Yan Fei chose to take it that way.

The next day there was an outing to the old people's association, which after years of indecisiveness, Ah Suk had finally decided to join. The occasion, along with the physical exertion, for it was a very long walk, promised to make this an especially nice day. By early morning, however, it became clear that they were not going. Ah Suk had decided to return to Hong Kong, several days ahead of schedule. Baat Guh was to accompany her.

When Yan Fei discovered this change in plans, she confronted Ah Suk and demanded to know if she was leaving in anger. Without directly addressing her, Ah Suk mumbled that she was not. Not satisfied, Yan Fei demanded she swear this before the Buddha. Ah Suk refused. At that point, Yan Fei grabbed Ah Suk's arm and began pulling her up the stairs to the shrine room. Half way up Ah Suk broke free and started back down. Yan Fei caught her and threw her against the wall, and struggled to pull her up the stairs. Ah Suk pushed Yan Fei against the rail, trying to get free. Yan Fei threw her against the wall again and continued trying to drag her upstairs. Then Yan Fei scratched Ah Suk, digging her fingernails into her arm to keep her hold. Ah Suk screamed in pain and others tried to separate the women. All this time Yan Fei continued to scream, "You must swear before Buddha." Some people led Yan Fei upstairs and tried to calm her down; others followed Ah Suk out onto the porch. Her arm had long scratches and deep punctures. Ah Suk left soon after for Hong Kong.

Aftermath and Analysis

The story of the fight quickly spread throughout the Buddhist community. Nuns in other jaai tongs said Yan Fei would suffer in the afterlife for each wound she had inflicted. The aftermath of the fight lasted for several months. As it played itself out, many of the underlying relationships and tensions among the members surfaced.

Yan Fei based her defense of her conduct on two levels. Rather than confronting the inappropriateness of her behavior, she sought to deflect her critics by bringing into question the legitimacy of the jaai tong. First, she invoked the orthodoxy of Buddhism, casting the conflict as one concerning appropriate ecclesiastical behavior, which she said was not being observed in the hall. She tried to remove the conflict from the realm of gossip and elevate it, by having the Buddhist Association mediate. The others refused to accept this view of the basic conflict and insisted on a personal interpretation. Failing at this, Yan Fei drew on the basis of long-felt ties of sororal loyalty. This gave her more hope, for her ties as a sister went back for decades. In her reformulation of the dispute, she made Sifu's management of the hall's ceremonial, social, and financial affairs the central issue of contention.

Yan Fei's interpretation of the conflict focused on the sisters' weakest form of relationship, hall membership. Hall membership was the most recent form of association and consisted of several overlapping sisterhoods. Hall members who at first opposed Yan Fei for her disruptive and highly inappropriate behavior, now faced a larger conflict within the religious community, the issue of hall membership. The dynamics and structures at work in this conflict can be viewed as types of relationships, although, in actuality, their content and practice were very fluid.

Sisters and Brothers

Hall members were not all sisters. In fact, I found only one case where an intact sisterhood formed a vegetarian hall. If a sisterhood remained together 30 to 40 years and there were enough members (usually five or more) to make it financially feasible to retire together, the women generally chose a secular lifestyle for old age. If the sisterhood was smaller and the members desired the spiritual, financial, and social security of hall membership, they usually joined an established jaai tong as a group, although sometimes religious preferences caused members of the same sisterhood to join different halls.

The members of this hall were made up of several overlapping sisterhoods. The core group had been together in during the war. Other members had been recruited through sisterhood relationships formed later in Hong Kong or through the activation of old associations from girls' houses re-met after the chaos of the war. Sifu, the head nun, was the last to join: Because she was the least connected with the others, she was the most vulnerable to attack.

Because this group had varying degrees of attachment and commitment to each other, the acknowledgment of religious brotherhood among the members was a key symbol tying them together. After they had moved in and taken possession of the hall, the members gathered before a portrait of the founder and performed a posthumous *gwai-yih* ceremony. Usually the gwai-yih ceremony is a non-binding acknowledgment of the master-follower relationship. It can be acted upon, sustained, developed, and infused with content. It then becomes significant and binding. Alternatively, it can be ignored and forgotten. Although only Ah Sam and Ah Poon had actually met the founder, the members chose to take this vow together. Through commitment to the founder, they hoped to strengthen and make explicit their commitment to each other.

The commitment was needed because the members' relationship would be expected to carry more weight than at any other time in their lives as they aged. The members tried to establish mutual financial security for old age, provide care and comfort in decrepitude, and to perform ancestor rites for members after death. As the only form of security and succor left for the women, it was essential that the bond be functional. It was this bond, and the long-range consequences of maintaining it, that caused members to side against their old sister, Yan Fei, once she had succeeded in recasting the conflict as an issue concerning the legitimacy of their hall.

Sisters and Sisters

The sisterhood bond was also not to be forsaken. Ultimately, it cut across and helped to resolve the conflict. Since adolescence, the sisterhood bond had been important in the women's lives. These sisterhoods had helped some women avoid a marriage arranged by a woman's parents. Even when parents acquiesced to the women's not marrying, the sisterhoods remained important in their lives. When women left the area in search of domestic work, they often did so in the company of a sister. From the time they had forsaken the life of marriage and the family, the sisterhood had been the main social and emotional bond for most of the women. Its importance increased as the tumult of war and revolution separated many women from their natal families and local communities.

Although the sisterhoods and the relations arising from them were generally accepted by the local communities where marriage resistance evolved the presence of a significant number of unmarried women was not unproblematic. In some cases families encouraged a daughter to take the sou hei vow so they could benefit from her earnings. The strong emotional and physical relationships which sometimes developed among the girls were not questioned unless they threatened to prevent a woman from marrying or from consummating a marriage. Thus, relationships among marriage-resisting women developed without community censure. The presence of unmarried women within a community, did, however, constitute certain problems. The women were thought to pose a serious sexual threat to married men. Chinese commentators have described the "lewdness" and "bold ways" of the women and speculated on their liaisons with married men. My informants identified sexual relationships with men as the single worst transgression a sou hei could make. It is possible that sexual accusations aimed at the sou hei were less a response to actual transgressions than to the threats which these women posed.

The sou hei vow, which a woman took to declare her intentions to remain single and to achieve adulthood without marriage, served three purposes. First, it freed her parents from their obligation to arrange her marriage. Second, it secured her soul so that she would not become a Hungry Ghost after death. This problem of life-after-death constituted the single greatest cultural hurdle a woman had to overcome if she were to remain single. Because a woman did not belong to the family of her birth, they were not obliged to worship her soul when she died; indeed, they were not supposed to have her soul tablet within the house. However, without anyone to carry on her ancestor rites, she would become a Hungry Ghost and come back to haunt her family. Third the woman vowed to remain chaste, i.e., not engage in sexual relations with men. To symbolize this vow, women ate hard boiled eggs at the sou hei banquet, for the yellow of the yolk was also the symbol for king. Thus, the woman declared that she would govern her own emotions much as a king must govern his people, and not behave in such a way as to bring disrepute to anyone.

Breaking the sou hei vow could mean explusion from the sisterhood, and according to my informants serious consequences for the woman. One woman who visited the hall frequently while I was there suffered this fate. After taking her vow, she had lived with a man in Hong Kong, where she worked as a servant during the war. She never married, but had two children. The man ran off and left her, and the two children were killed in the war. "A hard fate, but that is what happened when you broke the vow," was the unsympathetic response.

It was not heterosexuality per se that created the problems, but the willingness to participate in sexual relationships with men. Yaan, who had been married and borne a child before she ran off to rejoin her sisters, was welcomed back because she had been forced into marriage before she knew how to resist. Willingly going with a man as Yuk Sim had done, however, was an immediate threat to the sisterhood. Further, it was a threat to the larger social order of the district, which was exceptional in Chinese history in tolerating a large group of unmarried women of no organized religious calling. For the movement to maintain its social acceptance and for the sisterhood to retain its strength and supremacy in tying women together, heterosexual relationships could not be tolerated.

An unstructured social movement such as this contained a wide range of behaviors. No doubt, some of the stories about immorality were based on fact. But such stories might also be an indirect recognition of the economic threat which the women posed. Non-marriage was feasible because women could support themselves with wages earned in the silk industry. The ability for women to earn wages dated only from the mid-nineteenth century. At that time women took the jobs of men when steam power was introduced into the silk filiatures in 1846. The hostility toward the filiatures was so great that riots broke out; the filiatures were vandalized and had to be closed. Six years later, when they reopened in another town, women instead of men were employed. This economic advantage for women was a key factor in resisting marriage; it also constituted a real threat to family security.

The economic incentive was not the only motivating factor behind the sisterhoods. In other silk growing areas of China women made more money in the silk industry but no such movement developed. Many women in the Pearl River Delta already resorted to the practice of mh lohk ga, not residing with husbands after marriages. Most of the money they made during this time went to their new families, but some of it remained with their natal families, and any unpaid labor in the family's own silk production efforts was to their natal families' benefit. Once the silk wages became significant, this period of mh lohk ga became longer. Many women decided they did not want to reside with their husbands. This was a highly unusual practice, and one which received official government criticism. However, it is and still remains a singular cultural practice in this area.

As wages increased, an intermediate phase of marriage resistance evolved. Sisterhoods which had formed, sometimes in the girls' houses, sometimes in the factory dormitories, pooled their earnings to buy concubines to replace the women in their roles as wives and mothers. The sisterhood remained together, sending a portion of the members' earnings to their husbands' families, while the members continued to work. After menopause the members returned to their husbands and took up the position of first wife. This return could have disastrous outcomes. The concubines who had been senior wives for 20 years or more refused to cede their places to the returned mh lohk ga wives. The mh lohk ga wives became little more than servants in their own homes. Eventually many women chose not to marry at all. They took the *sou hei* vow and most lived permanently with their sisters; others chose to remain with their brothers' families. Lineage elders probably excepted this bold departure from traditional mh lohk ga because of the significant financial contribution these women could make to the lineage if they remained unwed. By no means did all women choose to follow this model. Some instead kept their earnings for their own use.

The presence of unmarried women within the community posed a threat to the security of the family, but it was probably more economic than sexual. Because the sou hei were able to make significant contributions to their natal families and to the lineage as a whole, the nature of the threat was ambivalent. The same family who could not attract the daughter-in-law into permanent residence may also have benefited from the wages of the sou hei daughter. Thus, the community tolerated these women and only voiced a warning about their potential moral threat to married men.

Sisters and Lovers

Sometimes sexual relationships formed among two or three sisters, creating physical as well as emotional bonds. Larger sisterhoods may have contained several couples or ménages à trois. The lesbian aspects of marriage resistance caught the attention of western writers and commentators, yet it was barely mentioned in Chinese sources. Lesbianism, unlike male homosexuality, was not something proscribed culturally.

Male homosexuality, because of the threat it posed to the continuation of the family, was severely rejected by Confucians. Lesbianism, on the other hand, was ignored or tacitly condoned. In fact, some Confucian tracts suggested it as a way for a gentleman to keep his wives content (van Gulik, 1961).

Although lesbian relationships may not have been subjected to outside social pressures, they faced serious problems. The relationships I observed were often unstable.[2] The ménage à trois was the most problematic form, and tended to become increasingly difficult as women aged. Two of the partners would gradually draw closer together and move away from the third. Sometimes this withdrawal was quite sudden and violent; one informant was literally kicked out of the communal bed and told never to return. Others broke up established living arrangements, thus threatening everyone's security in retirement.

Although a lesbian relationship within a larger sisterhood could provide continuity and a source of commitment, it could also threaten the group as a whole if its priorities competed with those of the group. According to many women, this conflict was the real story behind the fight. Ah Suk, always a difficult person, was the lover of Luhk Guh, a powerful and extremely devout and long-time member of the jaai tong. The others had long tolerated Ah Suk's disagreeable and passive-aggressive behavior because of her lover Luhk's position and the considerable contributions she made to the hall. Ah Suk's personality collided with the other most difficult personality, Yan Fei. Ah Suk had a double tie to the other sisters, of sister and brother, and had to be tolerated, but Yan Fei had only the tie of sister. Yan Fei knew this and chose to attack Sifu, who was the weakest sister and brother.

Yan Fei's relationship with her lover, Gong Lung, was also a threat to the group. She had helped Ah Sam establish the jaai tong because she suspected, with good reason, that Ah Sam would never live there. Ah Sam, while officially the successor and head of the jaai tong, could not bear to leave her lively life in Hong Kong and retreat to the contemplative life, at least not yet, and she was then 68. Unfortunately for Yan Fei, Ah Sam was extremely responsible and resourceful and made plans for maintaining the hall despite her absence. According to my informants, this action ran contrary to Yan Fei's plans. She had hoped to become manager in Ah Sam's absence and to live there with her lover, Gong Lung, away from the tumult and intrigue of the monastery. It was said she even planned to rename the hall in honor of her lover.

Ah Sam, however, took her vow seriously, especially with the urging and counsel of the senior nuns of the monastery, some of whom may have known of Yan Fei's plans. Ah Sam began to recruit members and to take control of the hall. Sifu, not then a nun, was the one she recruited to be cook and manager. Having her plans, or the "plot" as it was called, disrupted, Yan Fei began a rumor campaign to drive Sifu away, accusing her of being an incompetent manager and of having a "mean" face which drove worshippers away. At this point Sifu decided she must shave her head, take her vows, and become the legitimate successor of the founder.

These events had all taken place some years before the fight. Yan Fei was still struggling to maintain a place for herself in the hall and hoped that her influence in the religious community would eventually undercut Sifu and force her to leave. The extreme impropriety of her behavior in the fight discredited her efforts, however, and within the year she was no longer seen as a threat. The wider religious community accepted Sifu and the other sisters as legitimate members of the jaai tong and the Buddhist community.

CONCLUSION

The fight exposed the overlapping and conflicting commitments among the members. The weakest bond, that of jaai tong membership, or brotherhood, was the one under attack by Yan Fei, who sought to discredit the legitimacy of the group as a religious association. It was the jaai tong bond that had to be maintained, however, if the women were to achieve security in old age. The strong and enduring sisterhood bond among the members of the sisterhood formed in the war might have been sufficient to secure Yan Fei's place at the jaai tong and allow her to successfully challenge Sifu if her strong allegiance to Gong Lung, her lover, had not threatened the jaai tong's stability. By attempting to introduce an outsider, Gong Lung, who was neither sister nor brother, but who was strongly committed to Yan Fei, into the jaai tong, she upset the group's fragile sense of mutuality.

The lesbian relationships among the women in the jaai tongs were more volatile than other forms of relationship. In traditional Chinese culture marriage was for production, reproduction, and the maintenance of ancestor worship. Parents or relatives arranged marriages because they understood that it was important for marriage partners to have a successful life. They believed such business was too serious to be left only to sexual attraction. Folk wisdom warned against the instability of love matches, which were also the themes of some modern Chinese novels dealing with the problems of western influence.

In a similar fashion, the larger sisterhoods were not characterized by the women as fulfilling women's sexual needs. Sisterhoods were necessary to resist marriage, support oneself, and to secure work and retirement. Nevertheless, the strong group identities which often formed among adolescent girls in girls' houses had held sisterhoods together prior to marriage resistance. Then, as women acquired economic strength, the sisterhoods often bitterly resisted losing their members to marriage. Folk songs tell of women who longed to go to their husbands but were too intimidated by their ''fierce'' sisters to do so. A strong bond among the girls helped to later maintain the group's commitment to resist marriage.

In addition to the positive force of the sisterhood bond, the negative factor of the marital relationship also prompted marriage resistance. The Pearl River Delta area was one of the few places where single-surname villages existed. It was known for inter-clan warfare, especially aimed at control of valuable alluvial lands where the mulberry leaves for the silk worms were grown. A woman did not only marry out of her village; she often married into enemy territory. Numerous other factors included the existence of sou hei sisters-in-law who had unusually significant power in the family and could make the life of a young bride miserable. If a sou hei chose to remain at home and contribute her wages to the household, she could be quite tyrannical. These factors helped make marriage a frightening prospect for many women, perhaps more frightening than it customarily was in Chinese society.

The move away from the family and marriage was not one to be taken lightly or made simply for sexual attraction. Although sexual relationships were part of sisterhood life for some of the women, few chose to base their future security on such bonds. Instead, they worked at strengthening and supporting their larger sisterhood networks, hoping that, in the long run, a history of reciprocity and affection would provide them security.

NOTES

1. The term *spinster* is used because the women fit the literal definition: spinners of thread.

2. My data on the role of lesbian relationships within larger sisterhoods are constrained by the nature of my sample. Stable lesbian relationships tended to choose the more traditional form of retirement, the spinster house or its Hong Kong equivalent. These groups were by their intimate and private nature not easily located. Of the seven such groups I did contact, only one had decided to join a jaai tong made up primarily of lesbian couples and ménages à trois. Because they feared religious persecution from the Chinese Communists if their location became known, I was unable to continue my work with them. The non-jaai tong affiliated groups which I met often came to my attention because of some serious problem which plagued the relationships. Because jaai tong associations, and not sisterhoods per se, were my focus, I did not seek out the variety of relationships which might have existed.

REFERENCES

Gulik, R. van. (1961). *Sexual life in ancient China.* Leiden: Brill.
Sankar, A. (1978). *The evolution of the Sisterhood in traditional Chinese society: From village girls' houses to Chai T'angs in Hong Kong.* Unpublished doctoral dissertation, University of Michigan.
Topley, M. (1975). Marriage resistance in rural Kwangtung. In M. Wolf and R. Witke (Eds.), *Women in Chinese society.* Stanford: Stanford University Press.

The Lesbian Community:
An Anthropological Approach

Denyse Lockard, PhD (cand.)

University of Arizona

ABSTRACT. Visible lesbian communities, a recent social development in the United States, have received relatively little research attention. This article defines the ''lesbian community,'' as distinct from both the lesbian population and the lesbian subculture. The important features of the lesbian community are the social networks of lesbians, their group identity, shared subcultural values, and the institutional base, the organizations and places where community members can interact. One lesbian community is described and directions for future research suggested.

The existence of social networks of lesbian friends and acquaintances in the United States dates from the 1920s and 30s (Bullough & Bullough, 1977; D'Emilio, 1983; Katz, 1976). The rise and greater visibility of lesbian meeting places and organizations, however, are later developments. Gay bars that included women among their clientele first appeared in the 1930s, and by the '50s there were lesbian bars and a well-established lesbian and gay bar scene in places such as Greenwich Village in New York City. These bars were the visible setting for many social networks of friends, and for the developing gay subcultures of many cities. The bar subculture maintained well-defined norms of behavior, which included feminine and masculine role-playing. The '50s also saw the beginning of lesbian organizations. The Daughters of Bilitis, the first exclusively lesbian organization, was founded in 1955 in San Francisco as an alternative to the bar scene and the drinking and role-playing associated with it (D'Emilio, 1983).

It was not until the advent of the Women's and the Gay Liberation Movements in the late '60s, however, that gay bars and organizations increased in numbers and became more publicly visible in many urban areas. These institutions developed rapidly and many of them were not only oriented to lesbians, but were also based in feminist ideology. Currently they provide a wide variety of functions for lesbians, and include

---

Ms. Lockard is a doctoral candidate in the Department of Anthropology, University of Arizona, Tucson, Arizona, 85721.

83

not only the traditional women's bars, but also women's centers and bookstores, self-help groups, information and referral hotlines, concert production groups and musicians, theater groups and plays, record companies, feminist presses and writers, political organizations, and newspapers and journals. These institutions, the functions they provide, and the activities they support, form a widespread lesbian subculture, in which basic values are communicated and shared by many women. This subculture is manifested in the active and visible lesbian communities of many cities. Although these various communities share the basic values of the subculture, they are also shaped by the individuals who participate in them, and by their local, urban environments.

In recent years there has been an increase in the number of studies of lesbians, primarily in the fields of psychology and sociology. Few of these studies have examined lesbian interaction, their lifestyles, or the values they share in their communities. Fewer still have examined the internal structures and workings of those communities, and the importance they have in the lives of lesbians (the exceptions in anthropology are Barnhart, 1975; Wolf, 1979). The purpose of this article is to provide an explicit definition of the term *lesbian community* and to distinguish it from the related concepts of the lesbian population, subculture, and social networks. This will be done by first discussing the term lesbian community, and, secondly, by examining a particular lesbian community.

THE LESBIAN COMMUNITY

In order to define adequately what a lesbian community is, it is necessary to distinguish it from related concepts. The lesbian community is distinct from the lesbian population. It is composed of social networks of lesbians, although such networks may exist outside and independently of a community as well. Through the vehicle of the lesbian community women learn and share the feminist-based values of the lesbian subculture, and develop and maintain community institutions.

The lesbian population can be defined as those women who identify themselves as lesbians. Accordingly, a lesbian is anyone who says she is. Previous definitions, and the popular understanding of what a lesbian is, have focused on sexual behavior; that is, lesbians are women who engage in sexual activities with other women. Both identity and behavior, however, are important in the formulation of sexual preference. There are women who have engaged in same-sex activities and who do not identify themselves as lesbians, and women who identify themselves as lesbians who are not currently, or who have never been, sexually active with another woman. Lesbian identity is not solely dependent on sexual feelings and activities; it is also a response to emotional feelings, psychological responses (Kinsey, Pomeroy, Martin, & Gebhard, 1953), social expectations and pressures (Blumstein & Schwartz, 1974), or the individual's own choices in identity formation (Ponse, 1978).

The lesbian population can be viewed as a pool or reserve from which a smaller number of women draw together, forming the lesbian communities found in many cities today. Neither the size of the lesbian population, nor that of any lesbian community can be known with certainty. Nevertheless, observation indicates that only a minority of the total lesbian population of a city are active members of the community at any one time, although individuals may withdraw or re-enter at different times in their lives.

The first discussion of the lesbian community in the literature compared it to an ethnic community and defined it as "a continuing collectivity of individuals who share some significant activity and who, out of a history of continuing interaction based on that activity, begin to generate a sense of a bounded group possessing special norms and a particular argot" (Simon & Gagnon, 1967, p. 261). According to these authors, such a community did not require a formal character or a special geographical location, although they saw gay bars and organizations as segregated settings in which lesbians could portray their self-identification.

In a study of a specific lesbian community, that of Portland, Oregon, Barnhart defined the community as "a way of organizing and stabilizing relationships between members, implicitly establishing and enforcing rules for behavior. In fact, the Community may be seen as a partial alternative form of family unit for Community members" (1975, p. 93). The Portland community provided its members with a psychological kin group, as well as homes, work, and leisure activities, and the opportunity to form pair relationships. Membership was based on being a lesbian, identifying with the counterculture youth movement and its ideals, and participating in, and showing a commitment to, the community and its activities. Barnhart described the community as united by an intensive interpersonal communication network through which information about the community's social activities, and the activities and feelings of its members were exchanged on a regular basis.

In her study of the lesbian community of San Francisco, Wolf postulated that it was not a community in the traditional sense of being geographically bounded. Although her study focused on only a segment of the community, the radical lesbian-feminists, her definition is still pertinent. Wolf defined the community as:

> the continuing social networks of lesbians who are committed to the lesbian-feminist lifestyle, who participate in various community activities and projects, and who congregate socially. The concept "socio-psychological unity" is to them an important part of their

sense of what a community is and who belongs to it. (Wolf, 1979, p. 73)

These authors did not find that a territorial base or geographical boundaries were a necessary feature of a lesbian community, beyond the fact of its existence in a particular urban milieu. Instead, four features emerge as important in the definition of lesbian community. First, the community consists of social networks of lesbians who have a "history of continuing interaction" based on the assumption or knowledge of a shared sexual preference. These networks of friends and acquaintances are based on common interests and affection, and are fluid and overlapping, with continual changes in membership. The interaction of lesbians in these networks leads to the second feature of lesbian communities, shared group identity. The members of particular social networks may share feelings of unity among themselves, but the shared group identity, or "socio-psychological unity," extends to the larger lesbian community, which becomes the unit of identification, beyond the individual social networks, for the women who are active in it. This sense of unity and identity is apparent in the way that lesbians refer to "the community" as a real entity, whether they perceive it as including potentially all the lesbians of the city, or only those who are socially active members.

Within these social networks, there arises the third feature of the community, the shared values and norms of the lesbian subculture. Fine and Kleinman define a subculture as "a set of understandings, behaviors, and artifacts used by particular groups and diffused through interlocking group networks" (1979, p. 18). These elements exist among those members of the lesbian population who share a group identity, who communicate and interact with each other in social networks of friends or "interlocking group networks," and who share certain basic values. Not all lesbians share in the communication of the subcultural values and, thus, not all members of the lesbian population are part of the lesbian subculture. In general, the values of the subculture are shared among lesbians who are present or former members of a lesbian community, since it is the community which provides the means and the settings in which the values and norms of the subculture are learned, shared, and expressed as the visible "on the ground" behavior and activities of individuals.

The values of the lesbian subculture are synonymous with feminist values, as expressed in the most active and visible segments of the lesbian communities and held to some degree by other participating members. Lesbian-feminism rejects the traditional female role in which women are seen only in their relationships to men. It asserts equality for women, and attributes primary importance to women, and their needs, concerns, and activities. The lesbian subculture provides a women-oriented alternative to the values and concerns of the heterosexual world.

Although these core values are widely held by the members of lesbian communities, the subculture is by no means homogeneous. Other less fundamental values are not shared among all lesbians. The lesbian-feminists described by Wolf (1979) in her study of San Francisco in the early '70s, for example, were the most visible and active segment of that community. Their values and lifestyles were more radical than those of many other women who might also have described themselves as lesbian-feminists and who participated in the community's activities.

The identification of the individual lesbian with the interacting group, the lesbian community, serves as motivation for socialization into the subculture. A number of factors influence this identification, including the availability of access to a community and the attitudes of outsiders (Fine & Kleinman, 1979). Considerable differences exist in the degree of identification with or interaction in communities. Many women have no access to a community because they live in smaller towns. Other women do not identify with other lesbians or feel any need for support from them, or do not find their identification of sufficient importance in their lives to make the effort to seek entry into a community. These lesbians may not share the feminist views of the lesbian subculture, or think of their sexual preference as a common bond and the basis for a shared group identity, or be conscious of themselves as an oppressed minority group. Such a consciousness or group identity is a relatively recent phenomenon, and one that has, as yet, reached only a minority of gay people (D'Emilio, 1983).

The attitudes of outsiders and the stigma that is attached to lesbianism also affects the degree of the individual's identification and interaction with a community. Many women avoid socializing in the community or with other lesbians, because of their fear of becoming identified as lesbians and losing their jobs and families. This behavior is particularly true of older women and women in professional occupations. Professional women are more likely to have considerable investment in a career which they prefer not to risk, while older women may remain closeted because of fear and caution learned in the years before Gay Liberation, when homosexuality was never discussed openly.

The interaction and communication by which lesbians share group values occur both locally, within the social networks of the lesbian community, and nationally, among communities. On the local level, lesbians interact on a face-to-face basis within their social networks and with other members of the community. Individuals who maintain ties with members of other networks, and the local gay or feminist media provide the communication links through which cultural information is exchanged. Nationally, cultural information is exchanged by means of individual ties among the women of different communities, by relatively mobile women who travel and move around the country, by women who attend events such as national and regional women's music festivals and conferences, by musicians and speakers who travel from one community to another, and by the exchange of ideas among a ''gay intelligentsia'' (Blackwood, 1984), the writers and thinkers developing theories and models about lesbians. Information is also disseminated through the media by means of lesbian and gay newspapers, journals, books, and to a lesser extent, slide shows and films. Information is not uniformly distributed, however, and there are regional variations in the subculture, with the East and West Coasts at the forefront of cultural innovation.

The fourth feature of the lesbian community is its institutional base, the gay-defined places and organizations which characterize a community and provide a number of functions for community members. It is this institutional base that provides the means by which a community can mobilize its members for action as a minority group in the larger society, and that is visible, at least to some degree, to the outside world. Lesbian communities are not territorially based. However, they exist in the context of their urban environments, which provide the settings where activities take place and members or organizations meet. Settings may be either relatively permanent, such as a bar or a women's center, or temporary, such as a rented dance hall or a picnic area in a park. Organizations can also be short-lived or long-lived, but they are relatively fixed and visible landmarks in the lesbian social scene. These institutions may parallel those of the larger, heterosexual urban environment, or they may provide functions unique to the lesbian community. Bars, women's centers and bookstores provide places where lesbians can meet and exchange information. Organizations can provide medical services and counselling, cultural and social activities, and political activities and campaigns. Whatever their function, the existence of these institutions is tangible evidence of the feelings of identity and unity of a community.

The institutional base of a community serves an even more important function, however. Unless such an institutional base is present, what exists in any given city is more properly a social network of lesbians, not a lesbian community. There may be feelings of community or unity among individuals arising from their common identity in such a network, and the values of the subculture may be shared among its members. However, a network suffers two major shortcomings in comparison to a community, shortcomings that the presence of an institutional base can alleviate. First, a network of friends depends on the participation of its individual members; if these members disperse or lose interest, the network ceases to exist. In a community, on the other hand, if one institution fails, there are others to provide continuity. Bars, for example, are often short-lived, but as one closes down, another may open up (Achilles, 1967). If a political organization disbands, its members may fall back on the local women's center as a place to socialize.

Secondly, potential new members have no access to a network unless they encounter a member under circumstances that would allow the shared identity to be revealed and an invitation to participate extended. This process can be long and difficult if the women involved are closeted or if contact between them is relatively infrequent. The time required to build up to such a revelation increases correspondingly. In a community, the institutions are open to all, and new members can locate them through a variety of means. The lesbian who is newly out or new in town can contact the local women's center or bookstore, or a hotline or gay guide to find the name of the local mixed (gay) or women's bar. Further, with enough institutions in a city, and some degree of persistence, if one institution does not provide entry another one will.

This is not to deny the importance of social networks to lesbians. For lesbians in small towns, networks of friends may provide the only possible contact with other lesbians. Even in cities with a community whose institutional base provides a variety of visible activities and some means of entry, many women are unaware of the presence of these activities or the means of entry available. Other lesbians, because of their need to remain closeted, do not extend their social activities beyond their networks of friends. Within communities, most socializing takes place among friends who form a network or clique, united by common interests and affection. The presence of gay-defined places and organizations, however, facilitates interaction and the exchange of information among different networks. Because of their greater visibility and accessibility, they serve as the means of entry to the networks and the rest of the community's activities. They also provide an important element of continuity and structure for the fluid and everchanging relationships of the individuals and their networks.

The lesbian community can thus be defined through its four features. It consists of the interacting social networks of lesbians, who share a group identity or consciousness based on their sexual preference along with certain basic values, and who gather together to create and maintain institutions that support their social interaction, and which also serve to support the group identity and the shared values. Communities can be described and compared in terms of the variety of their institutional bases, and the degree of support they receive from community members. The remainder of this article is devoted to one particular lesbian community, as an example of how such discussion might proceed.

An Ethnographic Example

The community I studied is located in a large city in the Southwest with a population of over a quarter million. The study included participant observation over a period of five years, and structured interviews with 81 women who were active in the community to varying degrees. Overall, the sample was very similar in its demographic characteristics to the samples of lesbians in previous studies (e.g., Barnhart, 1975; Krieger, 1982; Ponse, 1978; Wolf, 1979). The women were young, primarily in their twenties and thirties, white, and college-educated.

During the five-year period, the community provided evidence of both an institutional base and socializing among networks of friends and acquaintances. Places included gay spaces, such as bars and a private gay club, and feminist spaces, which included privately owned land outside the city, a women's center, and a women's bookstore. Organizations included feminist groups such as a local chapter of NOW and committees for Take Back the Night marches, and a gay rights organization that published a newsletter.

These institutions were relatively short-lived and did not all exist simultaneously. The number of bars open to women ranged from none to three, including one women's bar open for a few months immediately before, and another one open after the field period. Although the women's center and bookstore were open the entire period, the private club was opened and then closed again, and the women's land was sold. The gay rights organization disbanded shortly after observation began, and nothing similar appeared to take its place. Although the lesbian community allied itself with the gay male community for a demonstration against Anita Bryant, and with other feminists for two successive annual Take Back the Night marches, sustained interest in political issues was relatively low. This lack of interest was due in part to the conservative atmosphere of the city and state. The women of the lesbian community maintained many ties with other feminists, but few with the gay male community, and there was little interaction or socializing with gay men.

Organized social activities in the community included occasional concerts by nationally known lesbian performers or by local musicians, community-wide parties, dances, plays, and sports teams, particularly softball teams organized within the city's softball leagues. The private club provided similar social activities for its members. Aside from the softball games, the number of organized activities averaged from six to eight a year.

In spite of the variety of institutions and activities available, this community was not as stable as some of the more established communities in other cities. The histories of the various institutions illustrate some of the reasons for this situation. The women's center and bookstore were able to survive because they drew much of their financial support from other feminists outside the community. Lack of financial support was the reason neither the women's land, the private club, nor the women's bars were able to remain in existence. The life of the club was further complicated by conflicts among women of varying lifestyles it attracted as members and differences of opinion about the way it was run.

The softball teams, on the other hand, were a successful community institution. The number of teams grew from one to three, with new players every season. The games attracted many fans and provided an opportunity for socializing on a regular basis during the summer. Their success was partly due to the fact that the games were free for fans, relatively low-cost for team members, and organized by the city. Thus, they did not lay a heavy financial or organizational burden on the community or on individual women. As women, lesbians have relatively low incomes, and many lesbians, in this community as in others, deliberately choose unskilled or lower-paid jobs to avoid working for the patriarchal and heterosexual establishment. Thus, finances are always a problem in the lesbian community. Furthermore, because of the relatively small size of this community, when individual organizers became "burned out," there were frequently not enough new people to take their places. The gay rights organization and newsletter, which was the work of a few men and women, met its demise because of the "burn-out" and changing interests of its founders.

Most socializing in the community took place at parties, dinners, picnics, and poker sessions. Groups of friends or networks, united by their common interests and mutual affection, composed the internal structure of the community. The women who were regular bar-goers were a different "crowd" than the members of the private club, which did not serve alcohol. Radical feminists were not usually club members, since few of them could afford the membership dues, and many disagreed with its policies. The club was supported by a number of regulars, including some professional women who rarely appeared anywhere else, and by a constantly changing stream of newcomers to the city and to the community, who used the club to acquire a group of friends or a lover, and who then let their memberships lapse while they socialized elsewhere. The softball teams and their fans usually met after games and practices over beer, while the women involved in organizing concerts or marches were likely to socialize with women similarly involved. Groups were fluid, however, and there was considerable interaction and overlap among them. Communication was facilitated by the many individuals who were involved with more than one group, or who had varied friends and interests.

The number of women who participated in the activities of the community was relatively low because of a number of factors. Out of an estimated population of several thousand lesbians, there were nearly 800 who had been members of the club at one time or another, while concerts of well-known musicians drew audiences of 200 to 300 women. The number of women who participated in the community's activities with any regularity can be set somewhere around 500 to 600 women. Age was one of the most important factors in determining individual participation in the community. Most of the women interviewed were in their 20s and 30s with only a quarter over 40. This reflects roughly the proportion of older women who actually participated in community activities. Their lower participation arose partly from lifelong habits of being closeted, the greater number of years that older women have invested in their careers, and also to a lack of interest in the social activities that the community had to offer. A frequent complaint heard among these women was the absence of other women their age in the community, and the different interests of the younger women who were often perceived as too radical, or too concerned with partying and drinking, or in looking for a lover.

Some younger women, on the other hand, perceived older women as too conservative, both in their lifestyles and in their feminist (or non-feminist) attitudes. Groups of elder women were occasionally referred to by some women as "the polyester pants suit crowd." Women of different ages did socialize together, however. Furthermore, the relatively small number of older women who did participate in the community provided important resources for the community out of proportion to their actual numbers. These resources included financial backing for the club, organizing and coaching the softball teams, hosting parties open to everyone in the community, and providing stability and role models for younger women.

Ethnicity was another important factor in participation. All but two of the sample were white, in spite of the fact that one-third of the city's population is Mexican-American. This sample bias reflects the fact that Mexican-American lesbians did not, for the most part, interact with the white lesbians of the community. The data indicate that these women maintained their own social networks, which are closed to white women. Only a few Mexican-American women interacted in the community with any degree of regularity, and they occupied a marginal position among Mexican-American lesbians, rather than serving as a bridge between the two groups. Cultural and language differences, and a continuing history of prejudice and discrimination have created a barrier that is not overcome by the bond of a common sexual preference. Given the strong family ties and Catholic heritage of Mexican-Americans, it is also likely that Mexican-American lesbians find themselves in a position similar to that of the black lesbians in an unpublished sociological study (Hunter, 1969). The black women could not be open about their sexual preference because of the fear of bringing shame on their families and being ostracized from the black community, both of which they were psychologically dependent upon and committed to from birth, as a means of survival in the hostile white world. Those few black lesbians whom Hunter observed participating in "public gay life," which then consisted mainly of gay bars, were already alienated from the black community. While the Mexican-American community may provide a family structure and an ethnic identity that is important to Mexican-American lesbians, it also makes it more difficult for them to come out as lesbians because they risk the loss of that family and ethnic community support for the less certain support of the white lesbian community. The result is that Mexican-American lesbians interact primarily with each other in their own social networks. These networks do not constitute a community because they lack the institutional base that is one of the features of a lesbian community. In this city, the lesbian community is dominated by the feminist-oriented white lesbians who have created its institutional base.

The limited direction and leadership that can be found in this essentially undirected and acephalic community came from those women who organized the activities and events of the community. The lives of these core members revolved almost entirely around the community. Core members socialized almost exclusively with other lesbians, and a few of them even chose jobs that allowed them contact primarily with other lesbians at work. They could be expected to show up at almost every scheduled event or activity. Theirs were the faces that everyone recognized, whether they were typed as party-goers or as organizers.

Core members usually became known for particular activities or roles which they filled, in addition to the large amount of time they spent in the community. These women were artists and writers, counselors, athletic stars of the softball teams, political organizers and speakers for the "Take Back the Night" marches, or hosts of the occasional community-wide parties. Others were well-known because they had been community members for many years, or because they were vocal and out-going individuals who showed up at every event and had an opinion on every issue.

Most community members were fringe members, women who were moderately active. Fringe members made up the majority of the community. They learned the norms and the values of the subculture, considered themselves to be members of the community, but did not have any desire to "run the show," or submerge themselves completely in it.

Potential members could gain entry into the community and become fringe members, while fringe members could become more actively involved and become core members. The reverse could also occur. Often a woman will withdraw from community activities when she enters into a relationship in order to spend more time with her lover. This occurs frequently enough that it has become enshrined in lesbian folklore as "disappearing into the sunset." Core members are particularly vulnerable to "burn-out," the result of too much organizational activity with too few rewards, and they may choose to become less active. Other women become disillusioned and alienated because of unrealistic expectations of mutual support and idealistic views of "sisterhood." In spite of changing personal relationships, however, the institutional base of the community and the values of the subculture provide a structure and some degree of continuity, making this community more than just a network of friends, and creating the foundation for ongoing activities that have the potential to reach an ever-widening number of women.

CONCLUSIONS

The lesbian community has four characteristic features: (1) interacting social networks; (2) a group identity based on sexual preference; (3) sub-cultural values, which are basically feminist in origin; and (4) an institutional base of organizations and settings which provide places and structures for lesbian interaction. This institutional base also serves to support the group identity, spread the values of the subculture, and provide some degree of continuity and structure beyond the social networks.

This definition of the term lesbian community provides a basis for further anthropological research. Based on this definition other communities can be compared in terms of the number and form of their institutions and the functions their institutional bases provide. Rather than criticizing previous researchers for having focused their studies on primarily white, young, well-educated, and middle class women (Krieger, 1982), studies should recognize the difference between the lesbian population, which undoubtedly includes a wide variety of women, and the lesbian community, which is limited in the kinds of women it attracts as members. Researchers need to focus on the reasons for, and the levels of, participation of other lesbians, such as older women or minority women. Other vital areas are the roles of community core members, the links between different networks, and the ways in which those networks facilitate socializing and the exchange of information.

Comparisons of communities will serve to point out other differences among them, and perhaps illuminate some of the external factors that help create a community. One would expect that communities in larger cities would have a larger population of lesbians to draw on, and thus would be able to support a greater number and variety of institutions. However, the population of a city is not the only factor that would influence the size and structure of its lesbian community. The presence of a university, the existence of a gay rights ordinance, or a reputation for a liberal and tolerant attitude in the city may be other contributing factors.

This article represents an attempt to clarify the term "lesbian community," so that researchers will be better able to study them. Eventually, such research should provide lesbians with a better understanding of themselves and of the ways in which they may successfully build their communities and provide themselves with the mutual support they want and need.

REFERENCES

Achilles, N. (1967). The development of the homosexual bars as an institution. In J. Gagnon & W. Simon (Eds.), *Sexual deviance* (pp. 228-244). New York: Harper & Row.

Barnhart, E. (1975). Friends and lovers in a lesbian counterculture community. In N. Glazer Malbin (Ed.), *Old family/new family*. New York: Van Nostrand Press.

Blackwood, E. (1984). Personal communication.

Blumstein, P. W., & Schwartz, P. (1974). Lesbianism and bisexuality. In E. Goode & R. R. Troiden (Eds.), *Sexual deviance and sexual deviants* (pp. 278-295). New York: William Morrow.

Bullough, V. L., & Bullough, B. (1977). Lesbianism in the 1920s and 1930s: A newfound study. *Signs: Journal of Women in Culture and Society, 2,* 895-904.

D'Emilio, J. (1983). *Sexual politics, sexual communities: The making of a homosexual minority in the U.S., 1940-1970.* Chicago: University of Chicago Press.

Fine, G. A., & Kleinman, S. (1979). Rethinking subculture: An interactionist analysis. *American Journal of Sociology, 85,* 1-20.

Hunter, E. (1969). *Double indemnity: The Negro lesbian in the "straight" white world.* (Available from Archive of Contemporary History, University of Wyoming, P.O. Box 3334, Laramie, WY.)

Katz, J. (1976). *Gay American history: Lesbians and gay men in the U.S.A.* New York: Thomas Y. Crowell.

Kinsey, A. C., Pomeroy, W., Martin, C. E., & Gebhard, P. E. (1953). *Sexual behavior in the human female.* New York: W. B. Saunders.

Krieger, S. (1982). Lesbian identity and community: Recent social science literature. *Signs: Journal of Women in Culture and Society, 8,* 91-108.

Ponse, B. (1978). *Identities in the lesbian world: The social construction of self.* Westport, CT: Greenwood Press.

Simon, W. & Gagnon, J. (1967). The lesbians: A preliminary overview. In J. Gagnon & W. Simon (Eds.), *Sexual deviance* (pp. 247-282). New York: Harper & Row.

Wolf, D. G. (1979). *The lesbian community.* Berkeley: University of California Press.

"Mummies and Babies" and Friends and Lovers in Lesotho

Judith Gay, PhD

Episcopal Divinity School

ABSTRACT. This paper examines an institutionalized friendship among adolescent girls and young women in southern Africa. Lesotho's economy is based on migrant male labor which leaves the women dependent on male earnings or subsistence from the land, and also creates unstable marital relations. Young girls in the modern schools develop close relationships, called "mummy-baby," with slightly older girls. Sexual intimacy is an important aspect of these relationships. Mummy-baby relationships not only provide emotional support prior to marriage, but also a network of support for married and unmarried women in new towns or schools, either replacing or accompanying heterosexual bonds.

This paper examines a type of institutionalized friendship in Lesotho, an independent migrant labor exporting country in southern Africa. These friendships most often occur among adolescent Basotho girls, who refer to each other by the English terms *mummies* and *babies*. They are closely related to heterosexual courtship that becomes dominant in late adolescence. Few ethnographic accounts give details about social and emotional relationships during adolescence. During this critical period girls usually experience three of the most profound bodily changes of their lives: Puberty, loss of virginity, and first childbirth (Hastrup, 1978). Furthermore, few ethnographic accounts discuss "homosexual" physical and emotional relationships, nor the adolescent shift from primary association with same-sex playmates and workmates to opposite-sex lovers and marital partners. Lionel Tiger (1969) argues in *Men in Groups* that women, in contrast to men, "do not form bonds. Dependent as most

An earlier version of this article was published in *Cambridge Anthropology*, 1979, Vol. 5, No. 3, the "Issue on Sexuality." Data for this article were collected while doing field research concerning the impact of migrant labor on rural women in Lesotho during 1976 and 1977. The author acknowledges the Smuts Memorial Fund and Sir Bartle Frere's Memorial Fund at Cambridge University for financial assistance which helped to make this field work possible. Gratitude is also expressed to Dr. Susan Drucker-Brown for invaluable suggestions on the preliminary draft of this article, and to Judith Ennew and members of their seminar on Kinship and Structuring of Sexuality for their comments. The author may be contacted at the Episcopal Divinity School, 99 Brattle Street, Cambridge, MA 02138.

women are on the earnings and genes of men, they break ranks very soon'' (p. 216). His argument is based on a lack of cross-cultural data concerning female friendships, which not only precede, but also exist alongside heterosexual relationships. It is my hope that this paper will contribute to the studies of female sexuality and the social roles of women, which are beginning to fill this ethnographic gap.

In such studies it is important to examine the nature of the sub-cultures girls create in adolescence, in order to see how they handle their physical maturation, emotional growth, and broadening social relationships. It is also necessary to break free from the ethnocentric polarization of homosexual and heterosexual relations that is such a marked feature of western culture, and take a fresh look at the neglected topic of affective relations among members of the same sex. Furthermore, any such inquiry into the structuring of sexual relations must be considered in light of the particular socio-economic conditions which dominate the lives of the individuals concerned.

SOCIAL AND ECONOMIC CONTEXT OF FEMALE FRIENDSHIPS IN LESOTHO

Lesotho is a country completely surrounded by the Republic of South Africa. The dominant feature of its socio-economic life is male migrant labor. About half of Lesotho's adult male labor force migrates to South Africa, leaving women in Lesotho for most of their lives as daughters without fathers, sisters without brothers, wives without husbands, and mothers without sons. In the rural lowlands village of 1,484 people where my fieldwork was conducted, 82% of the men between the ages of 20 and 39 were away as migrant workers for some portion of 1977.

Employment opportunities for women within Lesotho's towns are few and poorly paid, and most women are excluded by South Africa's ''influx control'' measures from living and working in The Republic. This forces them into increasing dependence on male earnings and on subsistence agriculture in impoverished rural areas. At the same time that the migrant labor system has increased female economic dependence, it makes marital relationships unstable. It prevents the establishment of close conjugal relations and encourages adultery, non-support, desertion and divorce. Marriage within a patrilineal family system remains the norm, but it is devalued in contrast to continuing close ties with mothers and siblings, who provide women with security in times of marital failure and economic distress.

Despite the importance of close ties with natal kin, fosterage arrangements are often made for children when marriages fail, extra-marital or pre-marital pregnancies occur, or mothers must seek employment. Many children are also separated from their mothers in order to attend school, or to provide help with child-care, house-work, or herding for relatives. Later, at the time of marriage, girls must leave their natal kin and move to their husband's homes. After just a few weeks of marriage they are often left with an unfamiliar mother-in-law and new neighbors when the husband goes off to his distant place of work. Young wives are eager to establish independent neo-local residence, but then they may spend the early years of marriage in lonely little homes waiting for the occasional visit of migrant husbands. Wives who are left alone in the rural areas, and unwed mothers and deserted wives who seek employment in towns, have to be self-reliant and independent in order to survive and to support their children.

Churches, schools, and a modern cash economy have undermined many social traditions. Sesotho initiation for girls is no longer practiced in most lowland villages, where about half of the nation's population lives. In the village I studied, there had been no girls' initiation conducted for twenty years; and only 10% of the women between the ages of 20 and 39 had been initiated. A western style education is highly valued, particularly for girls; 91.1 per cent of the girls and 65.7 per cent of the boys from ages 7 to 16 were attending school during 1977. Most aspects of the life of children, as well as of adults, are segregated by sex, but the common culture that develops in the co-educational schools provides a meeting ground for the sexes over which parents can exert little control. Traditional *rites de passage* and adult social control having declined in importance, modern youth culture plays an increasingly important role in socialization and regulation of adolescent interpersonal relations.

ORIGINS OF MUMMY-BABY RELATIONS

Basotho girls engage in three types of activities which they call *papali* (games), in which they act out different aspects of adult female roles. In playing house they pretend to cook and perform other domestic tasks without the drudgery of regular responsibility; in elaborate mock wedding festivities they celebrate marriages without husbands, in-laws or bridewealth; and in dyadic mummy-baby friendships they experience the nurturing aspects of mothering and being mothered, without the risks of childbirth or the responsibilities of child-care. This stands in contrast to the major role girls have in the care of younger children within their households.

In each of these activities young girls are gradually socialized into adult female roles and relationships by slightly older and more experienced girls. In Sesotho custom there is a strict prohibition against discussing sexual matters by a woman who has borne children with one who has not.

Where such a barrier is created by discourse taboos, and where mothers advocate a sexual morality of marital fidelity which is at variance with their own conduct, it is unlikely that a girl can obtain sexual information and advice from her own mother. Thus, it is particularly significant that these mummy-baby relations have developed as a way in which a fictive mother can provide what a biological mother cannot.

John Blacking (1959) first pointed to the existence of fictive kinship relations among Venda girls 20 years ago. In a more recent article he described Venda and Zulu school-girl friendships as "part of a common Black South African culture . . . associated with modern school education," perhaps diffused from a single source or "invented more than once" (1978, p. 104). Martha Mueller (1977) reported similar relationships in two villages in Lesotho, and my own investigations have documented their presence in many parts of Lesotho, as well as in Johannesburg and Durban. Girls regard these relationships as very personal, however, and only discuss them reticently with a stranger whose disapproval they fear. Hence, my study is limited to observations and to interviews with 14 village women, who were willing to discuss their own relationships and those of other women in the village, the larger towns and in more distant boarding schools.

The origin and diffusion of these institutionalized friendships are not clear. In Lesotho, as in the areas Blacking discusses, these relationships seem strongest in the modern school culture, yet have their roots in traditional institutions and practices.

The dyads in Lesotho are almost invariably described by the English words mummies and babies, whether embedded in English or Sesotho sentences. The use of the English terms bears out the assertion of several of my informants that the mummy-baby game is relatively new, first occurring during the 1950s. It apparently spread rapidly through the secondary schools, which drew pupils from diverse parts of Lesotho, as well as from South Africa. Prior to South Africa's rigid apartheid laws, there was considerable movement of Basotho women and children in and out of South Africa, as well as circulation of the educated elite among mission schools and training institutions. Quite likely free movement between towns and schools of southern Africa was a mechanism for the development and diffusion of a common black southern African culture in which these relations are just one ingredient. However, it seems clear that there were features of traditional female society which provided basic models.

First, elderly informants told me that special affective and gift-exchange partnerships among girls and women existed in "the old days" of their youth. Informants said that these were known simply by the Sesotho terms: *ho ratana* (to like or love one another), *Lechako* (from the verb *ho chaka*, to visit) *sethaka* (a relationship between agemates, *lithaka* usually referred to girls who had been initiated together), and *mechaufa* (from *ho chaufa*, meaning to fall in love or to flatter). This last word is not in the standard Sesotho dictionary, but my two oldest informants said it refers particularly to a love affair between girls.

Secondly, there is the underlying influence of female initiation traditions, though none of my informants acknowledged a connection between the mummy-baby relations and the initiation-sponsor relationships that Blacking describes for the Venda (1959, 1978), and Krige for the Lovedu (1953, pp. 111-125). Certainly, wherever initiation is practiced, small groups of girls spend an intense period of time in the company of agemates and are prepared for adult sexual lives by female teachers who are not their own mothers. Modern female friendships, at the very least, help to fill a vacuum created by the decline of female initiation, even if, as Blacking believes, there is little evidence of direct cultural continuity (1978, p. 101).

An additional feature of traditional female sexuality in Lesotho, which may have an indirect relation to this institution, is the practice of lengthening the labia minora. This is still practiced by many girls, as a matter of female pride, and is believed to enhance sexual pleasure during intercourse (Longmore 1959, pp. 40-41). The process of lengthening is done alone or in small groups, but is not directly tied to initiation. The process is said to heighten *mocheso* (heat) and appears to provide opportunities for auto-eroticism and mutual stimulation between girls. This practice stands in sharp contrast to taboos against masturbation in our own society, and to the practice of clitoredectomy in other African societies. It is also true that girls are warned by adults to avoid eating eggs and the inside parts of sheep, for these are believed to heighten *mocheso* and to lead a girl prematurely to desire sexual relations with boys. Thus, in these two contradictory customs female sensuality is both encouraged and restrained, but it is never denied.

THE PARTICIPANTS IN MUMMY-BABY RELATIONS

Mummy-baby relations in the village I studied are most common among pre-adolescent and adolescent school girls, although pre-school girls occasionally form pairs in imitation of their older acquaintances. Older unmarried girls who have dropped out of school and remain in the village, and those who have gone to the towns to seek employment or to attend distant schools, often maintain old ties, and form new ones in the urban environment. One informant said that she thought these relationships were most common among *ma-hippi* (plural of the English term "hippy"), meaning smartly dressed, single students or young working women in the towns, who often live with other women in rented rooms apart from their families. But mummy-baby relationships are also important in the lives of many older women who have gone to the capital city to take up work as domestic servants. These women form their own urban community while living in tiny servant's quarters apart from kin and former friends. Within the village I studied and the villages in which Mueller worked, some young wives maintained old, and formed new intimate friendships. Some married women said that former "childish" types of relations had matured to become "real adult friendships." Informants stated that in villages that are near the main road and the South African border, most adult women are no longer involved in intimate female friendships. In these villages men often come home on leave and women appear to be more interested in adulterous male lovers than in women friends.

I only began asking about these relationships after living for a year in the village. I told my research assistant that I had never heard anybody mention them. She chided me by saying that if I observed, and listened to the way girls and women sometimes addressed each other, saw how they sat together in a concert or a beer hall, or seemed startled when we found them together when we arrived for an interview, such relationships would have been apparent. She was right, of course, but my oversight can be attributed to the privacy that is an essential aspect of these relations, and points out the women's fear of condemnation by an outsider.

A conversation on female friendships with three older women was interrupted by the arrival of a 24-year-old daughter-in-law, who gasped and clapped her hands in amazement when she heard the topic of our discussion. "Why are you clapping so?" asked the straightforward 97-year-old woman. "Haven't you ever fallen in love with another girl?"

INITIATION OF A RELATIONSHIP

Relationships are always initiated voluntarily by one girl who takes a liking to another and simply asks her to be her mummy or her baby, depending on their relative ages. Real kin are rarely chosen, except by very small girls whom older girls say "don't know what the game is all about and are only playing at it."[2] Girls sometimes ask a village acquaintance or a sister's friend, but often choose a newcomer to the village, a schoolmate from another village, or an attractive older girl or woman from the nearby town where most of the shops, churches and schools are located. Thus, the initiation of such a relationship is a recognized means whereby a girl can extend the range of her social relations.

The most frequently given reason for initiating a particular relationship was that one girl felt attracted to the other by her looks, her clothes, or her actions. When I suggested that girls might approach an older girl or woman as a patron, thinking of the gifts or material help they can gain from the relationship, some informants expressed shock, saying that such an attitude would spoil the relationship, which should be based on sincere love, not on selfish calculation. Other informants admitted that some girls, particularly in the towns, do use the relationships as a calculated means to gain patrons, but they felt this practice debased the meaning of the bond.

The fictive kinship terminology used by the girls derives from the central mother-child bond of Basotho families, a bond that is often disrupted by fosterage and schooling. It is an accepted rule that a mummy may have several babies, but no baby may have more than one mummy at the same time. However, such rules do not prevent the formation of ties outside the village or school community, nor limit the number of relationships an individual may enter into as partners move away or marry. One of my informants reported having had six mummies between ages 12 and 18; and one of Mueller's cases, Clorina, was an unmarried mother still atttending school, who had had nine mummies although never any fictive babies (see Case 1). Some girls declined new relations because of previous commitments; Clorina's case was unusual. Other girls said they had not been particularly attracted to the person who proposed the relationship but they hadn't wanted to hurt her feelings by saying so. Others said they didn't know the other well, so they accepted the offer just to see how the relationship would develop.

THE NATURE OF A RELATIONSHIP: ENCOUNTERS AND EXCHANGES

Once two girls agree to be mummy and baby, the relationship develops through arranged encounters and by material, nurturant, and emotional exchanges which vary with relative age and marital status of the partners. Arrangements to meet somewhere or to do something together are almost always initiated by the older, dominant member of the dyad, and are generally arranged secretly so that others will not know of the arrangement or what they do when they meet. "You, as baby can't just go and visit your mummy," an informant explained, "for you respect her and would feel ashamed to do so. She must invite you." Thus, the deferential behavior appropriate towards older women is expected. A mummy may see her baby on the way to school and suggest that she come to visit and play cards on Saturday afternoon, knowing that her real mother will be away visiting that day. Or the mummy may hand the baby a letter suggesting that they meet at the football field, an evening concert, or that they go to collect firewood. Since letter writing is an essential means by which Basotho migrants keep in touch with their families and friends, it is not surprising that the exchange of letters is a feature of the mummy-baby game. Schoolteachers say that they often find "love letters" awkwardly scribbled by one school pupil to another. These children practice one of the principal uses to which literacy is put in Lesotho, and master the stock phrases used in such letters (see Blacking, 1959).

Gift-giving is an essential part of the mummy role. Mummies most often provide sweets, cosmetics, headties, or inexpensive items of clothing. One girl said that, whenever she is shopping and sees something nice, she will think of her baby and want to buy it for her. When one village woman married and then delivered her first child, it was her former mummy of many years back who was the first village woman to visit and bring her gifts of soap and baby clothing. Babies will reciprocate if they can with a few peaches or vegetables from their homes, or any small thing they may have, although it is understood that they are normally on the receiving end of the transactions.

For those girls who go away to boarding schools, gift giving and other material help becomes much more important, as Blacking points out in his study, because of the regimented living conditions, limited recreation, and poor food (1978). Informants who had attended such schools in Lesotho not only had school girl mummies or babies, but mummies who were older married women from a nearby village who gave tinned biscuits, cooked food, clothing, soap, or creams and occasionally even loaned money to their babies. Some would invite the baby along with a few friends to a Sunday afternoon party in the village. Girls who had been unable to find dormitory accommodations were given rent-free housing by married women who became their mummies in the sense of an adult foster-mother rather than a partner in an adolescent friendship.

Other important help given by mummies was in the form of advice and protection concerning love-relationships with men. Among the Basotho, as among the Zulu whose youth culture is discussed in detail by Reader (1966), love-relations are not directed at first towards marriage but towards establishing one's personhood in society. Boys see sexual conquests as a mark of achieving manhood, and conquests are a dominant preoccupation of migrant men of all ages home on leave from the single-sex compounds where they live and work. Sexual relations are problematic for girls during adolescence when they realize the risks of premarital pregnancy. Yet they are anxious both to learn the rules of the heterosexual game and to have female support when they begin to play it in earnest.

A girl's own mother can rarely give realistic advice or protection because of traditional prohibitions on sexual discourse. Mothers advocate old-fashioned norms of premarital chastity and marital fidelity which few people follow, and the attitude that love between a boy and a girl should never be displayed in front of adults. But an adolescent mummy can provide advice on sex and protection from aggressively courting young men which a mother cannot give. For example, informants said that, when girls go to play netball, hold mock weddings or participate in dancing and singing contests in other villages, their older mummies often go along for protection and to enjoy the fun of the inter-village female activities which they have outgrown.

The most important aspect of mummy-baby relations is the exchange of affection and sensual satisfaction. My informants talked openly about gifts, letters, visits, and advice, but were invariably reticent in discussing the emotional and sensual aspects of the relationships. Yet, when conversation became intimate, they said that, yes, this was what these relationships were really about and why they were different from ordinary friendships. One informant explained:

> Friends may visit, love each other, even give gifts now and then. But between mummies and babies it is like an affair, a romance, and being alone together to hug and kiss each other is always a part of it. (Field notes, 1976-77)

Every informant agreed that this aspect is essential, except in those cases where there is a great age differential which makes the relation more like that between a foster mother and her ward, or between very little girls who are really too young to "know what it is all about" and are just "playing at it."

Physical relations between females in Lesotho appear to fall into three distinct levels of intimacy. First, there is the common, public form of greeting when Basotho friends and relatives of either sex meet after a period of absence and kiss (*ho suna*) each other on the lips. At this level also friends or relatives of the same sex, who have lived all their lives with inadequate furniture in crowded households, often share a bed or sleep side-by-side in blanket rolls on the floor. The second form is distinguished from the public form as the way mummies and babies kiss and hug each other (*ho sunana* and *ho tsoarana*, with reciprocal verb endings) and rest together on the bed when they meet in private, or when one calls the other out in the dark at a concert or a dance to embrace. A third and more intense level of genital sexuality may exist between females. However, when I asked about "people of the same sex making love like a man and a woman," most women said they disapprove of it and regard it as quite distinct from the normal "hugging and kissing" of the mummy-baby game. Several informants said that the Bible forbids people of the same sex sleeping together and making love like a man and a woman, and cited sermons they had heard against homosexuality. Some said they had heard of men in mines who do such things, but they could not imagine how it could happen between women. But several younger unmarried informants said matter-of-factly that certainly it does happen, that some school girls learn to make love in that way, and that they personally see nothing wrong with it. My limited facility in the language, as well as my hesitance in asking, prevented clarification. The two types of responses may indicate that informants perceived my questions in quite different ways, in addition to affirming separate opinions about very subtle and personal matters.

It is the second level of physical contact which is the recognized norm in these fictive kinship relations. Although the informants were reticent in discussing their own present involvements, if they continued to have them, they were willing to discuss the relationships in general and their own past experiences. All expressed pleasure in remembering, and they insisted that they saw nothing wrong in such physical involvement with other girls. One girl said that at 15, when asked to be somebody's mummy, she had felt too shy to kiss although she realized that having accepted the senior role, she should have taken the initiative. The next year, an older girl became her mummy, and then, she said with a smile, "I was not too shy." Another informant told with pleasure of a church youth group outing where the bus had broken down in the night and couples rested together on their blankets, some girls with their boyfriends, and some with mummies or babies, while the teacher in charge and the bus driver were preoccupied with repairs. Although informants experienced these relationships as normal and enjoyable, and said their mothers usually permitted them if they knew, girls who had attended mission schools said that the nuns and matrons strongly disapproved and attempted to prevent them.

It is clear that these structured friendships provide opportunities for adolescent girls to discover and enjoy with other girls their own developing sexuality within a parentally tolerated relationship. They fill this need at an age when heterosexual relations are forbidden by adults and carry with them the risks of non-marital pregnancy and termination of schooling. Such mummy-baby relations also provide opportunities for girls to experience both dominant and receptive sexual roles, just as the experiences of real childbirth and childcare involve females first as dependent daughters and sisters and then as nurturing mothers. In courtship and marriage, on the other hand, it is always the Mosotho male who is expected to take the initiative in suggesting sexual encounters, in the act of sex, and in jural, ritual and economic matters as head of the family. Within mummy-baby relations, as within mother-centered female society generally, a girl passes from junior to senior roles as relationships change. She may even be engaged in both at the same time, passing on to her baby by words and actions what she has learned of love-making, and nurture, from her older mummy.

The emotional appeal of these relations is not merely in the sensual intimacy. It is present equally in the drama of making, breaking and re-creating relationships. This aspect appears in several recurrent themes in the accounts by informants. One theme is that girls take the initiative to propose love (*ho fereha*), an otherwise male prerogative and a dominant preoccupation of village men and boys. In heterosexual affairs, girls can only flirt and make themselves attractive (*ho iteka*) but in the mummy-baby game they can propose love with all its attendant excitement and anxiety. A second theme is secrecy, the idea that clandestine meetings must be arranged and that detection by critical adults, jealous age-mates, and prying youngsters should be avoided. Another is that of jealousy: hurt feelings when neglected, painful times of not speaking to one another and perhaps parting, or tender moments of apologizing and forgiving. Jealousy among partners and potential partners is also common. One woman proudly said that, when she had moved as a new bride to the village, many young women had asked her to be mummy or baby to them. They had, however, troubled her a lot because they were so jealous of each other, so she used to beat her babies when they squabbled. Another woman, Malerato, said that, when she had gone away from home to attend high school, still unmarried at the age of 20, she had two babies who loved her very much but were jealous of each other, a problem she finally solved by "giving" one of them to become the baby of a friend (see case 2).

Thus, romantic dramas of attraction, proposal, jealousy, estrangement, reconciliation, and restructuring of relationships are features of this game. This is important to recognize as we try to relate these fictive kinship relations to real kinship and marriage: the mother-child dyad, and the husband-wife dyad.

Mother-child bonds are biologically determined and immutable. Although they can be shared through child-minding and fosterage arrangements, they cannot be fundamentally altered. The structure of husband-wife relations is also relatively unchangeable once it is established and sealed by bridewealth, the birth of children, and the economic interdependence of the family. But pre-marital and marital relations also have dramatic aspects in courtship, jealousy, infidelity, confession, reconciliation, wife beating, fighting and separation. These instabilities are deeply threatening to the conjugal bond which is vital for reproductive and economic security; but they are also foci of passion, and a dominant preoccupation of village life. Their centrality is expressed in the adulterous alliances in which most adult Basotho are involved. It is significant that in mummy-baby friendships, as well as in adulterous affairs and real mothering relationships, women are able to exercise a great degree of initiative and autonomous action. This stands in contrast to the formal rules of marriage, where women are constrained by both the male-dominated family system and by the modern male-dominated economic system.

ADULT HETEROSEXUALITY AND FEMALE FRIENDSHIP

In addition to the female-to-female interactions so far considered, mummy-baby relations provide a training situation through which older girls help to introduce their juniors into the world of heterosexual relationships. In order to discuss this aspect we must first consider the rules that govern these fictive kinship relations, the common extensions of simple mummy-baby dyads, and the interlocking of these fictive kinship relations with heterosexual relations.

It is accepted that a mummy may have several babies who are then like sisters who may argue or feel jealous if one thinks she is being unfairly treated. Such jealousy is considered perfectly normal among sisters, despite the problems it creates. Likewise, it is permissible to have multi-generational chains: A girl plays the mother role in one dyad and the baby role in another at the same time. In such cases the junior girl may call the oldest "grandmother," but such a second-order link does not involve any specific obligation since each dyad is uniquely created by affection and voluntary choice. What is distinctly not allowed is for a girl to have more than one mummy; this only happens if done secretly, or in the case of consecutive relationships.

The rules of the game appear to be based on the biological nature of the uterine (mother and children) family group. However, the transactional aspects of the relation are equally important and suggest a parallel with conjugal as well as maternal bonds. Since a baby receives more in terms of gifts, help, advice and protection than she gives, and since long-term rearing reciprocities (see Goody, E.N., 1971) are not entailed, what she is expected to return is undivided loyalty and affection. Attempts to capitalize on the situation by accumulating many mummies are regarded as unfair because the loyalty with which a girl can reciprocate is thereby diluted. Should too many girls select the same wealthy or very attractive girl to be their mummy, they know that they must still give her their undivided loyalty even though they cannot expect undivided attention or a monopoly on gifts. Thus, the case of Malerato (case 2) is much more typical than that of Clorina (case 1).

The asymmetrical gift exchange, the dependency and loyalty of the junior to the senior, as well as the affective sensual relations between partners who are usually close in age, suggest a similarity to conjugal relations. In Lesotho, marriage is generally based on emotional attraction between peers. It is initiated by a dominant male who proposes to a receptive female, and involves economic ties and sexual relations initiated by the husband, to whom the wife is expected to be unfailingly loyal. This same loyalty is not expected from husbands. Women who do have other lovers must keep these affairs secret. Thus, there are enough similarities to conjugal relations to suggest that girls are learning the dynamics of the heterosexual relations within the mummy-baby game.

In fact the girls' game provides explicit opportunities for initiation into heterosexual relations. There are opportunities for older girls who have boyfriends to tell about their experiences to younger girls. Parents generally approve of the bonds between girls as a way of postponing heterosexual affairs, but distinctly disapprove of male participation in the game. However, the very same institution which helps to protect adolescent girls and to meet their emotional and physical needs also stimulates sexual interest and introduces girls into heterosexual affairs. This situation corresponds with the socialization pattern described as "transitional overlap" among the Xhosa youth groups (Mayer & Mayer, 1970), and also relates to the institutionalized Zulu courtship relations in which groups of girls advise, protect and control their younger members in early heterosexual affairs (Eastrup, 1978; Krige, 1968; Reader, 1966).

In Lesotho, where education is now generally coeducational and girls normally engage in adolescent affairs with boyfriends, female friendships are always spoken of in mother-daughter, never in husband-wife terms. This arrangement is in contrast to situations Blacking (1978) describes in single-sex boarding schools in Natal, and Giallombardo (1966) describes in a female prison in America. In these cases affective relations between females are constructed as fictive marriages. In Lesotho it is biological males, not females in male roles, who introduce the heterosexual dynamic.

A girl may become involved with a boyfriend, become pregnant or even get married, while still a mummy to a younger girl. Sometimes an older girl may actually invite a girl to be her baby in order to assist a boy in arranging an affair. Occasionally boys participate in the game as "sonnys" or as "daddys." A girl may take a fancy to a younger boy and invite him to be her sonny. Usually such a sonny is simply an appealing little boy in town. Older girls may choose a schoolboy or even a single young man home from the mines. This differs from the West African "God-ma" type of relation between a mature woman and a young boyfriend whom she finances (see the novel, *Jagua Nana*, Ekwensi, 1961). Most Basotho informants were shocked at the idea that sexual relations could exist between a fictive mother and son. But one informant said that a sonny might come to love another female baby of their common mummy. This too is considered wrong since "they should be like brother and sister to each other"; they should observe family respect rules (incest taboo) since love between them would cause their mummy to be jealous. Another informant said that if a sonny is nearly the same age as the mummy he might "get a promotion" to the status of real boyfriend as he matures, apparently causing considerable confusion of role. Sonny relations were rare in the village and were considered to be a new and intrusive feature of the game.

The more common involvement of males occurs when the older mummy acquires a boyfriend. When this happens, he usually knows about the girl's female friendships and may give sweets now and then to the baby and be called daddy by her. The case of Makhotso shows how boyfriends of mummies may become involved in a girl's life (see Case 3). When Makhotso was 13 and in the baby role, her mummy had a boyfriend who gave her sweets and was protective of her at school, and polite when he visited her at the mummy's home. She said that being with the couple had opened her eyes to what loving a boy is all about, something she had not learned in her own family because her mother had long been divorced from her migrant father. Not all daddys, however, were friendly and protective as this one was. They may use the game as a way of making sexual advances towards the younger girl and so destroy the female dyad. Because they are not actually part of the game, they are not bound by its incest rules. Makhotso's third mummy had a boyfriend who said he wanted to be the daddy to Makhotso, but in fact attempted to seduce her. She wanted to finish secondary school and so retreated from the relationship, engaging in a series of friendships with like-minded girls before she returned at a later age to heterosexual affairs.

Thus, although the mummy-baby game can postpone or replace relations with boys for a time, it can also introduce participants to heterosexuality. For most women, the game fades in importance or ceases as attention turns to the romantic dramas of adult life: to heterosexual courtship, marriage, childbirth, and the responsibilities of family life.

In many cases, however, the relations established with other girls are transformed, but do not cease altogether. Ties may be maintained by letters and visits and occasional gift exchanges. Such contacts can provide women with important assistance in finding work, new friends, or sleeping accommodations if one moves or travels to where the other lives. Thus, the game helps to maintain bridges across the geographical distance and status shifts which have brought its intense phase to an end. And if the pair remain resident in the same village, the relationship may become an adult friendship without romantic contact. Informants spoke of adult female friendships as more stable, dependable, and long-lasting than the mummy-baby relations, which some come to think of as childish and silly (Blacking, 1978). In such adult friendships, village women continue to exchange visits without the romantic uncertainties or the sensual exchanges. They discuss problems, give advice and consolation, and provide help and companionship in their domestic tasks.

In some cases, particularly for women in lonely, unfamiliar situations, the game itself may be continued and new relationships established. By finding new mummies or babies, the young bride in a strange village or the lonely domestic worker or clerk in the city can quickly become in-corporated into a female social group where she finds emotional and material support. She can create a "family" which she selects for herself, no matter what strains may exist in her relations with male lovers, in-laws, co-workers or employers. These affective female relations also pro-vide an important alternative to heterosexual affairs for married women who face possessive in-laws and jealous husbands. As one woman said, "if a husband comes home and finds you in bed with a woman, he won't mind. But if he finds you in bed with another man, he may kill someone."

Fictive kinship relations among females never replace the kinship rela-tions with mothers and children, nor the heterosexual relations with lovers and husbands. However, they do provide important alternative bonds at critical moments in the women's lives.

SIGNIFICANCE OF MUMMY-BABY RELATIONS

Much more ethnographic data are needed to extend our understanding of the structure of female relations under variable socio-economic cir-cumstances, and the nature of affective relations between members of the same sex. This paper, as well as the studies by Blacking and Mueller, suggests that certain features of the social and economic structure of southern Africa are significantly related to the form which female friend-ships take.

Segregation of the sexes in play and work, and the absence of the ma-jority of adult men, encourage the development of close bonds among girls and women. Traditional female institutions have largely been destroyed, but new forms of female association have developed.

The mummy-baby game points to features of female sexuality and affective relations between same-sex partners which challenge some of our western assumptions. First, the compatibility of these intimate female relations with heterosexuality challenges our western insistence on polar-izing homosexuality and heterosexuality. Both Blacking and Mueller in-sist that there is nothing essentially homosexual (Blacking, 1959, 1978) or lesbian (Mueller, 1977) about the relations they report, because they do not replace heterosexual relations with boyfriends and husbands. Scha-pera, on the other hand, discusses southern African groups in which homosexual relations among both men and women may have been "quite an ordinary occurrence" (1930, pp. 242-243). Rather than deny any homosexual aspects, I would argue that these relations point to the nor-mality of adolescent homosexuality that is so rigidly censored in western societies. The fact that close physical and emotional relations between women often have a significant place, even after heterosexual relations have begun, suggests that the growing recognition of bisexuality in psycho-sexual studies may find support in studies of non-western societies. As one Mosotho woman said about the physical side of these relationships: "It's not wrong. It's just another part of life."

Second, there is a growing body of literature on the nature of female sexuality and the difference between male and female attitudes, again limited by the lack of non-western data. These female mummy-baby relations are structured differently from sexual relations among men in the enforced all-male living conditions of South African mine compounds. The reported male homosexuality of the mines seems to be solely for the purpose of obtaining sexual release when intercourse with women is not available. Younger male migrants who sell their favors are considered as "women of the compound" (*Another Blanket*, 1976), and there is no evidence that male sexual relations continue when migrants return to their women in Lesotho. The female relations, however, are compatible with heterosexuality and involve fictive kinship, not fictive marriage. They represent a broader kind of romantic-sensual relationship which has closer affinities to the physical and emotional pleasures of mother-child and perhaps sister-sister bonds, than to the genital pleasures of heterosexuality. In fact, girls do not consider genital contact essential to mummy-baby relationships. The contacts which may be involved in lengthening the labia minora are apparently not regarded as emotionally significant, whereas falling in love with a girl and simply caressing her is. One girl wondered if boys ever loved as seriously as girls, or if boys only wanted sexual satisfaction.

Recent research by women scholars is beginning to explore the broader concept of female sexuality. Smith-Rosenberg describes "emotional and sensual" same-sex relations which were accepted as normal for many 19th-century married American women, and were sometimes regarded as more emotionally satisfying than their stiff Victorian marriages (1975). Speaking specifically of female sexuality, Irigary argues that *touch*, rather than intercourse, is primordial for females (1977, p. 65). She makes particular reference to mother-daughter relations, arguing that most women in our western social system are "totally censored in the carnal relationships with their mothers and other women" and thus towards themselves. This situation leads to guilt and "narcissistic distress which the little girl suffers because of the devaluation of her relationship with her mother, and her own sex" (1977, p. 75). Perhaps the Basotho combination of warm, affectionate, early mothering, genital manipulation in childhood, and institutionalized female friendships which blend mother-daughter emotions with growing adolescent sexuality, are cultural features that spare Basotho women from some of the psychic distress of western women. Basotho women, however, experience more than their share of economic, social and psychic distress, because they live in one of the world's poorest countries as heads of households, workers or insecure dependents of underpaid migrants laboring in South Africa, one of the world's richest countries.

CASE STUDIES

In the following cases I have utilized a modified form of anthropological kinship diagram to show graphically the changing friendships of three adolescent girls. I have used circles to indicate females, triangles for males, lines for relationships, and levels for relative age and status. However, I have superimposed a series of circles representing "ego" in order to show successive relationships with female friends (single lines) and male friends (double lines). The age at the time of the particular relationship is writen inside the relevant circle. Lines indicating mummy-baby relationships are crossed out with three bars if known to have been terminated; a question mark indicates uncertainty of the status of the relationship. The dotted lines in case 3 indicate relationships between "ego" and the male friends of her mummies.

Case 1—Clorina

(My diagram and summary of a case reported in Mueller [1977, pp. 155-157].) Clorina is 25, unmarried, and has a year-old daughter. She was living at home and attending a nearby home economics school when interviewed by Mueller. She never had a fictive baby but had nine mummies most of whom live some distance from her home. Only two or three of these relationships have been maintained. Mueller's detailed account shows that five of the relationships since she was 16 were with married women 5 to 12 years her senior and primarily involved visits, letters, and gifts. Two of the bonds were established with close friends of Clorina's older sisters who lived away from home. Two mummies gave gifts to their "grandchild" when Clorina's own baby was born and one decided on the baby's name; thus as young married women they provided support for Clorina as an unmarried mother. The relationship established when she was 21 is the only one with a girl who also remained unmarried. In only this case were kissing and resting together said to be important aspects of the relationship.

Case 2—Malerato

Malerato is now 30 years old, married with three children. She states that she has not had time or interest in mummy-baby relations since her marriage at age 23. The first relationship lasted for three years, then faded out when the mummy married. The second mummy has remained a

Clorina's
mummies

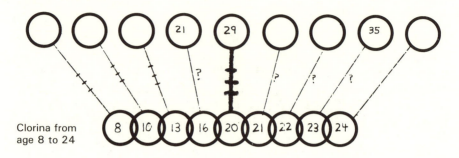

Clorina from
age 8 to 24

Makhotso's
mummies and
their boyfriends

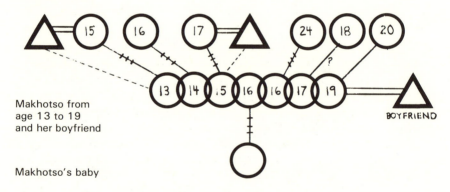

Makhotso from
age 13 to 19
and her boyfriend

Makhotso's baby

friend whom she occasionally visits in the distant capital city. Malerato
said the two babies loved her very much but were jealous of each other,
so she gave one of them to a friend of hers.

Case 3—Makhotso

Makhotso is now 21, still unmarried and working far from her home
and family. She is busy with her work, part-time studies, and boyfriends.
She appreciates the companionship of female friends whom she no longer
considers in terms of mummy-baby relations. The boyfriend of her first
mummy was simply a friend and occasionally considered as her daddy but

Malerato's
mummies

Malerato from
age 12 to 20
plus friend
and husband

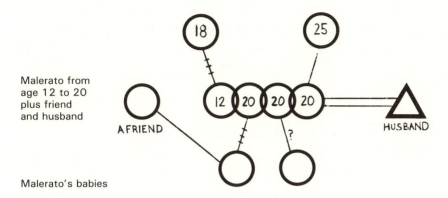

Malerato's babies

the relationship ended when the couple married and moved away. The boyfriend of the third mummy attempted to seduce her and the relationship with the couple ended abruptly. Her other relationships ended as she or the girls moved to different schools or jobs.

NOTES

1. Variants of the root word Sotho are as follows:
Lesotho: The nation;
Basotho: people of Lesotho;
Mosotho: singular of Basotho;
Sesotho: The language and culture.
2. Quotes are from the author's field notes (1976-77).

REFERENCES

Basotho Theological Students. (1976). *Another blanket*. Lesotho, Agency for Industrial Mission.

Blacking, J. (1959). Fictitious kinship amongst girls of the Venda of the Northern Transvaal. *Man, 59,* 155-158.

Blacking, J. (1978). Uses of the kinship idiom in friendships at some Venda and Zulu schools. In J. Argyle & E. Preston-Whyte (Eds.), *Social system and tradition in Southern Africa.* Cape Town: Oxford University Press.

Brain, R. (1976). *Friends and lovers*. London: Hart-Davis, Mac Gibbon.

Ekwensi, C. (1961). *Jagua Nana*. London: Hutchinson.

Friday, N. (1978). *My mother, myself*. London: Fontana.

Giallombardo, R. (1966). *Society of women: A study of a women's prison*. London: John Wiley & Sons.

Goody, E. N. (1971). Forms of pro-parenthood: The sharing and substitution of parental roles. In J. R. Goody (Ed.), *Kinship*. London: Penguin.

Hastrup, K. (1978). The semantics of biology: Virginity. In S. Ardner (Ed.), *Defining females: the nature of women in society*. London: Croom Helm.

Irigary, L. (1977). Women's exile (C. Venn, Trans.). *Ideology & Consciousness, 1,* 62-76.

Krige, E. J. & Krige, J. D. (1943). *The realm of a Rain Queen*. London: Oxford University Press.

Krige, E. J. & Krige, J. D. (1968). Girls' puberty songs and their relationship to fertility, health, morals and religion among the Zulu. *Africa, 38,* 173-198.

Longmore, L. (1959). *The dispossessed*. London: Johnathan Cope.

Mayer, P. & Mayer, I. (1970). In P. Mayer (Ed.), *Socialization: The approach from social anthropology. ASA Monographs, 8,* London: Tavistock.

Mueller, M. B. (1977). *Women and men in rural Lesotho: The periphery of the periphery*. (Doctoral dissertation, Brandeis University, Boston.)

Reader, D. H. (1966). *Zulu tribe in transition*. Manchester: Manchester University Press.

Schapera, I. (1930). *The Khosian peoples of South Africa: Bushmen and Hottentots*. London: George Routledge and Sons.

Smith-Rosenberg, C. (1975). The female world of love and ritual: Relations between women in nineteenth-century America. *Signs, 1,* 1-29.

Tiger, L. (1969). *Men in groups*. London: Thomas Nelson and Sons.

Mexican Male Homosexual Interaction in Public Contexts

Clark L. Taylor, PhD, EdD

The Institute for Advanced Study in Human Sexuality

ABSTRACT. In western societies, homosexuals must solve problems of how to recognize one another, meet and socialize while avoiding hostility and punishment. In the United States a preferred approach is to establish exclusive homosexual locales; but in Mexico, interaction problems are solved primarily in heterogeneous situations. The article shows how this is accomplished. The material is analyzed using game theory, a perspective which assumes that homosexual interaction exhibits qualities generally associated with games and can be analyzed utilizing concepts such as players, teams, rules, points, winning, and losing. The article also illustrates ways in which cultural determinants shape homosexual social organization in different western societies.

Exclusive homosexual businesses and gathering places (much less neighborhoods) are exceedingly rare in Mexico and an overt gay world such as we have in the U.S. is almost nonexistent. Essentially, in urban U.S. ''gaylife,'' social interaction is ghettoized; in its Mexican counterpart (*Ambiente* in homosexual slang) such interaction often takes place in heterogeneous locales. For example, between 1960 and 1984 in Mexico City, one of the largest cities in the world, while there was abundant homosexual social life, there were never more than six or seven exclusively homosexual establishments in operation at any one time, and there were no exclusively gay baths. This situation takes on particular significance when compared to such cities as New York and Los Angeles which have long had hundreds of homosexual establishments each (Dameron, 1974).

It could be assumed that this difference between gaylife and Ambiente results from relatively greater homosexual oppression in Mexico. However, while Mexicans treat homosexuality as deviant, there are other cultural variables (many of them positive) that contribute to the difference

The material presented here is from the author's doctoral dissertation, *El Ambiente: Male Homosexual Social Life in Mexico City*, University of California at Berkeley, 1978. The research was made possible by grants from the Department of Anthropology and Center for Latin American Studies at Berkeley and the Tinker Foundation. The author may be contacted at the Institute for Advanced Study of Human Sexuality, 1523 Franklin St., San Francisco, CA 94109.

in Mexican homosexual interaction. These variables will be explored in this article and will point to ways in which homosexual social worlds adapt to different cultural values and conditions.

HOMOSEXUAL PUBLIC INTERACTION AS PLAY

> . . . play is not "ordinary" or "real" life. It is rather a stepping out of "real" life into a temporary sphere of activity with a disposition all its own. . . . What the "others" do "outside" is no concern of ours at the moment. Inside the circle of the game the laws and customs of ordinary life no longer count. We are different and do things differently. (Huizinga, 1964, pp. 8-12)

Much insight can be gained by looking at Mexican homosexual behavior in public from the analytic framework of *play* or *games*. Homosexual activities contain a strong element of play, as do many "love games"; and Mexican Ambiente, like gaylife in the United States, primarily exists during play or leisure time.[1] Further, Mexican participants themselves use language common to games when speaking about their activities.

Approaching homosexual public interaction from the theoretical point of view of play allows the use of familiar game concepts such as players, teams, points, fouls, winning, and losing. This perspective is loosely called "game theory" in sociology (Lyman & Scott, 1970). Its particular usefulness for understanding Ambiente is that it allows one to create a framework for comparing behavior in many individual homosexual interactions, analyzing the structural similarities of these "gaming encounters" (Goffman, 1961), and rendering them as an organized account.

The terms "play" and "games," as they are used here, should not be mistaken to mean only light or frivolous entertainment. Rather, they are used in the metaphorical sense of "the great game of life" where the stakes can be high and participants may become enmeshed in the entire range of human experience—comedy, tragedy, mystery, suspense, and boredom.

The Players

In games, many of the ordinary world's roles and rules are exchanged for "game-generated roles or identities" and "game meaningful events" (Goffman, 1961). Although game-meaningful events, with their appropriate strategies and combinations of players, differ with each gaming encounter, the teams and types of players recognized by seasoned Mexican participants are fairly limited.

Males within the Mexican urban homosexual world divide players into two categories: those who engage in homosexual activities and those who do not. Furthermore, they have special names for the many types of people within these two categories or teams.[2]

Players Who Take a Homosexual Role

In Ambiente, seasoned players distinguish between those committed to a homosexual identity and socialized into the homosexual milieu (*los de Ambiente*), various independent operators, and those who use sex or the promise of sex to exploit other players. These various roles are subdivided as follows:

Los de Ambiante

1. *Pasivos* (passives) are insertees, those who receive the penis of others in their orifices (particularly the anus). This role is considered unmanly—fit only for women—and is therefore a stigmatized homosexual identity. However, while shunned by many people, insertees are also greatly sought after, desired, and loved by inserters.
2. *Activos* (actives) are inserters, those who insert their penises into the orifices of other males (particularly the anus). Such players are expected to be manly, at least more masculine than their partners. Activos are sometimes called *mayates*, particularly if they are extremely masculine, engage in hustling or are from the lower classes.
3. *Internacionales* (internationals) are those who take on both of the above roles. This humorous term indicates that males who do not take just one sex role are a "bit foreign," not like Mexicans.

Independent Operators

1. *Jaladores* (swingers) are those who enjoy homosexual relations (particularly bisexuals), but whose other sexual interests keep them from identifying themselves or being identified as true members of Ambiente.
2. *Bugas Que Jalan* (straights who swing) are bisexual or heterosexual men who occasionally enjoy a homosexual relation as well as homosexuals not yet socialized into the homosexual world.
3. *Pollos* (chickens) are boys who may or may not take a sex role, and who often are either too naive or considered too dangerous because of laws against corrupting minors to be allowed to play.

Sexual Exploiters

1. *Mayates*—see activos above. In addition to engaging in occasional prostitution, mayates sometimes rob and extort other players. The difference between mayates and chichifos (below) is that the latter, "rough trade," are more violent.
2. *Chichifos* (rough trade) are males who use sexual games to rob, blackmail, beat and/or murder their victims.
3. *Madrinas* (decoys) are young attractive males who are used as entrapment lures by police agents, or by others intent upon theft or blackmail. Often, madrinas are inexperienced pollos who have been caught and are then forced into helping catch more lucrative game.

Players Who Take a Non-Sexual Role

A. *Bugas* (straights) are people naive about homosexual games (usually heterosexuals) whose simple presence has the power to determine the game in progress and game strategies. When Bugas become aware of homosexual activity, they may show no interest, become scandalized, or melt over into the role of swingers, bugas que jalan.
B. *Agentes* (agents) are various agents of social control: security guards, plain clothesmen, detectives and uniformed police.
C. *Entendidos* (those who understand) are people who know what is happening and are generally sympathetic to homosexual activity.
D. *La Administracion* (the administration) are business owners and employees in locales of homosexual interaction who may be "wise" or naive, act as informal agents of social control, or facilitate homosexual interaction through their collusion.
E. *Ladrones* (literally, thieves) are those who rob or blackmail participants. Quite often, ladrones impersonate police.

In actual play, teams are in constant flux, and roles blend into one another as players frequently change roles and at times manage several roles simultaneously. Often, homosexual players enact a buga role in deference to bugas present in a game; they pass as straight, while also managing a sexual role with a prospective partner. For example, Mexican males may rub knees under a table while carrying on an ordinary buga conversation for the benefit of buga friends present.

Police and thieves often enact the roles of bugas, entendidos or mayates in the early stages of homosexual games, only to switch into their roles as agentes or ladrones when the strategies and moves of those in homosexual roles make such a revelation "profitable." This role flexibility adds an important element of tension to the games and makes their outcome par-

ticularly unpredictable. As Humphreys (1970, p. 49) observes of homosexual interaction in U.S. public restrooms, "Only after the game has
ended in payoff or disaster can others label most of the participants."

Types of Games Played

Mexican homosexual interaction can best be described using a game
typology devised by Lyman and Scott (1970), who in turn drew heavily
upon the work of Erving Goffman. According to Lyman and Scott:

> Although game situations are subject to abrupt or gradual shifts, and
> although one game may interpenetrate another, it is possible to dis-
> tinguish four game types: face, games, relationship games, exploi-
> tation games, and information games. (p. 36)

A brief description of the four game types follows:

1. *Relationship Games.* "In relationship games, the participants seek
   to create, maintain, attenuate or terminate personal relations"
   (Lyman & Scott, 1970, p. 37). Relationship games will occupy the
   central position in this analysis since they are the main reason for
   Mexican public homosexual interaction and the impetus for other
   types of games.
2. *Face Games.* In face games, people attempt to maintain a valued
   identity and make it possible for others present to do the same. If
   one's valued identity, or face, is challenged, remedial steps are
   often taken to restore social equilibrium (Goffman, 1955).
3. *Information Games.* "In information games, the participants seek
   to conceal and uncover, respectively, certain kinds of knowledge"
   (Lyman & Scott, 1970, p. 37).
4. *Exploitation Games.* In exploitation games, individuals try to exert
   power and influence over others in order to maximize personal gain
   or achieve and/or maintain personal or group dominance over
   others.

THE CONTOUR OF HOMOSEXUAL RELATIONSHIP GAMES

There are many similarities between homosocial relationships and
homosexual relationships among males (intimacy, commitment, jeal-
ousies, and shared adventures). However, the major difference is not the
sexual conduct which distinguishes the latter. The world of homosexual
relationship games consists of a tradition of cultural meaning absent from
other male friendships. In many ways their contour reflects that of erotic

heterosexual relationship games. Indeed, much of the language used to describe homosexual relationships is the same.

Mexican homosexuals distinguish between anonymous encounters (*fichas*) and romantic encounters (*ligas*). These terms reflect social values, for a ficha is a poker chip given by a client to a prostitute for sexual services in a very cheap brothel, while liga comes from the verb *ligar*, meaning "to alloy precious metals." Some males prefer *fichando* or "tricking" to "*ligando*," forming lasting romantic relationships. They consider the latter to be *muy puto*, "very queer." Other males consider ligando the only socially acceptable way for a good homosexual to behave.

This differential assignment of values to ligando and fichando creates additional tension in homosexual relationship games. In such encounters, participants must accurately surmise the feelings prospective partners and others present in order to avoid an incident and to "score" a liga or a ficha. Further, the differential values assigned give rise to games concerned with reputation and image management (information games and face games). This situation reflects Lyman and Scott's (1970) observation of heterosexual games (though they completely ignore male reciprocity):

> . . . the girl herself modifies her value if she bestows emotional or sexual gratification too soon or too late. Thus, in romantic societies . . . a girl may lose the man she desires by giving in too quickly, or not at all to his requests for increased intimacy. (pp. 45-46)

While homosexuals share problems of romantic involvement and promiscuity with heterosexuals, there are also rules particular to male homosexuality, especially with regard to the division of males into various sexual and social types. While in heterosexuality men are supposed to be manly and women womanly, in Ambiente there is a strong cognitive division of sex roles into the purported "manly" activo and "womanly" passivo. Further, a firm belief exists that males who play the same role cannot satisfy one another sexually. A humorous saying of Ambiente which refers to two passive males in bed goes, "It's better to die than have lesbian sex" (*"primero mortis que tortis"*).

Mutual interest and desire result in flexibility, and of course, some participants are internacionales. But, as Carrier (1972) notes, even where there is flexibility, participants feel that the inserter should be more masculine than the insertee. In some instances guessing another's sex role is easy, but often it is not. To further complicate relationship games, one must be careful about revealing "passive" inclinations or in assigning them to others lest unpleasant, or extremely serious consequences arise. Consider the opening gambit and ensuing complications of sex-role identity in the following example from my fieldnotes:

Once, during carnival in Veracruz, because of crowded conditions, they [Arturo and his Gay cousin] agreed to share their hotel room with another young man, a stranger. . . . During the night, Arturo got into bed with the stranger, but it turned out that they wanted to be both activo, and the stranger wound up masturbating in the bathroom. The next morning, the stranger informed them that he was on the first string of a Guadalajara soccer team (a very masculine role). Arturo, an internacional, had misjudged the stranger's true masculine identity. He said, "I had the chance of a lifetime and flubbed it. Ah, I didn't know what I was missing."

POINTS AND FOULS: INTIMACY AND POLLUTION

To understand homosexual interaction games, it is particularly important to study transformation rules by which behavior, considered a violation in the ordinary world, is changed into desired ends—points—in the world of meaningful homosexual game events. These rules derive from what Goffman (1971, p. 44) calls "territories or preserves of the self" and include rights or claims for respect for the sacredness of one's person. Such claims are commonly expressed as concern about proper physical proximity, bodily contact, visual scrutiny, exposure to body excreta (saliva, semen, fecal matter) and odors. Territories of the self perform a dual function in social life. As Goffman (1971) notes:

. . . the very forms of behavior employed to celebrate and affirm relationships . . . are very close in character to what would be a violation of preserves if performed between wrongly related individuals. The same can be said for acts performed as a means of signalling the initiation or extension of a personal relationship. (pp. 58-59)

Behavior between men which is defiling in ordinary Mexican social life becomes an expression of intimacy in homosexual relationship games. For example, in ordinary life "kiss my ass" (*besame culo*) is a grave insult, but in el ambiente between partners, such an act is called *un matrimonio* (a marriage). This dual aspect of preserves of the self holds for most sexual intimacy and accounts in part both for the aesthetics of sex and for the shock which can occur when one is improperly importuned or when sexual acts are accidentally witnessed. Thus, a felt stare, improper touch, or unexpected invitation for sex can have dire consequences. It is this uncertainty and risk-taking in relationships, whether one will score a point or foul with a prospective liga or ficha, which helps create the game.

WINNING AND LOSING

A final important consideration in the overall contour of Mexican homosexual relationship games is the "settlement phase," the part of a game "beginning when the outcome has been disclosed and lasting until losses have been paid up and gains collected" (Goffman, 1967, p. 154). In terms of Ambiente, a gaming encounter is a positive relationship game if it produces euphoria and participants score compatible homosexual relationships while avoiding social embarrassment, loss of face, or exploitation. It is a negative relationship game if nothing happens, relations worsen or are broken off, a negative incident occurs, face is lost or participants turn out to be opponents such as chichifos, or agentes, and exploitation games ensue.

GAMING LOCALES AND STRATEGIES

Even in those cases in which the weaker party secretly plays a different game with its own risks and stakes, he must take into account the game defined by the more powerful person and in the process mobilize his sign equipment to satisfy the requirements of the dominant game. Thus, while several games may be going on in the same encounter, it is certainly relevant to enquire into the hierarchy of domination that governs the engagement and the modifications on game play imposed by this hierarchy. (Lyman & Scott, 1970, pp. 66-67)

Since there are extremely few locales where obvious homosexual interaction is within the proper public decorum, parameters of homosexual games are provided considerable structure by the interaction rules of the dominant Mexican society.

An important rule of social life, one central to Mexican homosexual games, is that behavior must ultimately be subordinated to and in accordance with the decorum appropriate to "the overriding social occasion" (Goffman, 1963, p. 21). Thus, for example, if all present in a gaming locale are indifferent or in accord that homosexual interaction may take place (such as flirtation in a department store, or a sexual encounter in a public bath or a movie house), then it can occur without negative sanction. However, if there is not a consensus, then the rules of shopping, bathing, or movie attendance prevail and no obvious homosexual activities are permitted. As Goffman observes of public interaction, "Potentially competing definitions in the situation then give way to a kind of public decorum" (1963, p. 21). Accordingly, the best locales for homosexual games are those in which competing audiences can be easily segregated, such as movie theaters and plazas. Participants can often accomplish this feat through the creative use of time and space (see Carrier, 1972).

Movie Theaters

Homosexual games take place throughout Mexico in movie theaters, especially during the late show, when families have gone home. Smoking areas at the back or side aisles are the preferred spots. Since smoking is generally a male activity, and the area is out of audience view, these are places where men can loiter and mingle inconspicuously with many possible companions without making themselves obvious. Vestibules and restrooms are also used to advantage. The darkness of theaters enhances homosexual interaction, of course, just as steam obscures homosexual activities in Mexican baths.

Plazas

Plazas lend themselves particularly well to homosexual activities because many of the special rules of interaction common to parks are in force. Regardless of class, financial status, sexual orientation or social respectability, in the plazas citizens are free to mingle with one another, loll, and loiter as they please.

As in movie theaters, men use time and space to advantage when cruising plazas. While some homosexual activity takes place during the afternoons, when people are usually at home eating or taking siestas, most adventures take place in the evenings. A Mexican custom, the *paseo*, affords an important occasion to look for possible partners during the early evening. For at this time on Sundays or other days when a band plays in the central plaza, residents of Mexican cities gather to stroll, visit, and flirt.

During the paseo, the elderly, married couples, their young children, groups of girls and heterosexual couples walk in one direction or sit on benches in the center of the plaza. Unattached males walk in the opposite direction, and congregate or sit on benches at the outer edges of the plaza. Single males and females have the opportunity to exchange glances and remarks as they pass and to gossip with companions about their favorites. Boy friends and girl friends (*novios*), whose relationships are approved by the community, are allowed to walk together. The division of the crowd coupled with the expectation that males will socialize and meet new friends greatly facilitates homosexual flirtation.

Discrete homosexual friendship networks are generally indistinguishable from other male groups to Bugas. However, to former sex partners of network members, rival homosexual cliques, and others ''in on the game,'' such groups stand out. Males interested in homosexual company or those who explicitly want sex, often try to gain entry into such groups, lure a possible liga or ficha away on the spot, or make a date to meet later when the paseo is over and it is possible to detach more easily from families, girl friends, and companions.

More commonly, males simply look over the crowd, watching until the families and couples have gone home, to see which interesting (and interested) stragglers remain in the plaza. In Mexico, men commonly look for male companionship and adventure in plazas late at night. To many, an alluring aspect of plazas and other such public locales is that, in the initial stages of interaction, one often does not know what games will unfold: simple conversation or other socially polite pursuits, a drinking bout, clandestine marijuana smoking, a homosexual encounter, a trip to a house of prostitution, an exploitation game, or a face game—to name some of the common activities.

Occasionally in plazas, particularly late in the evening, a male group will develop in which all present realize that everybody has been together sexually with someone in the group. At such times they relax their usual reserve and enjoy themselves in homosexual conversation, flirting and joking.

Glamour Locales and Proper Involvement

To examine further how aspects of the dominant social order structure homosexual games, it is useful to shift attention to a favored area of urban Mexican homosexuals, shopping-recreational zones. These areas are the kind Strauss (1960) calls "glamour locales" in his spacial typology of cities. Here, the focus will be on Mexico City's most famous glamour locale, the Zona Rosa.

One social rule which strongly contours gaming strategies in such places is "proper involvement." Essentially, it is the requirement that people at least appear to be involved in the overriding social occasions in which they find themselves (Goffman, 1963). Since overtly looking for homosexual partners or engaging in homosexual activities in public is not considered proper in Mexico, participants must generally conceal their behavior and effect appropriate involvement in activities such as shopping, dining, and drinking. Thus, the "main involvement" for others present becomes a "subordinate involvement" for players, one they attend to in abstract fashion while actually concentrating on the game (Goffman, 1963).

A basic problem created by the requirement of proper involvement is how to remain in a costly locale long enough to meet a partner. The solution depends upon factors such as the number of props and activities available in the environment which can be turned to advantage in the game—become "realized resources" (Goffman, 1961), and one's economic ability to participate. The most common game strategy requires the transformation of ordinary objects and activities within the glamour locales into "involvement shields," those areas and activities which serve as barriers to perception and "behind which individuals can safely do the kind of things that would ordinarily result in negative sanctions" (Goffman, 1963, pp. 38-42). Economically, those with little money are usually limited in game resources to places such as waiting areas, streets, restrooms and park benches along the boulevards. Their involvement shields include waiting for a friend, waiting for a toilet stall, combing hair, washing hands, window shopping, strolling, and resting. Affluent players use all of these resources and, in addition, utilize restaurants, cabarets, cafes, department stores, and hotels. In such places involvement shields can be eating, drinking, purchasing magazines and other merchandise, or watching night club acts.

Men use these poses (*posturas*) not only for the benefit of bugas or police, store managers, and possible exploiters, but also to hide their identity from obvious homosexuals. Such individuals might spoil a player's buga role and reputation if he were to become too friendly, or might reveal the player's game to unsympathetic parties. Equally important, many in Ambiente feel that nice homosexuals do not go looking for encounters; it should happen fortuitously, and between persons properly introduced. Thus, when players who know one another accidentally meet in a gaming area, they may pose as though they do not know they are in a homosexually active locale, give excuses for their presence in such a "notorious" place, and then gossip to friends about one another's questionable habits. In effect, both for personal safety and for one's reputation in Ambiente one must maintain a "respectable" involvement.

INFORMATION GAMES

In the process of maintaining face by meeting obligations players become involved in information games. For, just as members of Ambiente must hide the game from some people, they must also uncover the roles and games of others and reveal their own game and roles to potentially desirable players. Such situations call for "team collusion," namely:

> Collusive communication which is carefully conveyed in such a way as to cause no threat to the illusion that is being fostered for the audience. (Goffman, 1959, p. 177)

Perhaps the most common forms of team collusion, at least in opening gambits, are the careful use of body idiom, particularly modes of expression which are ambiguous. Of these, use of the eyes is the most important. As Goffman (1971) observes:

> Given that a rule exists against seeking out a stranger's eyes, seeking can then be done as a means of making a pickup or as a means of making oneself known to someone one expects to meet but is unaquainted with. (p. 61n)

When handled carefully, non-players are unaware that anything unusual has occurred, or, at best, are mildly confused; but prolonged eye contact to the Ambiente signals homosexual recognition or interest.

In team collusion communication signals can be combined into sets or "protective disclosure routines" (Goffman, 1959). A common disclosive routine involves the exchange of glances while proceeding in a gaming locale from one area of popular involvement shields to another. In this sequence of moves one partly lets the other party know that he is in on the game and playing. For example, in a popular department store, players at a soda fountain can watch other players make the rounds as follows: stopping at the entrance to adjust their clothes or wait for a friend, then stopping at the magazine racks to browse, and then going past the tables in the restaurant to the toilet and so forth. If mutually interested, players will try to make eye contact, then also begin "making the rounds," and eventually try to meet.

In addition to the use of body idiom and sequence of positions, there are also verbal protective disclosure routines. Use of the term Ambiente is one of the most common. It is an ambiguous term with various meanings such as "environment," "atmosphere," "ambience," and "gaity," but in the homosexual subculture it means "having to do with homosexuality." If the person fails to understand the innuendo, no harm is done and the player can look for another likely candidate. Mexican homosexuals also use other terms skillfully to obfuscate conversation. In addition to ambiente, there are the special names for players such as *buga, chichifo, mayate,* and *pollo,* and other terms such as *cuchiplanchar,* to have homosexual sex, and *la tira,* the police, or literally, "the throw away," from the language of marijuana smokers.

There are other means of team collusion, some spontaneous, others formalized. Collusion with employees in gaming locales is particularly important. Because Mexicans tend to keep their jobs for many years and are in the same locales daily, employees are in a particularly good position to inform players which roles people are taking—who are homosexual, swingers, trade, police, or extortionists. They can also help or hinder people in meeting. Though employees sometimes dispense such information and services out of general good will or because they themselves are homosexual, more often it is obtained for the good tips they receive. Indeed, in some locales, employees actively compete for the best paying homosexual customers.

Employees are also in a good position to be collusive members of other teams such as the police, or thieves involved in exploitation games. Thus, though workers often have a relatively low status in the overriding social occasion of a locale, they have very high status in the other more subtle or hidden games.

INCIDENTS, FACE GAMES AND EXPLOITATION GAMES

Under the best conditions, with good players and no unexpected complications, Mexican homosexual interaction takes place successfully in heterogeneous locales. However, the occurrence of serious problems, or "incidents," outline most clearly the boundaries of public homosexual interaction as well as the political, and economic implications of "the rules of the game."

In this discussion it is useful to consider the homosexual relationship game with its various bases of operation and players as constituting a self-contained unit, cut off from the overriding social occasion by its secret, learned, shared and spontaneous strategies.[3] Incidents can occur within the boundaries of the game, as when lovers discover one another *fichando* in a notorious place. More importantly, when the game leaks into the "real world" or when the outside world intrudes into the game, homosexual interaction comes to an abrupt halt and the players are labelled cheaters or spoil sports in "the great game of life." As Huizinga (1964) writes:

> . . . as soon as the rules are transgressed the whole play-world collapses. The game is over. The umpire's whistle breaks the spell and sets "real" life going again. (p. 11)

Homosexual interaction in public places obviously requires considerable ingenuity and skill to prevent discovery, but of course, not all players are talented. Further, players sometimes become so involved in the game that they fail to observe and conform to changing requirements of the overriding social occasion. Still other players have little regard for the feelings of non-players and behave in an obvious fashion. In Goffman's terms they "take a high line" (1955). For example, in the bathroom of a department store which does not employ fulltime attendants,[4] events such as that described in the following entry from my fieldwork journal are common:

> When I entered, there were six men masturbating at the urinals. My arrival startled them and caused them to scatter as the young man

against the wall who was supposed to be guarding the door had become too absorbed in watching the activity. I smiled and the men returned to masturbating.

On the floor of the same department store, one would occasionally hear homosexual remarks between men such as, "Maria, where is my cosmetic bag?" One could see men eyeing one another and nearly tripping over customers in the "following" moves. Furthermore, throughout the Zona Rosa, one occasionally observed what Mexican homosexuals call *bolas de locas* (clumps or nests of queens), such as the group described below in my field notes:

> One group of six was particularly fetching in their highly original costumes with handbags and purses. One individual wore a white leatherette duster that went all the way down to his exaggerated platform shoes. All were wearing cosmetics and perfume. I don't think they made a single movement or sound that was not a homosexual stereotype.

Such occasional failures to maintain the boundaries of the game do not usually result in harsh sanctions brought against players. The serious problems occur when (as often happens on weekends, particularly late in the evening) homosexual players outnumber non-homosexuals in a locale. At the entrance to popular places, for example, there are often as many as 30 to 80 males in a "waiting" involvement shield which can only accommodate 10 or 15 skilled players convincingly.

When homosexual participants in a locale strongly outnumber others, they tend to redefine the situation as *de Ambiente* rather than *Buga*. Even when a crowd observes most of the rules of Buga interaction, the number and flirtation of the homosexuals give the game away. Such flooding out of the game into the social occasion can constitute a felt offense which initiates the opening move in a face game, a call for an accounting, the application of social sanctions to restore the boundaries of the game, or destroy the game completely. For Bugas, to be outnumbered by people considered deviant, exposed to so much perceptible deviant behavior including body motions, conversations, flirtations and even sexual acts requires extraordinary mental work and coping strategies. It is a breach of Buga etiquette, a violation of their sense of territorial preserves (of *Bugalandia* or "Bugaland" in homosexual slang). Both Bugas and homosexuals concerned about their reputations tend to avoid such situations, which result in a loss of business and social status for the establishments involved.

From the viewpoint of *los de Ambiente*, on the other hand, since homosexual acts in private are legal, the social rules which prohibit homosexual males from "acting gay" or meeting, courting and expressing the regard they have for one another are unjust and unwarranted. When homosexuals are in the majority in a public place, they feel that they should be able to do what feels natural, and have the same right to define acceptable behavior as heterosexual people do in other public places.

Flooding out of the game boundaries or the game's accidental discovery may result in a call for an accounting, although sometimes overtly homosexual situations will last for many months with few incidents. At those times a mass "counterfeit secrecy" (Ponce, 1976) prevails. At other times, simple warnings such as stares and glares or disparaging remarks are deemed sufficient to control the game. Occasionally, players are dealt what *los de Ambiente* call a *guemadura* ("a burn," are branded socially, as for example, when homosexuals are denied service and told to their faces that they are "*gente anormal*," abnormal people. Sometimes, the police are called to deliver more serious sanctions; and at still other times there are massive raids which net hundreds of people.

It is hard to say when such social sanctions are the result of an actual felt offense to face, or when flooding out of the game is used to advantage in other, more important games (particularly games of economic exploitation). As Lyman and Scott (1970) observe:

. . . face games may be undertaken for their own value, or for the payoffs they have in the context of wider strategies in other games. (p. 43)

For example, massive raids in the Zona Rosa are often applauded by business people because the tactic seriously disrupts all the games which do not require spending money in the legitimate business establishments of the expensive glamour locale. These include loitering, both homosexual and heterosexual pickup games, prostitution games, and recreational drug games. The raids return people's activities to "proper involvement," that is, activities which are lucrative for established businesses.

Raids are good business for the police. At times, the police may cordon off whole areas and threaten to arrest all those present on ambiguous charges. They let off the affluent with a *mordida* (bribe) while beating the poor and taking them to jail. As one affluent respondent stated, "In the United States you have policemen's balls, here we just have raids." At other times, the targets of raids are simply the poor. In such instances, police work is made easy by the economic segregation of involvement shields noticed earlier. When the police arrive, those who are properly dressed and possess money escape into the nearest business establishment.

The ambiguity of face and exploitation games is particularly evident in locales where sex occurs on the premises. Rare is the homosexual who does not have at least one tale of extortion by police or ladrones in such places. In some instances police insist they are acting out of a commitment to the laws and professionalism; in others real agentes and ladrones, posing as police claim that they are truly upset by homosexuality. But much of the time, economic profit seems clearly the objective. For example, in an encounter witnessed outside a steam bath, one "agent" (either a policeman, or vigilante/petty-thief) berated the person being held, saying he was a puto, a degenerate, that he was going to tell the victims family and throw him in jail. It would be in all the papers and he would lose his job. However, the "agent's" partner interrupted and said, "We are wasting our breath, he doesn't have any money. Let's let him go and catch another one."

Whether the motives of the police and thieves are personal or moral, the interaction ritual is standardized. The formula closely resembles the moves of a face game as described by Goffman (1955) and Lyman and Scott (1970). There is an opening move (an action which can be interpreted as an infraction of the rules), a negotiation in which the nature of the offense and appropriate recompense are agreed upon, and a settlement or an exchange of money, or, more simply, a loss of face. There can be more serious consequences such as a beating or jail. Whatever the reasons, economic exploitation, enforcing the law, or vigilante action, the formula is the same. The reasons become unimportant, for the effect of losing one's valuables, being beaten, going to jail or being murdered is equally devastating.

DISCUSSION AND CONCLUSION

Some of the differences between public homosexual interaction in Ambiente and in United States gaylife are attributable to the social forces which repress homosexuality in Mexico. However, many of the contrasts in sexual expression are a manifestation of cultural differences. Homosexual Mexicans often prefer their way of interacting to the U.S. forms because of cherished, cultural values.

In some ways, Mexican homosexual interaction in public resembles that of homosexual people in small towns in the United States and in some heterogeneous locales of our large cities. The number of people involved in this activity in Mexico, however, is far greater than in this country. Overall, the penalties for being caught in Mexico are generally much lighter. Here, the penalties can be quite severe in comparison to the usual Mexican shake-down, fine, or 15 days in jail, although very serious dangers do exist.

The difference reflects traditional Mexican values concerning the importance of personal sexual freedom. According to a study by Ramos

Frias (1966, pp. 69-70), Mexicans feel that law should not "invade the terrain of the individual moral conscience, in order to protect the precious concerns of sexual freedom and security"; the law should limit itself "to the minimum ethics indispensable to maintaining society." In thus limiting itself, Mexican jurisprudence is "obeying the Latin tradition of indifference concerning these problems."

Considering how liberal the Mexican legal attitude towards sex is, how can we account for the constant repression of overt homosexual expression? Why must Mexican males play such complicated interaction games to achieve their goals and stay out of trouble? The answer lies in the nature of "the minimum ethics indispensable to maintaining society." For the laws state that overt behavior must conform to the prevailing norms, values, folkways, and mores. Whether homosexual, bisexual or heterosexual, people must not engage in behavior which disturbs the peace, scandalizes others, or is generally considered immoral conduct (*falta de la moral*). Thus, sex in private is inviolate, but public manifestations of sexual interests are subject to prevailing customs and values.

The system makes the existence of places such as homosexual bars, baths or restaurants extremely difficult because, as public businesses, they must be open to all people, many of whom are offended by homosexual conduct. Thus, the system makes little provision for freedom of assembly for potentially offensive or nontraditional minority groups, be they swingers, homosexuals, nudists, hippies, punks, or devotees of rock-and-roll. This situation has two sides, however. In 1982, Mexico City police allowed homosexual activists to put up signs for their equivalent of a Gay Pride Parade and paint slogans on walls as a gesture of political protest, while street sweeps and raids of homosexual bars were being carried out to prevent homosexuals from assemblying for entertainment.

The Mexican situation illustrates a striking paradox when compared to the United States. For in Mexico, where consensual homosexual acts have been legal in private for more than a hundred years and personal sexual freedom is considered very important, overt homosexual institutions and most forms of freedom of expression are traditionally repressed. In the United States, where private homosexual relations are often a felony, there is relatively greater freedom to be publicly homosexual. Certainly the paradox calls into serious question the notion that when homosexual acts are legalized, there is a dramatic increase in overt homosexuality.

Having looked at limiting factors, let us now examine the advantages of the Mexican system. Mexicans familiar with U.S. gaylife often express a strong preference for Ambiente. They usually point out that, in the United States, homosexual activity is cut off from the rest of society. Homosexuals live away from their families and there are few babies, children, or elderly people in their lives. Where they mingle, they seldom see anybody but homosexuals. On the other hand, the Mexican system keeps homosexuals centered in their identity as humans and prevents them from becoming isolated from the mainstream of life. Whether in a plaza, a glamour locale, or boulevard, people flow into and out of homosexual encounters as well as many other kinds of experiences. This Mexican (indeed Latin) emphasis focuses on remaining centered in one's total identity while exploring many social roles. In the typical Mexican Ambiente homosexual men with lesbian dates and Buga friends, entendidos, ligas, fichas, family groups, shoeshine boys, lottery salesmen, waiters, bathroom attendants, and many others create a diverse, rich social network.

In addition to its rewards, there remain certain other reasons for Mexican homosexual interaction in public places. Laud Humphreys (1970), in studying sex in public restrooms in this country (perhaps the closest analogy to sexual activities in movie theaters, baths, and other public places in Mexico), proffers the suggestion that in the United States homosexual individuals engage in these activities because they like the danger involved. Mexican homosexuals suggest that, while some enjoy danger, for the most part Humphreys' analysis is not really applicable to them. As one respondent stated:

> We endure the risks and dangers simply because there are no suitable alternatives, especially for the poor who cannot afford to live apart from their families or rent a hotel room.

The statement focuses on an important paradox in Mexican life: while private homosexuality is legal, there is very little privacy in Mexico. Even the rich have to be careful not to bring someone home while the family is present or scandalize the servants. Further, Mexican homosexuals avoid discovery and gossip by *porteros*, people who guard the entrances to apartment buildings and other places. They also avoid being seen entering hotels or private baths where sex is known to take place.

There is another important reason why Mexican males engage in homosexual interaction in public places. Besides the occasional thrill of a dangerous encounter, or necessity created by the general lack of privacy, public homosexual encounters provide factual knowledge about what type of people are in reality homosexual and what types of sexual activities these men actually like to perform. In a society which keeps homosexuality hidden from view, many homosexuals have tremendous curiosity and need to know the truth about common stereotypes about homosexuals. In the process of playing or observing homosexual games, especially explicit sexual games, many stereotypes are broken and the often severe anxiety caused by folk beliefs collapses in the face of knowledge. Although Mexicans have ideal types, and judge one another on criteria such as personal beauty, age, masculinity, femininity, physical shape, and social class, in the baths they find that these ideals may have little connection with what people actually do sexually. As one respondent in my study philosophically remarked, "The Mexican baths are our schools about homosexuality. They teach us things about each other that foreigners often learn at gay bars, in magazines, and sex movies."

Finally, regardless of the reasons Mexicans participate in homosexual games, regardless of the positive or negative aspects of these games, their socialization into the rules and strategies of homosexual public interaction have profound significance for the existence of homosexual subculture. For as Huizinga (1964, p. 12) states:

> A play-community generally tends to become permanent even after the game is over. Of course, not every game of marbles or every bridge-party leads to the founding of a club. But the feeling of being "apart together" in an exceptional situation, of sharing something important, of mutually withdrawing from the world and rejecting the usual norms, retains its magic beyond the duration of the individual game.

NOTES

1. One might protest such statements on various grounds. For example, in contemporary U.S. urban gaylife, there are social and political institutions which exist in everyday life and furthermore, many people have come out of the closet and are integrating their worlds to varying degrees. However, such objections are true as yet only for a small number of homosexual people and most homosexual individuals both in the United States and Mexico must still relegate their homosexual interaction to leisure time.

2. The definitions or roles presented here are based upon observation, fieldnotes and a subsequent written questionnaire administered to 30 homosexual males in Mexico City.

3. Goffman (1961) provides a useful organic analogy, comparing encounters within a broader social setting to a cell and referring to the ongoing strategies to exclude the external world and maintain the gaming world as an "interaction membrane."

4. Because of poor plumbing and cheap labor, most large businesses employ attendants in restrooms to keep the facilities in order, dust off customers' clothes while they urinate, turn the water on and off for clients to wash their hands, and furnish them with a towel. For these services they receive a tip from which they derive their livelihood. Because of their presence and the need to respect their sentiments, little sexual activity takes place in most public restrooms unless the attendant is in collusion, or absent at the moment.

REFERENCES

Carrier, J. M. (1972). *Urban male homosexual encounters: An analysis of participants and coping strategies.* Unpublished doctoral dissertation, Social Sciences Department, University of California, Irvine.

Dameron, B. (1974). *Bob Dameron's address book.* San Francisco: Bob Dameron Enterprises.

Goffman, I. (1955). On face work: An analysis of ritual elements in social interaction. *Psychiatry* *18*, 213-231.

Goffman, I. (1959). *The presentation of self in everyday life.* New York: Doubleday.

Goffman, I. (1961). *Encounters: Two studies in the sociology of interaction.* New York: Bobbs Merrill.

Goffman, I. (1963). *Behavior in public places: Notes on the social organization of gatherings.* London: Collier-Macmillan.

Goffman, I. (1967). *Interaction ritual.* Chicago: Aldine Press.

Goffman, I. (1971). *Relations in public: Microstudies of the public order.* New York: Basic Books.

Huizinga, J. (1964). *Homo ludens: A study of the play element in culture.* (Trans.). Boston: Beacon Press.

Humphreys, L. (1970). *Tearoom trade: Impersonal sex in public places.* Chicago: Aldine.

Lyman, S. & Scott, M. (1970). *A sociology of the absurd.* New York: Appelton-Century-Crofts.

Ponce, B. (1976). *Secrecy in the lesbian world.* Unpublished paper, Dept. of Sociology, University of Southern California.

Ramos Frias, J. A. (1966). Estudio Criminologico y Medico—legal de la Homosexualidad. Masters Thesis in Law, Universitad Nacional Autonomo de Mexico. Mexico D. F.: Virginia.

Strauss, A. (1960). Spatial representation and the orbits of city life. *The Sociological Quarterly, 1*(3), 167-180.

Taylor, C. L. (1978). *El ambiente: Male homosexual social life in Mexico City.* PhD dissertation, Anthropology Department, University of California, Berkeley.

Taylor, C. L. (1974-1984). Fieldnotes and journal of the author (personal files).

Male Homosexuality and Spirit Possession in Brazil

Peter Fry, PhD
The Ford Foundation
Escritorio No Brasil

ABSTRACT. This paper examines the relationship between male homosexuality and the Afro-Brazilian possession cults in Belém do Parà. After a discussion of the literature follows a description of the cults' beliefs, rites and social organization. Male sex roles are then discussed and the two categories, *bicha* and man, analyzed. It is noted that there is no term which is equivalent to the western category of "homosexual" in this taxonomic system. After putting forward folk explanations for the presence of many bichas in the cults, an analysis is put forward of the social rewards available to bichas within these cults, and the structural relationship between homosexuality and these regions in terms of their congruent marginality vis-à-vis "normal society."

Writing on the Afro-Brazilian possession cults of Bahia in 1940, Ruth Landes asserted that the majority of cult leaders and followers were "passive homosexuals of note, and were vagrants and casuals of the streets" (Landes, 1940, p. 393). Much later, René Ribeiro reported similar findings in relation to the cults of Recife; of a sample of 60 male cult members and leaders, he claimed that "thirty-four (57%) showed various degrees of emotional imbalance and deviant behavior from overt and covert homosexualism to problems of sexual inadequacy" (Ribeiro, 1969, p. 113). Seth and Ruth Leacock found that in Belém there was "a widespread belief, both within and without the Batuque religion, that men who wear ritual costumes and dance in public ceremonies are either effeminate or, in most cases, active homosexuals. In part, this belief is based on fact—some of the men are indeed homosexuals" (Leacock & Leacock, 1972, p. 104). Public opinion was apparently similar with

This essay was originally written in 1974 for the Annual Meeting of the American Anthropological Association in Mexico City. I would like to take this opportunity to thank the Ford Foundation for financial assistance for my research in Campinas, and Professor Napoleão Figueiredo and Professor Anaíza Vergolino for their help in Belem. For comments on earlier drafts, I am grateful to Verena Martinez Alier, Mariza Correa, Gary Howe, Plínio Dentzien, Maria Manuela Carneiro da Cunha, Gilberto Velho, Yvonne Maggie, Leni Silverstein and Richard Parker.

Correspondence should be addressed to the author at the Ford Foundation, Praia do Flamengo No. 100, 22-210, Rio de Janeiro, Brasil.

　　　137

respect to the cults in other cities in the North and Northeast of Brazil, but not in the highly industrialized southern cities of Rio de Janeiro, São Paulo (Pressel, 1971), or Campinas.[1]

Roger Bastide also observed that "passive pederasty" was "very common" in certain cult houses in Bahia, but he brushed this aside as "pathological" (Bastide, 1961, p. 309). Male homosexuality and other stigmatized forms of sexual expression held a significant place in the cults in the North and Northeast of Brazil, and were certainly of more importance than their sparse appearance in the literature would suggest.

A relation exists between male homosexuality and the cults in Belém both at the level of collective representations and at the level of actual practice. Landes, Ribeiro and the Leacocks argue, in essence, that the cult houses represent a social niche where "homosexuals," otherwise despised, might find high status and prestige as respected cult leaders. It would seem, however, that in Belém, and probably in other parts of North and Northeastern Brazil, males who profess a sexual preference for other males and who are ascribed the status of bicha come to the cults not only because they are popularly defined as niches for bichas, but also for two other important reasons. First, both homosexuality and the possession cults share a common reputation as deviant in relation to dominant Brazilian values. Secondly, following the theoretical leads of Douglas (1966) and Turner (1969), to be defined by society as defiling and dangerous is often a positive advantage to those who practice a profession which deals in magical power. Persons who are defined and who define themselves as homosexuals find themselves classified as "perverts" and "deviants" and thus live on the margins of the formal social structure.

THE BASIC PROPERTIES OF THE POSSESSION
CULTS IN BELÉM

The raw materials which comprise the rituals, beliefs and social organization of Brazilian possession cults spring from origins as diverse as European spiritualism, as set down by Allen Kardec (Warren, 1968a, 1968b), Amerindian healing practices, astrology, West African religions brought to Brazil by way of the slave trade, and Roman Catholicism. While most of the early studies focused on the cultural genealogies of the various forms found in Brazil, it makes more sense to regard them as local responses to the social conditions in which they operate (Carneiro, 1964; Dantas, 1983a, 1983b; Velho, 1975).

The cults may be divided into two broad categories: those which follow more or less faithfully the Kardecist tradition, and those which approximate African and American Indian forms and are denominated "Afro-Brazilian." The former tend to occur in middle class milieux, while the latter are more commonly associated with the urban poor, whose magical services the affluent procure. The Afro-Brazilian cults are variously called *Umbanda, Macumba, Xangô, Batuque*, or *Candomblé*, but the subtleties of cult nomenclature can only be understood in the specific contexts in which they arise. The Kardecist cults allow for possession by the spirits of deceased persons in a relatively calm ritual atmosphere without singing or dancing or drumming, and emphasize the doctrine of successive re-incarnation based on an ethic of charity, education and hard work. Kardecists in general have little respect for Afro-Brazilian cults which they consider underdeveloped and which they call, pejoratively, *baixo espiritismo* (low spiritualism).

The number of terms used to discriminate between one cult group and another, or between one category of cult groups and another in Belém, relates to the way in which autonomous rival groups differentiate themselves from each other. It is, however, possible to discern the existence of two kinds of cult groups among the non-Kardecists, those whose meeting places are termed *searas* and those whose meeting places are called either *terreiros* or *barracões*. Those who meet in searas refer to their cult as Umbanda, and the others are Candomblé, Mina or Macumba. The critical difference between the searas and the terreiros is that only the latter use drums (*tambores*); this is partly why the ritual of the terreiros is more dynamic and colorful than that of the searas. It is the terreiros, rather than the searas, that are commonly associated with male homosexuality. Throughout this essay, the term *macumba* refers to these cults and *macumbeiro* for cult practitioner.[2]

The structure of the macumba groups follows the general pattern in the rest of Brazil. They are autonomous, and intercult rivalry is pronounced. The macumbeiros form an extensive communications network along which passes information relating to the activities of cult leaders and their followers. Although much of the gossip and scandal is malicious and expresses interpersonal and inter-group conflict, it nevertheless contributes to the formulation of common norms and values and, because the lines of conflict tend to be cross-cutting, guarantees a certain degree of solidarity amongst all macumbeiros in relation to the wider society (Gluckman, 1963; Silva, 1976). A significant part of such gossip concerns the supposed sexual activities of cult members.

Cult houses are led by either a *pai* or *mãe de santo* (father or mother in sainthood), each of whom has a number of *filhos* and *filhas de santo* (sons and daughters in sainthood) under his or her control and ritual guidance. Although the internal organization of cult groups varies in complexity, in most cases the mãe or pai de santo tries to maintain absolute control over his or her filhos. The most significant structural relations, therefore, are the dyadic ties linking followers to those who lead. In general, the competition between cult leaders and between individual mediums leads to a marked autonomy of the terreiros which prevents attempts at federation.

Although the cults are in principle monotheistic, God is otiose and of less importance than the hosts of lesser spirits (variously called *encantados, orixás, guias, entidades, santos*) which are believed to possess (*incorporar, arreiar, baixar*) cult members who act as their hosts (*mediuns, cavalos, aparelhos*). Each member owes a series of obligation (*obrigações*) to his possessing spirits and to his patron deities (*orixás*), the fulfillment of which guarantee his good fortune, health and survival. Such obligations consist of regular offerings, but, most important of all, in "receiving" (*receber*) the spirits in regular ritual seances.

The cult groups, apart from serving the needs of their members, also provide ritual and magical services for clients (*clientes*), non-practicing believers who approach the cults for assistance when necessary. Cult leaders recruit new filhos from clients whose troubles are diagnosed as being due to incumbent spirit-mediumship. The cult centers, then, offer magical services to their followers and the population at large. They are financed by the regular contributions of members, by fees paid by neophyte mediums for the ritual expenses of initiation, and by grateful clients.

Ritual varies from one group to another, but the basic pattern is for each to congregate at its terreiro where, to the singing of ritual songs (*doutrinas, pontos*), hand-clapping, dancing and drumming, they fall into trance, possessed by the spirits relevant to the occasion. With the exception of the most traditional candomblé cults of Bahia, the possessed mediums not only dance but also speak with the clients to whom they offer advice and ritual protection. Theatricality is important and great attention is paid to the mise-en-scène of the seances. The cult houses are elaborately decorated with statues of the spirits, paper flags and streamers, silver paper, and flashing fairy lights. Mediums must dress well, the women in long, wide skirts, the men in singlets and trousers. During trances, mediums dress and behave according to the personality of the possessing spirit. Rituals end with the departure of the spirits and a closing song, although it is not uncommon in Belém for a number of mediums to remain possessed after the ritual ends. Certain "carousing spirits," who enjoy drinking and making obscene jokes, may remain in possession of their mediums for many hours or even days (Leacock, 1964, 1965).

It is beyond the scope of this article to discuss the psychology and physiology of the trance state; spirit mediumship will be treated as a social role whose credibility is defined by the actors themselves (Fry, 1976; Leacock, 1966; Lewis, 1971). Thus a medium is possessed by a spirit for those who believe he is, and is a fraud for those who do not. In Belém, as in other societies which practice spirit-mediumship, the phenomenon follows what Lewis (1971) has called social grooves. In Belém, the majority of macumbeiros belong to what may be called the urban poor. Even though there are a number of mediums whose socio-economic status is much higher, they are numerically insignificant. Further, as in the rest of Afro-Brazilian cults, women members outnumber men about two to one.[3]

In Belém, as elsewhere in Brazil, the cults are held in low esteem by the majority of people, especially those who are wealthier and who have acquired an advanced, formal education. Negative attitudes are so strong that although a large number of middle and upper class persons are faithful clients of the terreiros, they deny it and make their visits outside of ritual hours. Police repression has been constantly reported (Carneiro, 1954; de Mattos, 1938; Ramos, 1934; Rodrigues, 1935) but, although it has to a large extent ceased, and although there have been attempts on the part of state and municipal governments to recognize the value of the cults for drawing tourists, the negative attitudes persist. In Sao Paulo, the *Jornal do Estado de S. Paulo*, which is the newspaper representing bourgeois opinion, described the cults as the haunt of "immorality, crime and corruption." (See also Herskovits, 1966.)

Throughout Brazil, the cults are associated with "immorality, crime, and corruption," in Belém they are also associated with male homosexuality. The word "homosexual" has multiple meanings in English which makes its use in a scientific context of doubtful validity. The term homosexual is rarely used in Brazil outside middle class and intellectual circles. The most common term is *bicha.* Other terms include *pederasta, fresco* (fresh) and *veado* (deer). To understand the relationship between male homosexuality and macumba, it is necessary to comprehend the true significance of the term bicha as it relates to male gender roles in Belém.

THE CLASSIFICATION OF GENDER ROLES IN BELÉM

There are two basic male gender roles in Belém, the bicha and the *macho* or *homem* (man). Since a bicha is also a homem in a biological sense (the word homem means man and male), this latter category is sometimes given as *homem mesmo* (a "real" man). The bicha can be understood, therefore, in relation to the homem mesmo and these two roles may be distinguished by the sexual and social behavior and status accorded to each.

In sexual encounters the bicha assumes the "insertee" role while the homem assumes the "insertor" role.[4] This sexual relation is expressed by the terms "give" and "eat" (*dar* and *comer*). The homem "eats" the bicha, who, for his part, "gives." The same terms refer to heterosexual encounters, in which it is the female who "gives." The homem/bicha relation is characterized by a power differential. The homem dominates the bicha as he dominates women. As one young bicha affirmed: "The bicha is always beneath the man's foot. He assumes this position.'' The terminology of giving and eating expresses this power relation quite clearly.

The homem is also distinguished from the bicha by certain behavior traits. Bichas are more extravagant in their gestures, and at the same time delicate. In describing bichas, most informants mentioned particular behavioral features, such as the way the bicha holds a cigarette or sits down; other said they were like women or *efeminadas.* Indeed, the bicha role approximates the standard female role and many bichas assume female pseudonyms, ''war names'' (*nomes de guerra*) or ''screen names'' as they are called.

This classification of male gender roles derives from two criteria— biological sex and the role in sexual encounters. The homem is a male who takes the insertor role and is dominant, be his partner male or female. The bicha is a male who takes the insertee role and assumes an inferior social stance vis-à-vis his male partner. The English word homosexual, defined as a person who prefers the sexual company of persons of his or her own sex, corresponds to none of the Belém categories (Young, 1973). In this paper, therefore, the Brazilian terms will be used to refer to the social categories involved, reserving the term homosexual as an adjective to refer to sexual encounters between persons of the same sex.

In practice, the males who are called bichas fall into two categories, those who define themselves as bichas and those who publicly define themselves as men. The former may be called *bichas mesmo* (''real'' bichas) or *bichonas* (the suffix *-ona* amplifies the noun). They may or may not conform, in actual practice, to their described role. It is not uncommon for bichas to assume the insertor role in sexual encounters, for example, and this behavior may occur either in sexual encounters with males who define themselves as men or with other bichas. Bichas regard sexual encounters between two bichas, however, as ''deviant'' and class it as lesbianism (*lesbianismo*).

Those who are called bichas but who define themselves as men are referred to as ''incubated bichas'' (a good translation might be ''closet queen''). This category is reserved for accusations and is one of the most common weapons used in Brazil in situations of attempted degradation.

BICHAS AND MACUMBEIROS

Public opinion both within and without the cults associates the role of medium and pai de santo with that of bicha. The evidence already presented is sufficient to demonstrate that at the level of collective representations these roles are linked; but whether or not this linkage corresponds to reality is another matter.

The Leacocks (1972) claim that some of the males in the cults "are indeed homosexuals. . . . There was often unanimity among our informants, both male and female, that some male mediums lived with other men with whom they had sexual relations" (p. 104). Of the 46 male cult members they interviewed, "the evidence seemed indisputable in only 14 cases. (. . .) Of these 14 homosexuals, several were pais de santo" (Leacock & Leacock, 1972, p. 104). Whatever the proportion of males ascribed either real bicha or incubated bicha status in the cults, the fact remains that most people believe that the two roles are linked. No one, however, has gone so far as to say that all males who danced in the terreiros were bichas. Nevertheless, a large number of the most expressive and important pais de santo in Belém fall into the category of real bichas; they not only accept this appellation but make a point of confirming it publicly. Whether or not, however, the proportion of bichas in the cults is as high as 80%, as well-informed official of the Federation of Afro-Brazilian cults of Para claimed, will never be known for certain. But, as one young bicha who was not a cult member pertinently observed, "*o povo aumenta mas não inventa*" (the people may exaggerate but don't invent).[5]

Folk Interpretations

The pais and filhos de santo who affirmed that the majority of male cult members were bichas were asked why they thought this to be the case. Many found difficulty in formulating their replies at first; it was clear that as far as they were concerned there was no question in the matter. After a certain amount of pressing, however, several suggestions were put forward. Cult members insisted that the presence of bichas in the cults was by chance, and they supported this argument by citing the dictum that cult life was not related to everyday life. The Leacocks make a similar observation:

> For those men who wear ritual costumes and dance and who are either alleged or actual homosexuals, the doctrine accepted by most Batuque leaders is that as long as they carry out their obligations and show respect during ceremonies, their sex life should be of no concern either to their fellow members or anyone else. (Leacock & Leacock, 1972, p. 106)

As one pai de santo said, "I am a bicha, everyone knows that I'm a bicha and I have never denied that I am a bicha. At the same time I'm a pai de santo and was initiated (*feito*) in Bahia. When I hold ritual (*festa*) these things are left aside."

In many terreiros this belief in a total separation between the religious life and a "sinner's life" (*a vida do pecador*) legitimizes what appears to the outsider as a considerable degree of sexual freedom. The only restrictions that the cult imposes on sexuality are on sexual activity before and after rituals but not on the type of sexuality nor the sex of the persons involved. Immediately after sexual intercourse and for a period varying from 24 hours to 3 days, depending on the terreiro, the partners are considered unclean; their bodies are "dirty" (corpo sujo). It is the female who "dirties," so a male may "clean" (limpar) his body by ritual means and thus enter the terreiro before the 24 hours or 3 days are up, but this is not possible for women. Informants claimed that sex between two males was also polluting even though there was no woman involved. They explained the apparent contradiction by saying that it was the act of insertion which polluted, suggesting that sex without insertion was not sullying. All informants agreed that bichas, like men but unlike women, could purify their bodies by bathing before the end of the proscribed period.

The fact that festas in many terreiros do, in fact, offer opportunities for homosexual and heterosexual encounters, led to the comment by some informants that bichas are common in the cults because of the opportunity they provide to "hunt" (caçar) men. Linked to this interpretation was the common observation that bichas like to show themselves off. By dancing in the cults, it was claimed, the bichas could dress up in fine clothes and dance, thus furthering an apparent desire to compete with other bichas ("Every bicha wants to be better than the others"—"Cada bicha quer ser maior que a outra") and also to attract the "men" present. Cult members, both male and female, do use fine clothes and the festas do attract a large number of people some of whom are on the lookout for possible sexual adventures of all types. Such adventures, however, are easier to arrange for non-participants than for the cult members themselves who have little opportunity to interact with persons outside the terreiro.[6]

Another interpretation offered for the presence of bichas in the cults was that bichas are more artistic than men and women and are therefore better equipped to organize and participate in ritual. One pai de santo, who claimed that if he had not been "called" by the spirits he would have become a successful transvestite (travesti), felt that "real men" did not have the "knack" (jeito) for dancing for the spirits. In fact the aesthetic side of ritual is important and, when judging a particular terreiro, the quality of the decor, dancing, drumming, clothing, food, drink and hospitality are all taken into account. The bichas were, in general, more extravagantly and expensively dressed than other cult members and they dominated the ritual scene. When possessed by female spirits such as Dona Herodina, Dona Mariana, or Dona Jarina, they were notably exuberant and luxuriously clad. Indeed, the existence of female spirits and the phenomenon of the transsexual trance led to a further interpretation of bichas in the cults. It was claimed by bichas and non-bichas alike that some males entered the cults in order to be possessed by female spirits so that they might give rein to their "feminine" tendencies. Although males were frequently possessed by female spirits, they also received male ones. In the case of the "real bichas," the most important of their possessing spirits, the ones they received most frequently and for the longest periods were male. It would seem, however, that bichas particularly enjoyed acting as mediums for female spirits. As one bicha commented shortly before a festa for Dona Mariana whom he was to receive, "I am so ugly and Dona Mariana is so beautiful."

A more malicious interpetation of transsexual trance was that many bichas feigned trance in order to exploit the authority of their spirits for sexual ends. Such spirits were refered to as *santos de pagação* or *santos de fechamento* (lit. "picking-up saints" or "showing off saints"). Such accusations of false trance, however, are usually made in the context of interpersonal rivalry and tend to occur between rival bicha pais de santo. One pai de santo told me that it was not uncommon for males to receive female spirits because they wanted to go after men but did not have the courage to do it in their everyday lives. They used their female spirits, he claimed, as a mask. "I know what their game is. Who likes me likes me for what I am. There is no need for me to mix my private life with my work [*trabalho*, i.e., as a pai de santo] for the simple reason that I am much more of a coquette than any of the female spirits which I receive."

All these interpretations given by the actors themselves stress the way in which bichas are supposed to exploit the cults for certain specific ends such as to "show off" or "hunt men." The only interpretation that a bicha might have a special quality advantageous to the role of pai de santo, was that regarding the artistic and theatrical talents associated with the bicha role. Not one person, however, volunteered the suggestion that bichas entered the cults because they wanted to be women or preferred the company of women, an explanation proffered by Ruth Landes for the presence of "passive homosexuals" in the Bahian cults (Landes, 1940).

On the contrary, the majority opinion was that the bichas entered the cults either to be with men or else to show off before other bichas. No cult belief accounted either for the statistically significant presence of bichas as mediums and pais de santo or explained why bichas were bichas at all. Most informants, both bicha and non-bicha, could offer no explanation and felt that bicha status was just a fact of life, something taken for granted and not worthy of further speculation. The only connection between cult beliefs and sexuality was that which Ruth Landes observed in Bahia, namely the tendency for bichas to have female deities as their patrons (Landes, 1940). Those who saw a link among such saints as Yansan, Oshum and the androgynous Osunmaré and bicha status, described it in terms of affinity rather than cause and effect. Others denied any connection between the sexuality of an individual and that of his patron deity.

In spite of this lack of consensus, however, males who are ''sons'' of female deities are often assumed to be bichas and it is not uncommon also to assume that a real bicha has a female saint as his patron.

Some Analytical Interpretations

Certain terreiros serve as a social niche for a number of bichas where they may interact with one another and with non-bichas in a congenial setting. The terreiros have a daily life of their own which is interspersed with ritual. They are made up of the pai de santo and a small staff of people who take care of the terreiro, cooking and cleaning in exchange for food, lodging and pocket money provided by the pai de santo. Very often these small communities contain a number of bichas who are out of work or short of money. Certain terreiros might act as sanctuary for young bichas who had problems with their families and had to leave home. Bichas affirmed that family relations improved after developing their mediumship. Successful pais de santo achieved considerable prestige both within and outside of the cults. Thus, the cult houses offer career opportunities to bichas that can provide them with important political, economic and social advantage. Even for those who do not make a career of their calling as spirit-mediums, the terreiros appear to be capable of absorbing young men defined as sexually deviant by their families. But why should the possession cults perform this function, and why should bichas find prestige and economic rewards in this area of social life while they are denied them in others?

Part of the answer to this question lies in the fact that the relation between the cults and homosexuality is something of a self-fulfilling prophecy. Once the cults have been labelled as a social niche for bichas, real men will avoid them for fear of being defined as bichas. At the same time males who have been defined as bichas and who choose to accept this definition may feel attracted to the cults. As the male population of the cults would, in this way, be recruited from bichas, it would not be surprising to note the high number of bichas among successful pais de santo. One informant went so far as to suggest that some males assume the bicha social role in order to get ahead in the cults. Bichas affirmed, however, that they were bichas before entering the cult. Some may enter the cult as incubated bichas and after joining change their strategies, redefining themselves as real bichas, thus laying claim to full membership. In this way the cults play an important role in the articulation of norms and values of the bicha community in Belém.

But the fact that the terreiros are labelled as a niche for bichas is itself still unexplained. In order to find some reasons why this should be so, it is necessary to look a little more closely at the role of pai de santo.

The pai de santo is above all a magician-counsellor, whose explicitly religious function is to listen to his clients' problems, provide explanations and offer solutions, both magical and practical. A successful pai de santo is also expected to possess a large and richly decorated terreiro, a large number of filhos, good drummers, resplendent rituals and, in the event of important feasts, to provide impressive quantities of food and drink. Clearly, magical efficacy and conspicuous consumption are mutually dependent, for while the former furnishes the cash necessary for the latter, the latter points to the former and attracts the clients who are the original source of income. A pai de santo who can boast the material attributes of a successful pai de santo must surely be a successful pai de santo. Thus the success of a pai de santo rests on the continued confidence of his filhos and clients. He maintains this confidence by continuing to prove his magical efficacy and by displaying the material signs of success. The situation is schematized in Figure 1.

The pai de santo, as Figure 1 shows, is the center of a redistributive network where magical services are exchanged for cash with rich clients, feasts are exchanged for recognition on the part of the filhos de Santo and the public at large, and cash is invested in the terreiro as a symbol of success. The crucial components of these exchanges are material and magical.

The model outlined above suggests that the more cash a pai de santo can invest in his terreiro and in his immediate followers, the more recognition and political support he can hope to gain. Any leakage of cash outside this circle will therefore diminish resources available for garnering prestige. Pais and mães de santo who are married and maintain ties with their kinship networks, are therefore obliged to divert resources in order to meet their social obligations outside of the cult. Clearly, those cult leaders who are not so encumbered can invest all their energies in social relations which are important in the cult context. Bichas find themselves in this situation. They rarely have children, and almost always maintain only the most tenuous links with their kinship networks. Forcibly cut off from family ties, the bicha must invest in new social relations. If he chooses to enter the cults, his social investment can be channelled solely within the cults, thus giving him an advantage over non-bichas.

In addition to these advantages, the bicha pai de santo also has other material advantages over other non-bicha cult leaders. His bicha role equips him with a combination of talents which are generally distributed between the two sexes on the basis of the sexual division of labor. Cooking and embroidery, for example, both of which are important for the daily life of the terreiro, belong to the female and the bicha role, but are taboo to the male role. Not only do bichas share advantages with women which are denied to men, but also they share advantages with men that are denied to women. Brazil is still very much a male-dominated society in which men command the majority of positions in the formal power struc-

148

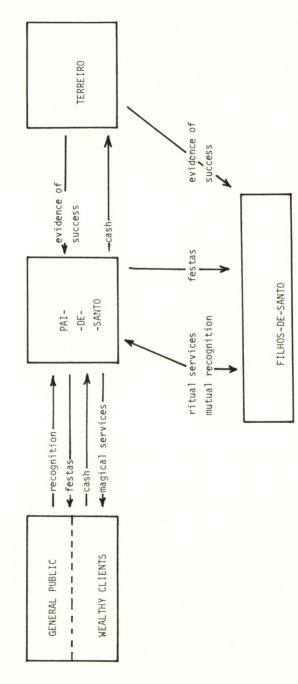

FIGURE 1. The Ritual Economy of Fathers in Sainthood.

ture. Regardless of a male's degree of commitment to the bicha role, he continues to benefit from certain male prerogatives. Bichas can, when necessary, assume the man role; they continue to interact with men and bichas and thus have easy access to the "world of men," in the form of institutions such as the police and judiciary. Similarly, they are in a better position to maintain links with doctors, lawyers, and politicians whose services they themselves may use or broker to clients for their own advantage. The cult leader who adopts the bicha role is not, as Ruth Landes claimed for the Bahian situation, a would-be woman (Landes, 1940); he is in a category apart, and can use the privileges associated with both the male and female role.

Having suggested ways in which bicha status is advantageous to cult leaders in their strictly non-ritual functions, it now remains to demonstrate how the status of sexual deviant, vis-à-vis the wider society, is of importance to cult leaders in their role as magician-counsellor.

People normally seek advice and counsel from persons who are considered well-informed and impartial. Institutionalized advice-givers and counsellors generally occupy positions which lie outside the formal power structure in any given society. Thus, unallied to politically compromised factions and other interest groups, they are in a position to obtain relevant information from all sides in any conflict situation. Most cases of misfortune which clients take to the pais de santo for explanation and cure are believed to be caused by the mystical attacks of enemies who are intent on destroying (*derrubar*) their victims. Further, clients expect the pais de santo to analyze these problems using the supernatural powers of their spirits or divining apparatus and not through questions and answers. The ritual system of the possession cults contains various symbolic mechanisms for ensuring that the analyses of misfortune are seen as provenant from an impartial outsider, through spirit-possession itself (the medium is substituted by a distant spirit), and various divinatory techniques.

The pais de santo, who also define themselves as bichas, are doubly "marginal" for the wider society. Defined as deviant in sexual terms, they are cut off from their kinship networks and thus become outsiders in social terms. Not only do they live encapsulated in a social network which is outside "normal" society, but also they ideally opt out of the conventional production process; the income which they derive from their magical services enables them to work exclusively "for the saints" (*trabalho no santo*).

While outsider status is associated with the role of secular counsellors, it is perhaps even more so in the case of holy men. The ethnography of prophets and holy men in general is that of the assertion and ascription of difference. Magicians and saints accrue to themselves characteristics which are classified as outside the formal structures of society. The holy men of Late Antiquity were set apart by their asceticism (Brown, 1971).

The *prophetae* of medieval Europe were classically strange figures, cut off from the political and ecclesiastical power structures. Like the cult leaders of Belém, they were often accused of "sexual licence and perversion" (Cohn, 1970, p. 39). The ethnographic examples are legion, and in the particular case of spirit-possession cults, Ioan Lewis has amassed a remarkable quantity of evidence to show how, especially in the case of peripheral cults, the membership is recruited from peripheral social categories (Lewis, 1971).

Mary Douglas (1966) observes that societies tend to develop very clear ideas in relation to order and disorder, form and formlessness. That which is classified as not pertaining to order is associated with regions beyond society. The inside is perceived as ordered and tidy; what is outside is defined as disordered and dirty. Sorcerers, prophets and healers, she notes, play on the symbols of disorder, associating themselves with those regions of the cosmos which are defined as outside society. "The man who comes back from these inaccessible regions brings with him a power not available to those who have stayed in control of themselves and of society" (Douglas, 1966, p. 95). While Douglas sees society as playing on the themes of form and formlessness, order and disorder, Victor Turner, in similar vein, characterizes society as an ongoing dialectic between what he terms "structure" and "comunitas" or "anti-structure."

> From the perspective viewpoint of those concerned with the maintenance of "structure," all sustained manifestations of comunitas must appear as dangerous and anarchical, and have to be hedged around with prescriptions, and conditions. (Turner, 1969, p. 109)

In Belém, males fill the categories of normal men and deviant bichas. The latter are nauseous (*nojentas*) and beyond the pale of normal society. But the possession cults also fill a marginal category. This categorization accords with Douglas' and Turner's arguments. Macumba owes its attributed magical powers to a position defined at the margins of society—in the regions of formlessness and comunitas. But if magical power is related to the outside, it is not surprising that it should be associated with those who are defined as marginal people.

Societies classify persons and objects into categories. In so doing they classify that which defies the correct categories as defiling and dangerous. But that which is incorrect is also part of the social system; it cannot be expunged. The magical powers which society believes inhere in these forbidden areas are the price it pays for its symbolic and social order. The ins define the outs, but in so doing they furnish them with an inherent power which they, by definition, cannot have.

If the bichas are attracted to the cult because of their sexual deviance, then the same should hold true for females; the cults should also attract those defined as lesbians (*lésbicas*), whores (*putas*) and sexually promiscuous women in general (*mulheres de programa*). The fact that a large number of informants perceived the categories of bichas, puta, and lésbica as linked provides evidence that it is sexual deviance in general, and not just male homosexuality, that is associated with the cults. It is not uncommon for informants, when asked to interpret the presence of bichas in the cults to comment spontaneously that there were also females defined as deviant. One pai de santo was more explicit. "In the whole of Brazil, you would find it difficult to find a pai or a mãe de santo who was correct (*correta*) sexually. The candomblé was born, you see, in part for homosexuality (*homosexualismo*)."

If macumba is associated with marginal people, why should sexual categories define this marginality? To suggest answers to this question it will be necessary to consider why this correlation between the cults and sexual deviance does not occur to the same degree in the cities of Rio de Janeiro, São Paulo and Campinas. There have been attempts to draw the cults from the social periphery in Rio and São Paulo and an increasingly large number of middle and upper class people frequent them (Brown, 1974). However, at the level of collective representations, the cults are still perceived as marginal and probably the vast majority of the adepts come from the urban poor. They key to the problem lies in the classification of gender roles.

Gender roles in the North and Northeast of Brazil are much more rigid than in the industrialized southern cities. To borrow Basil Bernstein's terms (1973), the sexual code of the North and Northeast is "restricted", while that of the southern cities is "elaborated." Whereas in Belém the roles of man, woman, bicha and lésbica are clearly defined and logically consistent, the same is not true in the southern cities. Once consensus breaks down about the correct roles of men and women, then the definition of what is incorrect necessarily becomes more blurred. Furthermore, the classification of gender roles is not only a function of regional differences but also of class differences. The sexual code of the working class in the southern cities is more restricted than that of the middle and upper classes, for example. Max Gluckman suggested that sexual roles would be more clearly defined where social networks were recruited largely on the basis of kinship and where mono-sex groups were the rule (Gluckman, 1971; xxii). These two conditions probably apply more in the North and Northeast of Brazil than in the southern industrialized cities where increased social mobility and massive labor migration have contributed to a situation in which kinship ascription is not the only basis for the structuring of social relationships or for the accumulation and maintenance of wealth and power.

These tentative concluding remarks are essentially exploratory and necessarily over-generalized. While the classification of gender roles is less rigid in the South than in the North and Northeast, it is much more so than in certain areas of North America and England, and is more marked at certain levels of the social structure than in others. Furthermore, it is not implied that a more elaborated sexual code is necessarily related to a greater degree of liberality and tolerance with respect to sexual matters.

NOTES

1. There were also hints that female homosexuality was not uncommon in the cults (Ribeiro, 1970). In fact, the earliest reference to homosexuality and the cults that I have been able to find is in the journalist João do Rio's articles on religion in Rio de Janeiro, published in 1905. He refers to a certain Maria Luiza, whom he describes as ''as seducer of honest ladies'' (Rio, 1905, p. 19) and later on announces that amongst the blacks there is a ''sinister propensity'' for lesbianism (Rio, *op. cit.*; p. 46)

2. The Leacocks employed the term *Batuque* to refer to this same set of cults. I choose the term macumba because it is commonly used in Belém and also elsewhere in Brazil. This term was also chosen because it is used pejoratively by detractors of the cult and yet proudly by its members.

3. In Campinas the ratio is two women for every one male; also in Araraquara (Delgado Sobrinho, 1974). Ruth Landes and Edison Carneiro maintained that the cult in Bahia was essentially female (Carneiro, 1954, 1964; Landes, 1940).

4. I adopt these terms following Laud Humphreys (1970) in order to avoid the value loaded terms ''active'' and ''passive.''

5. Quotations from informants throughout this article are from the author's field notes, 19--.

6. Ethnographic accounts of these kinds of religious festival often discreetly avoid mentioning that they are essentially entertaining and marvelous opportunities for ''cruising'' or ''hunting'' (*caçar*). After the ritual is over festivals often become quite simply parties with food and drink and much sexual play and comment.

REFERENCES

Bastide, R. (1961). *O Candomblé da Bahia*. [The Candomblé of Bahia]. São Paulo: Editora Nacional.

Bernstein, B. (1973). *Class, codes and control*. London: Paladin.

Brown, D. (1974). *Umbanda: The politics of urban religious movement*. PhD Dissertation, University of Columbia.

Brown, P. (1971). The rise and function of the holy man in late antiquity. *Journal of Roman Studies, LXI*, pp. 80-101.

Carneiro, E. (1954). *Candomblés da Bahia (2ª Edição Revista)*. [Candomblés of Bahia (2nd Edition Revised)]. Rio de Janeiro: Civilização Brasileira.

Carneiro, E. (1964). *Ladinos e crioulos*. [Creoles and Africans]. Rio de Janeiro: Civilização Brasileira.

Cohn, N. (1970). *The pursuit of the millenium: Revolutionaries, millenarians, and mystical anarchists of the middle ages*. London: Paladin.

Dantas, P. G. (1983a). Reprensando a pureza nagô. [Rethinking Yoruba purity]. *Religião e Sociedade, 8,* 15-20.

Dantas, P. G. (1983b). *Vovô Nagô e papai branco: Usos e abusos da Africa no Brasil*. [Yoruba Granma and white daddy: The use and abuse of Africa in Brazil]. Master's thesis, UNICAMP.

Delgado Sobrinho, A. T. (1974). *Practicas religiosas nos terreiros de Umbanda de Araraquara*. [Religious practice in the centers of Umbanda in Araraquara]. São Paulo: Master's Dissertation. Fundação Escola de Sociologia e Politica de São Paulo, mimeo.

De Mattos, D. B. (1938). As macumbas de São Paulo. [The macumbas of São Paulo]. *Revista do arquivo municipal, XLIX*, pp. 151-160.

Douglas, M. (1966). *Purity and danger: An analysis of concepts of pollution and taboo.* London: Routledge and Kegan Paul.

Fry, P. (1976). *Spirits of protest: The spirit mediums and the articulation of consensus amongst the Zezuru of Southern Rhodesia (Zimbabwe).* Cambridge: Cambridge University Press.

Fry, P. (1982). Da hierarquia à igualdade: A construção historica da homossexualidade no Brasil. [Hierarchy and equality: A historical construction of homosexuality in Brazil.] In Peter Fry, *Para Inglês Ver: Identidade e Politica na Cultura Brasileira.* Rio de Janeiro: Zahar.

Gulckman, M. (1963). Gossip and scandal. *Current Anthropology, IV,* 307-316.

Humphreys, L. (1970). *Tea Room Trade: A study of homosexual encounters in public places.* London: Duckworth.

Landes, R. (1940). A cult matriarchate and male homosexuality. *Journal of Abnormal and Social Psychology, XXXV,* 3, 386-397.

Leacock, S. (1964). Ceremonial drinking in an Afro-Brazilian cult. *American Anthropologist, 66,* 344-354.

Leacock, S. (1965). Fun-loving deities in an Afro-Brazilian cult. *Anthropological Quarterly, 3,* 94-109.

Leacock, S. (1966). *Spirit possession as role-enactment in the Batuque.* Paper presented at the 65th Annual Meeting of the American Anthropological Association.

Leacock, S. & Leacock, R. (1972). *Spirits of the deep: A study of an Afro-Brazilian cult.* New York: Doubleday Natural History Press.

Lewis, I. (1971). *Ecstatic religion.* Harmondsworth: Penguin Books.

Pressel, E. J. (1971). *Umbanda in São Paulo: Religious innovations in a developing society.* Unpublished doctoral dissertation, Ohio State University.

Ramos, A. (1934). *O negro Brasileiro.* [The Brazilian Black]. Rio de Janeiro: Editora Brasileira.

Ramos, A. (1942). Pesquisas estrangeiras sobre o negro brasileiro. [Foreign research on Brazilian Blacks]. In A. Ramos, *A Aculturacão Negra no Brasil.* Rio de Janeiro: Biblioteca Pedagogica Brasileira.

Ribeiro, R. (1969). Personality and the psychosexual adjustment of Afro-Brazilian cult members. *Journal de la société des Americanistes, LVIII,* 109-120.

Ribeiro, R. (1970). Psicopatologia e pesquisa antropologica. [Psychopathology and anthropological research.] *Universitas, 6/7,* 123-134.

Rio, J. do. (1905). *As religiões do Rio.* [The religions of Rio]. Rio de Janeiro: Garneiro.

Rodrigues, N. R. (1935). *O amimismo fetichista dos negros Bahianos.* [The fetishistic animism of Black Bahians]. Rio de Janeiro: Civilização Brasileira.

Silva, A. V. E. (1976). *O tambor das flores.* [The drum of flowers] [translation]. Master's Thesis, UNICAMP.

Turner, V. (1969). *The ritual process: Structure and anti-structure.* Chicago: Aldine.

Velho, Y. M. A. (1975). *Guerra de Orixá: Um estudo de ritual e conflito.* [War of the Gods: A study of ritual and conflict]. Rio de Janeiro: Zahar.

Warren, D. (1968a). Spiritism in Brazil. *Journal of Inter-American Studies, X,* 3, 393-405.

Warren, D. (1968b). Portuguese roots of Brazilian spiritism. *Luzo-Brazilian Review, V,*2, 3-33.

Young, A. (1973). Gay gringo in Brazil. In L. Richmond & G. Noguera (Eds.) *The gay liberation book.* San Francisco: Ramparts Press.

Masculinity, Femininity, and Homosexuality: On the Anthropological Interpretation of Sexual Meanings in Brazil

Richard Parker, PhD (cand.)
Department of Anthropology
University of California, Berkeley

ABSTRACT. This essay examines the anthropological interpretation of sexual meanings in Brazil as presented in the recent work of Peter Fry. Following Fry's lead, it places central emphasis on the study of male homosexuality and sexual ideology, suggesting that these cultural domains can be fully understood only when situated within the wider context of sexual meanings in Brazil. With this in mind, it traces the historical development of a series of analytically distinct, though practically interrelated, systems of sexual classification which structure the constitution of meaningful sexual identities in Brazilian life.

The Brazilian anthropological tradition is a long, sophisticated, and highly distinguished one. It focused in its early years almost entirely on the study of Brazil's indigenous peoples. Over the course of the 1960s, the '70s, and into the '80s, it has expanded its perspective to the full range of social and cultural life in contemporary Brazil. Writers such as Roberto Da Matta and Gilberto Velho linked the study of Brazilian society, in all its detail and diversity, to an increasing awareness of the importance of both gender and sexuality for a full understanding of Brazilian life (Da Matta, 1978, 1981, 1983a, 1983b; Velho, 1981, 1984). The emergence of feminist thought within Brazilian anthropology, in turn, has greatly extended this perspective through an increasing concern with reappropriating and understanding the lives and experiences of women within Brazilian society (Barros, 1981; Durham, 1980, 1983; Franchetto, Cavalcanti & Heilborn, 1981; Prado, 1981; Salem, 1981).

The most innovative and influential research yet carried out on gender

Richard Parker received his Bachelor's and Master's Degrees from the University of California, Berkeley, where he is currently a Doctoral Candidate in the Department of Anthropology. He can be contacted c/o the Department of Anthropology, 232 Kroeber Hall, University of California-Berkeley, Berkeley, CA 94720.

and sexuality in Brazil, however, focuses on the study of male sexual ideology, and, in particular, on the cultural construction of male homosexuality; it is perhaps most closely associated with the work of Peter Fry. First elaborated by Fry (1982a, 1982c [original 1977, see the English translation in this issue]) and presented in its most extended form by Fry and MacRae (1983), this work is motivated by the conviction that an adequate interpretation of homosexuality in Brazil can be possible only through a detailed analysis of sexual classification. Such an analysis explores the complex ways in which Brazilian society categorizes and classifies same-sex interactions, and, by extension, the ways in which those engaged in such interactions come to understand their own sexual identities. From this perspective emerges the insight that multiple systems of sexual classification exist simultaneously in contemporary Brazil, and that a full understanding of homosexuality in Brazilian life results only from the interpretation of the specific historic, geographic, and social interrelations which exist between these systems.

Fry's work on homosexuality in Brazil began, in many ways, as a logical extension of his earlier research concerns: originally trained at the University of London, he conducted his first fieldwork on ecstatic religion among the Shona of southern Africa. Upon taking up a teaching position in Brazil at the University of Campinas in 1970, his attention quickly turned to the many Afro-Brazilian religious groups that are highly active throughout urban Brazil. An important link between homosexuality and the Afro-Brazilian cults had long been recognized by Ruth Landes (1940) in her groundbreaking essay, "A Cult Matriarchate and Male Homosexuality." Although Landes noted an empirically verifiable phenomenon in the association between male homosexuality and certain Afro-Brazilian cult groups, she failed to interpret this phenomenon as a specific cultural construction. Taking "homosexuality" uncritically as a valid cross-cultural category, she based her analysis largely on a set of unexamined assumptions concerning the nature of sexual deviance (Fry, 1982c; Landes, 1940).

Seeking to rethink the connection first noted by Landes from a more critical perspective, Fry quickly came face-to-face with a number of important contradictions. First, he realized that the connection that Landes had noted in the northern city of Salvador did not hold true for Brazil as a whole in the 1970s. While such an association continued to be present in the less modernized regions of northern Brazil, it was considerably less pronounced in the more heavily industrialized and modernized cities of the south. Second, the category of homosexuality itself seemed inadequate for describing the situation in either region. These facts, in turn, seemed linked to the historical development of a fundamental diversity in the structure of Brazil's sexual ideology (Fry, 1982a, 1982c; Fry and MacRae, 1983).

Within the realm of traditional folk conception, Fry found that the sexual world in Brazil was divided not into the categories of homosexuality and heterosexuality, but into the hierarchically related categories of those who *comem* (from *comer* or "to eat"), and those who *dão* (from *dar* or "to give"): those who metaphorically consume their partners by taking the active role of penetration as opposed to those who passively offer themselves up to be penetrated in either vaginal or anal intercourse. The hierarchical structure of male-female sexual relations in traditional Brazil, which carries with it a sharply defined distinction between masculine *atividade* (activity) and feminine *passividade* (passivity), thus provides a conceptual model for same-sex relations among males as well. Those who comem, who take the active role, are defined as *homens* (men) and can enter into relationships not only with *mulheres* (women) but also with other males without sacrificing their fundamentally masculine identity (precisely because, as the active partner, their hierarchical dominance is preserved). Males who take the passive role are *bichas*, literally, "worms, internal parasites," and maintain a fundamentally feminine social role. Having adopted the female gender role in the sexual act itself, they come to be treated—and, in fact, treat themselves—as the symbolic equivalent of a biological female, finding work only in occupations traditionally restricted to women, being referred to as *ela* (she) rather than *ele* (he). To say that the bicha is a symbolic female, however, is not to say that the distinction between bicha and mulher is unimportant. The ideology itself gives different values to sexuality in social contexts and biological sex—to the social and the biological as classificatory criteria. Brazilians tend to see the bicha as a failure on both counts: no longer an homem due to his sexual behavior, he is unable to fully adopt the role of mulher because of biology. His social status is thus even lower than that of a woman in traditional Brazilian society.

Biologically male, yet socially female, the bicha is thus a highly ambiguous figure within the traditional Brazilian system of sexual classification. According to Fry, it is perhaps precisely because of this fact that the bicha has been traditionally linked to the Afro-Brazilian religious cults, which themselves exist on the margins of Brazilian society. The bicha is the most striking character in a system of sexual classification that had almost universal validity for Brazilians before the twentieth century and continues to be dominant today in rural areas, in the less modernized cities of the north, as well as among members of the lower classes in the more modernized and industrialized urban centers of southern Brazil (Fry, 1982a, 1982c; Fry and MacRae, 1983).

Within this first system of classification, same-sex relationships are, like extramarital male-female relationships, relatively unproblematic for the social condemnation and imputation of sinfulness which such activity invokes is aimed largely at the passive bicha rather than the active homem. This situation changes radically, however, with the gradual construction of a second system of sexual classification among the intellectual elite in Brazil. A so-called scientific or medical model emerged during the late 19th and early 20th centuries and drew heavily on developments in European psychology and sexology. This model is complex, and goes through a number of transformations as indicated in the works of Karl Heinrich Ulrichs, Richard von Krafft-Ebing and Havelock Ellis. In the writings of Brazilian scientists, such as the medical doctors Piers de Almeida (1906) and Leonídio Ribeiro (1938), it leads ultimately to a shift from gender (as a cultural construction) to sexuality (and, especially, sexual object choice) as the defining criterion for sexual classification, and, hence to the creation of *heterossexualidade, bissexualidade,* and *homossexualidade* as new categories in Brazilian sexual thought. With this new distinction, the popular opposition between the active homem and the passive bicha is simply ignored; both active and passive partners in same-sex interactions are included in the new category of the homossexual. This categorization, in turn, joins with a fundamentally new moral discourse in which any deviation from a heterosexual norm represents the external sign of an internal sickness (Fry, 1982a, 1982b, 1982d; Fry and MacRae, 1983).

The construction of homosexuality as a medical category in the 19th and 20th centuries can hardly be separated from the emergence of a closely linked, yet politically very different, discourse among writers such as Edward Carpenter and Magnus Hirschfeld of a ''homosexual consciousness'' and, subsequently, a gay liberation movement. As Fry and MacRae point out, this alternative discourse had relatively little impact in Brazil up until the late 1960s and the 1970s. In this later period, a third system of sexual classification emerged among members of the growing middle classes in the large cities of southern Brazil. Heavily influenced by both the women's and gay liberation movements, this model consciously rejected both the active/passive role playing and the hierarchical domination which are implicit in the traditional system of sexual classification. Like the medical model, it focuses on sexual object choice as its fundamental classificatory criterion, and thus tends to reproduce the distinction between heterossexualidade and homossexualidade. In the language of daily life this distinction is reflected in the terms homens and *entendidos* (literally, ''those who know, roughly coterminous with the English word ''gay'').[2] The homem is masculine, active and heterosexual. The entendido combines the social characteristics of masculinity and femininity; he is either active or passive in sexual intercourse, and is fundamentally homosexual in terms of his sexual object choice. If the traditional model of sexual classification is a model of hierarchy, this modern system consciously articulates the values of equality and egalitarianism, and rejects the accusation of sin as well as the diagnosis of sickness. Like Brazil's new feminist and black movements, the *movimento homossexual* has begun to work toward a radical reorganization of social relationships (Fry, 1982a; Fry and MacRae, 1983).

Combining an anthropological analysis of folk conceptions with an analysis of scientific discourse similar to the work of Michel Foucault and his followers, and situating this analysis within a historical framework and recognition of social inequality and social class, Fry's work offers a fundamental contribution not only to the study of homosexuality but also to the anthropological interpretation of gender and sexuality in general. One of its most important and innovative conclusions, which is crucial for those of us working in Brazil, as well as for anthropologists engaged in the study of other complex societies, is the extent to which multiple systems of sexual classification can co-exist and in fact intertwine within the context of a single social fabric.

A fundamental problem that must be raised is the nature of homosexuality as a category in anthropological analysis, and the caution with which this category must be employed in the interpretation of gender and sexuality in non-western societies. As the work of Boswell (1980), Foucault (1976) and Weeks (1981) clearly points out, homosexuality is itself a historical construct, a category which was quite literally created at a highly specific juncture in the history of Western civilization. Recent research on the structure of same-sex relationships in different historical contexts, as in the case of gender-crossing in native North and South Americans cultures has also called into question the validity of this construct in much cross-cultural research (Clastres, 1978; Desy, 1978; Whitehead, 1981). Peter Fry's work has similar implications for the Brazilian case. If homosexuality is to be used in describing certain aspects of same-sex relationships in Brazil, those aspects which are in fact historically congruent with the term itself, it cannot be invoked as a unitary analytic category for the interpretation of same-sex relations.

In order to avoid what, in the end, would be little more than ethnocentric reductionism, it is necessary to situate the study of homosexuality, specifically defined, within a wider context. As Fry has demonstrated, homosexuality in Brazil can be fully understood only in relation to those other same-sex interactions which, from the proverbial "native's point of view," cannot be described as homosexual, i.e., relationships between homens and bichas. And, by extension, same-sex relationships in general can be fully understood only within the wider structures of Brazilian sexual ideology and its definitions of masculinity and femininity and of heterosexuality and bisexuality. In post-structuralist fashion, then, the part can be understood only in terms of its historical relation to the whole. This process, in turn, opens the way for a fundamental advance in the anthropological interpretation of gender and sexuality. The emphasis it places upon temporal relationships allows an understanding of sexual classification as an ongoing historical process. It refocuses attention onto the meaningful practices that construct sexual identities.

One telling example of such an interpretive strategy comes from the construction of male prostitution in the large, highly differentiated urban centers of southern Brazil. Drawing its personnel largely from the impoverished lower classes, the world of male prostitution reproduces the traditional distinction which Fry has noted between homem and bicha. It draws a sharp line between *michês*, highly masculine individuals who are thought normally to take only the active role in sexual interactions, and *travestis*, who present an extreme version of femininity and are expected to take the passive role (though the ideology itself acknowledges that sexual practice may often reverse such a priori assumptions). Not surprisingly, the clients of both michês and travestis come from the more well-to-do segments of Brazilian society, who, as members of the middle and upper classes, are often the carriers of rather different systems of sexual classification. In many instances, it is the entendido who seeks out the services of the michê, while the heterosexually identified homem turns to the travesti. In all such interactions, there is a constant process of negotiation in which far more than money is changing hands. Systems of symbolic classification are consciously manipulated by the social actors who give them practical form. Indeed, it may be useful to conceive of these classificatory systems in dialogical terms, less as a collection of categories than as a chorus of voices engaged in an ongoing conversation that continually creates and recreates meaningful sexual identities (see Bakhtin, 1968, 1973, 1981).

The ability to fully realize such an interpretive project will both free the conception of same-sex relationships from the constraints placed upon it by our own cultural vision of the world, and advance and extend the anthropological understanding of gender and sexuality. Peter Fry's work in Brazil is clearly an important step along such a path. To the extent that it has drawn our attention to both the remarkable complexity of cultural particularity, as well as to the possibility of understanding more fully the nature of historical processes, his contribution provides us with an example which is well worth our careful consideration.

AUTHOR NOTES

Preliminary research in Brazil during July and August of 1982 was made possible by a grant from the Tinker Foundation and the Center for Latin American Studies at the University of California, Berkeley, as well as a Robert H. Lowie Scholarship from the Department of Anthropology at Berkeley. Research carried out from August, 1983, to July, 1984, was supported by a Fulbright Full Grant, a Graduate Humanities Research Grant and a Travelling Fellowship in International Relations from Berkeley, as well as a Grant-in-Aid from the Wenner-Gren Foundation for Anthropological Research. This essay was originally intended as a research report for the Anthropology Research Group on Homosexuality; I am indebted to Clark Taylor for suggesting the possibility of submitting it for publication as well as for his helpful comments concerning content. Thanks also to my friends, Adalberto Rodrigues da Silva, Jeanne Bergman, Roberto Da Matta, Samina Bashiruddin, and Vagner João Benicio de Almeida for many insightful comments and conversations. Finally, special thanks to Peter Fry for the great generosity which he has shown in encouraging me to explore the issues discussed in this brief essay.

NOTES

1. My concentration here will be almost exclusively on male homosexuality, as little work has yet been carried out on female homosexuality or the lesbian community in Brazil. It should be noted that Fry's work on male homosexuality has both drawn upon and inspired a good deal of related research on the part of a number of scholars (Guimaraes, 1977, 1983; MacRae, 1982, 1983a, 1983b; Mott, 1982a, 1982b; Mott and Assunção, 1982; and Perlongher, 1983). For a slightly more detailed discussion of these writers, see Parker, 1984.

2. Based on comments received following publication of *Da Hierarquia à Igualdade*, Fry now thinks that the term *entendido* was in fact used with reference to homosexuality earlier than the 1960s; it was only in the late '60s and the early '70s, however, that it began to take on a meaning roughly equivalent to the English term "gay" and was associated with the egalitarian homosexual relationships of members of the middle class in Brazil (Fry, 1984).

REFERENCES

Bakhtin, M. M. (1968). *Rabelais and his world*. Cambridge, MA: The M.I.T. Press.

Bakhtin, M. M. (1973). *Problems of Dostoevsky's poetics*. Ann Arbor: Ardis.

Bakhtin, M. M. (1981). *The dialogic imagination: Four essays*. Austin: University of Texas Press.

Barros, M. M. L. de (1981). Testemunho de vida: Um estudo antropológico de mulheres na velice. [Life testiment: An anthropological study of women in old age]. *Perspectivas Antropológicas da Mulher, 2*, 11-70. Rio de Janeiro: Zahar Editores.

Boswell, J. (1980). *Christianity, social tolerance, and homosexuality: Gay people in Western Europe from the beginning of the Christian era to the fourteenth century*. Chicago: The University of Chicago Press.

Clastres, P. (1978). O arco e o cesto. [The bow and the basket]. In P. Clastres (Ed.), *A sociedade contra o estado* (pp. 71-89). Rio de Janeiro: Francisco Alves.

Da Matta, R. (1978). *Carnavais, malandros e heróis: Para uma sociologia do dilema Brasileiro*. [Carnivals, rogues, and heroes: Toward a sociology of the Brasilian dilemma]. Rio de Janeiro: Zahar Editores.

Da Matta, R. (1981). *Universo do carnaval: Imagens e reflexões*. [Universe of carnival: Images and reflections]. Rio de Janeiro: Edições Pinakotheke.

Da Matta, R. (1983a). Notas sobre o masculino e o feminino no Brasil como uma questão relacional [Notes about the masculine and the feminine in Brazil as a relational question]. Paper presented at the Primeiro Encontro do Grupo de Trabalho Sexualidade e Reprodução, October. Rio de Janeiro.

Da Matta, R. (1983b). Para uma teoria da sacanagem: Uma reflexão sobre a obra de Carlos Zéfiro. [For a theory of *sacanagem*: A reflection on the work of Carlos Zéfiro]. In J. Marinho (Ed.), *A arte sacana de Carlos Zéfiro* (pp. 22-39). Rio de Janeiro: Editora Marco Zero.

Désy, P. (1978). L'homme-femme. [The man-woman]. *Libre: Politique-Anthropologie-Philosophie, 3*, 57-102.

Durham, E. R. (1980). A família operária: Consciencia e idiologia. [The working class family: Conscience and ideology], *Dados, 23*, 201-214.

Durham, E. R. (1983). Familia e reprodução humana. [Family and human reproduction]. In *Perspectivas Antropológicas da Mulher, 3*, 13-44. Rio de Janeiro: Zahar Editores.

Foucault, M. (1976). *La volonté de savoir*. [The will to knowledge]. Paris: Gallimard.

Franchetto, B., Cavalcanti, M. L., and Heilborn, M. L. (1981). Antropologia e feminismo. [Anthropology and feminism]. In *Perspectivas Antropológicas da Mulher, 1*, 11-47. Rio de Janeiro: Zahar Editores.

Fry, P. (1977). Mediunidade e sexualidade. [Mediumship and sexuality]. *Religião e Sociedade 1*, 105-124.

Fry, P. (1982a). Da hierarquia à igualdade: A construção histórica da homossexualidade no Brasil. [From hierarchy to equality: The historical construction of homosexuality in Brazil]. In P. Fry (Ed.), *Para Inglês ver: Identidade e política na cultura Brasileira* (pp. 87-115). Rio de Janeiro: Zahar Editores.

Fry, P. (1982b). Febrónio Índio do Brasil: Onde cruzam a psiquiatria, a profecia, a homossexualidade e a lei. [Febrónio Índio from Brazil: Where psychiatry, prophesy, homosexuality and the law cross]. In A. Eulalio, B. Waldman, C. Vogt, E. MacRae, G. Velho, M. D'olne Campos, M. Corrêa, P. Fry (Eds.), *Caminhos cruzados: Linguagem, antropologia, e ciências naturais* (pp. 65-80). São Paulo: Editora Brasiliense S. A.

Fry, P. (1982c). Homossexualidade masculina e cultos Afro-Brasileiros. [Male homosexuality and Afro-Brazilian cults]. In P. Fry (Ed.), *Para Inglês ver: Identidade e política na cultura Brasileira* (pp. 54-86). Rio de Janeiro: Zahar Editores.

Fry, P. (1982d). Léonie, Pombinha, Amaro e Aleixo: Prostituição, homossexualidade e raça em dois romances naturais. [Léonie, Pombinha, Amaro and Aleixo: Prostitution, homosexuality and race in two naturalist novels]. In A. Eulalio et al. (Eds.), *Caminhos cruzados: Linguagem, antropologia e ciências naturais* (pp. 33-51). São Paulo: Editora Brasiliense S. A.

Fry, P. (1985). Male homosexuality and spirit possession in Brazil. *Journal of Homosexuality, 11*(3/4), pp. 000-000.

Fry, P., and MacRae, E. (1983). *O que é homossexualidade.* [What homosexuality is]. São Paulo: Editora Brasiliense S. A.

Guimarães, C. D. (1977). O entendido visto por entendidos. [The *entendido* as seen by *entendidos*]. Tese de Mestrado. Rio de Janeiro: Museu Nacional.

Guimarães, C. D. (1983). O novo homosexual: Velhas teorias e novas praticas. [The new homosexual: Old theories and new practices]. Paper presented at the Primeiro Encontro do Grupo de Trabalho Sexualidade e Reprodução, October. Rio de Janeiro.

Landes, R. (1940). A cult matriarchate and male homosexuality. *Journal of Abnormal and Social Psychology, 35,* 386-397.

MacRae, E. (1982). Os respeitáveis militantes e as bichas loucas. [Respectable militants and crazy queens]. In A. Eulalio et al. (Eds.), *Caminhos cruzados: Linguagem, antropologia e ciências naturais* (pp. 99-111). São Paulo: Editora Brasiliense S. A.

MacRae, E. (1983a). Em defesa do gueto. [In defense of the ghetto]. *Novos Estudos Cebrap, 2*(1), 53-60.

MacRae, E. (1983b). O movimento homossexual em São Paulo: Representações da masculinidade e da homossexualidade. [The homosexual movement in São Paulo: Representations of masculinity and of homosexuality]. Paper presented at the Primeiro Encontro do Grupo de Trabalho Sexualidade e Reprodução, October. Rio de Janeiro.

Mott, L. R. B. (1982a). Escravidão e homossexualidade. [Slavery and homosexuality]. Paper presented at the Terceiro Congresso Afro-Brasileiro, September. Fundação Joaquim Nabuco. Recife.

Mott, L. R. B. (1982b). A homossexualidade: Uma variável esquecida pela demografia histórica, os sodomitas no Brasil Colonial. [Homosexuality: A variable forgotten by historical demography, sodomites in Colonial Brazil]. Paper presented at the Terceiro Encontro da Associação Brasileira de Estudos Populacionais. Vitória.

Mott, L. R. B., and Assunção, A. H. F. (1982). Os gays e as doenças sexualmente transmissíveis. [Gays and sexually transmitted diseases]. Paper presented at the Trigéssima-quarta Reunião Anual da Sociedade Brasileira para o Progresso da Ciência, July. Campinas.

Parker, R. (1984). A report from Rio: Notes on the study of gender and sexuality in Brazil. *Anthropology Research Group on Homosexuality Newsletter, 5*(1/2), 12-22.

Perlongher, N. (1983). Maculinidade y violencia en la prostitucion viril. [Masculinity and violence in male prostitution]. Paper presented at the Primeiro Encontro do Grupo de Trabalho Sexualidade e Reprodução, October. Rio de Janeiro.

Pires de Almeida, J. R. (1906). *Homossexualismo (A libertinagem no Rio de Janeiro).* [Homosexualism (Libertinism in Rio de Janeiro)]. Rio de Janeiro: Leammert & C.

Prado, R. M. (1981). Um ideal de mulher. [An ideal for women]. *Perspectivas Antropológicas da Mulher, 2,* pp. 71-112. Rio de Janeiro: Zahar Editores.

Ribeiro, L. (1938). *Homossexualismo e endocronologia.* [Homosexuality and endocrinology]. Rio de Janeiro: Francisco Alves.

Salem, T. (1981). Mulheres faveladas: "Com a venda nos olhos." [*Favelado* women: "With a blindfold over the eyes"]. *Perspectivas Antropológicas da Mulher, 1*, 49-99. Rio de Janeiro: Zahar Editores.

Velho, G. (1981). *Individualismo e cultura: Notas para uma antropologia da sociedade contemporânea.* [Individualism and culture: Notes for an anthropology of contemporary society]. Rio de Janeiro: Zahar Editores.

Velho, G. (1984). Novas propostas de relacionamento sexual-efetivo nas camadas médias urbanas. [New proposals for sexual relationships among the urban middle classes]. Paper presented at the Primeiro Encontro do Grupo de Trabalho Sexualidade e Reprodução, October. Rio de Janeiro.

Weeks, J. (1981). *Sex, politics and society: The regulation of sexuality since 1800.* London: Longman.

Whitehead, H. (1981). The bow and the burden strap: A new look at institutionalized homosexuality in Native North America. In S. B. Ortner and H. Whitehead (Eds.), *Sexual meanings: The cultural construction of gender and sexuality* (pp. 80-115). New York: Cambridge University Press.

Men and Not-Men:
Male Gender-Mixing Statuses
and Homosexuality

Charles Callender, PhD

Case Western Reserve University

Lee M. Kochems, PhD (cand.)

University of Chicago

ABSTRACT. Male gender-mixing statuses, such as Native American berdaches, consist of men who assume the cultural, symbolic attributes of
women to attain the status of not-men. Remaining distinct from women,
not-men are a culturally defined gender status whose indexing features include women's dress and behavior, occupational inversion, and some
cultural traits of men. Another indexing feature of not-men is the absence
of sexual relations with other not-men, which forces them to seek not-
status men or women as sexual partners. The frequent equation of gender-
mixing statuses with homosexuality is a misunderstanding: Sex with men
is a secondary and derivative characteristic.

The status of Native American berdaches rests upon a cultural construction of gender that differs significantly from gender construction in
the United States and the western tradition (Callender & Kochems, 1983).
As stated by Whitehead (1981), the two cultural traditions, Native
American and western, give very different weight to particular cultural
attributes of gender. At the ideological level, Western gender construction acknowledges only a dichotomy between two opposing gender
statuses, men and women. Many Native American cultures, however, accept a gender-mixing status.

The theoretical and methodological position embodied here involves an
analytical distinction between two gender levels, *gender category* and
gender status. Gender category, although culturally constructed, desig-

Dr. Callender is Associate Professor of Anthropology, Case Western Reserve University,
Cleveland, OH 44106. Mr. Kochems is a PhD candidate in the Department of Anthropology,
University of Chicago, Chicago, IL 60637. The authors wish to thank Cynthia Beall, Vishvajit Pan-
dya, and Harriet Whitehead for advice and suggestions during the writing of this article. Reprint re-
quests may be sent to Dr. Callender, Dept. of Anthropology, Case Western Reserve University,
Cleveland, Ohio 44106.

nates the biologically identified classes of males and females, which, except for the few clinical hermaphrodites, constitute a dichotomy between the two sexes. Gender status, also socially and culturally defined, is less directly tied to this anatomical basis, although ultimately limited by it. It similarly involves oppositional classes of men and women but does not have to be limited to these two statuses. At the gender-category level, classification as not-male necessarily means being classified as female, and vice versa. At the level of gender status, however, definition as not-men is not equivalent to identification as women (Kochems, 1983) because status depends on the cultural construction of gender. While women are, by definition, not-men, other social groups within a society may consist of males whose gender status is that of not-men but who are also defined as not-women. Gender-mixing statuses, whose members are neither men nor women, are an example. Throughout this article, the term not-men designates males belonging to a gender-mixing status. The terms male and female indicate the gender-category level; men and women denote the gender-status level.

As a gender-mixing status, the position of the male berdache among Native American cultures did not represent an attempt by males to achieve social recognition as females or to attain the gender status of women. Such a goal was impossible. Even if gender status is culturally defined, its biological foundations are an inescapable restriction. The anatomical maleness of a berdache could be denied only within these limits, even if the boundaries might have surprisingly wide breadth. Male berdaches could not bear children. The Hidatsa let them become mothers through adoption (Bowers, 1965), but most cultures did not. The Mohave rejected and ridiculed their claims to transcend their gender category by achieving pregnancy (Devereux, 1937). As males who displayed some cultural attributes of women, berdaches were not classed as women by their societies, but were assigned to a particular gender status designated by a special label. These not-men also differentiated themselves from women as well as from men in the behavior they displayed, and were similarly distinguished in their treatment by other members of their societies. Based on the ethnographic evidence, these males did not direct their behavior toward achieving the gender status of women, but rather toward appropriating some of its specific symbolic features. The berdaches thereby established a gender status that combined attributes of men and women, a status that was gender-mixing.

From this theoretical standpoint, the term "gender-crossing," often applied to such a status and its members, is misleading. It implies a division into two genders, with individuals crossing from one gender to the other. It also implies a complete crossover. Gender categories are necessarily limited to two, but their membership is fixed. Male berdaches, unable to alter their gender category, remained males. Thus, at this level gender-crossing cannot occur. A culture may recognize three or more gender statuses among which limited movement is possible. A male may move from a male gender status to a gender-mixing status, or the reverse, but he cannot move from the gender status of man to that of woman. Consequently, the term "gender-mixing" more precisely accords with the ethnographic evidence.

A further aspect of berdache status, closely linked with concepts of gender construction (cf. Whitehead, 1981), is its assumed connection with homosexuality. The very early use of such terms as the French *berdache* and the Spanish *bardaje*—words which connote male prostitute—for gender-mixing males in the New World evidences this equation of berdaches and homosexuals. The use of berdache also reflects the assumption that a homosexual orientation invariably accompanies transvestism and effeminate behavior, a folk belief that has historically characterized western gender ideology. The same assumption underlies many analyses by anthropologists who, in dealing with homosexuality, often accept the gender ideology of their own cultural tradition as established fact, a point noted by Callender and Kochems (1983), Carrier (1980), and Trumbach (1977).

A variant explanation of berdache status, based on perceptions of sexual behavior, defines berdaches as passive homosexuals who, during sexual intercourse, take the role of insertee or receptor. Western ideology equates this role to the role of women in the sexual act. Devereux (1937) foreshadowed this argument when he defined Mohave berdaches as homosexuals, while classifying their sexual partners, who did not cross-dress, as temporary bisexuals. In his survey of the status among northern Plains tribes, Forgey (1975) explicitly suggested that its functions included filling the sexual needs of so-called active homosexuals who retained their gender status as men. Trumbach (1977) argued that cultural traditions tending to accept homosexual acts still disapproved of adult males being receptors and assigned this role either to adolescents, for whom it is age-linked, or else to a special adult status such as that of berdaches.

Arguments that sex with males was a secondary and derivative feature of berdache status have been proposed by Thayer (1980), Whitehead (1981), and Callender and Kochems (1983). Differing in emphasis, their analyses concur on three important points. First, stressing the erotic or genital aspects of the berdache role distorts its nature. Second, evidence of homosexual inclination was not an important factor assigning individuals to that status. Third, sexual intercourse with males essentially grew out of the interstitial gender-crossing or gender-mixing status of berdaches.

This article applies the theoretical framework derived from an analysis of berdache status to male social statuses outside Native North America

whose members, like berdaches, have often been described as homosexuals or as men trying to attain the social status of women. It also examines the theoretical implications of such an analysis for anthropology.
These aims require an explicit presentation of the features defining the
kind of status we have labeled gender-mixing.

INDEXING FEATURES OF GENDER-MIXING STATUSES

Whitehead (1981), comparing gender ideology among Native American cultures and the contemporary United States, singles out three
crucial features of the berdache status, apart from the biological distinction of males and females. These behavioral features are occupation,
dress and demeanor, and choice of sexual object. The features postulated
here as defining a gender-mixing status are similar, but modified to fit a
slightly different context. Thus, we separate dress from demeanor and
conceive sexual behavior differently.

The four features which define gender-mixing statuses for males are:
(1) a distinctively non-male style of dress, usually a form of transvestism;
(2) expression of important traits of women's behavior; (3) occupational
inversion; and (4) the absence of sexual relations with others occupying
these statuses. The features of dress, social behavior, and occupation, in-
dexed by the gender status of women, also index male gender-mixing
statuses. Consonant with the mixed character of such statuses, individuals
seldom carry such symbolic features through to completion and offset
them by other features characterized by the gender status of men. While
the latter features are always present, they show variation, and their particular forms are probably tied more to particular cultures. The fourth
feature that defines gender-mixing statuses, sexual behavior, occurs with
persons belonging to other gender statuses, usually men but sometimes
women.

These four features combine to form a system, except that social
pressure against the public display of an indexing feature, such as dressing like women, may inhibit display. In these circumstances other
features often assume greater significance. Moreover, this constellation
of indexing features should appear consistently. Similar behavior may be
temporarily expressed, in very limited contexts and usually as a single
feature, by men who do not ordinarily display it. For example, Kehoe
(1983) describes a Blackfoot holy man who dressed as a woman only
when performing sacred rituals. Oglala contraries often dressed or spoke
like women (Powers, 1983). In several Siberian cultures, shamans,
whose gender status was that of men, wore women's garments only when
engaged professionally (Sternberg, 1925). The Moro of the Nuba Hills
included cross-dressing in male initiation rites (Nadel, 1947). Gender-

mixing behavior may also occur as a solitary practice of an eccentric individual, lacking significant cultural recognition as a status.

Each male gender-mixing status also has a distinctive label, separating it from the gender statuses of men and women. Moreover, the same inhibitions described above that prevented movement by Native Americans from the male to the female gender category seem to have been universal in societies with gender-mixing statuses, with possibly one exception. The genitals of gender-mixing Chukchee males were eventually supposed to assume female form. But Bogoras (1907), who credits these not-men with fathering more children than they bore, implies that, by the early years of this century, the Chukchee assigned gender metamorphoses to the past when they had greater power.

DRESS

A distinctive style of clothing, but not necessarily complete transvestism, is the most visible symbolic feature identifying the members of a gender-mixing status. This visibility, however, makes it the feature most vulnerable to social pressure against such display, usually introduced through exposure to other cultural traditions. In Oman, where cross-dressing is prohibited (Wikan, 1982), males of the *xanith* status wear clothing whose pattern style combine aspects of men's and women's dress. Tahitians belonging to the *mahu* status, who dressed like women in the past, now usually dress like men or in a traditional style regarded as gender-neutral (Levy, 1973). Metraux's description of gender-mixing Araucanians (1942) suggests that, even if transvestism is fully developed, not-men may subtly differentiate their clothing from that of women, aiming for similarity rather than complete identification. Cross-dressing may also be subject to contextual restrictions. Some Native American cultures made berdaches dress as men when going to war. The *bissu* of southern Celebes, normally dressing as women, combine men's and women's clothing when conducting ritual (Chabot, 1950). Contextual variation also marks the clothing of the Mombasan *washoga*, who dress like women when publicly associating with them, but otherwise signal their status by a distinctive style of tight and brightly colored men's clothing (Shepherd, 1978). If transvestism is abandoned or forbidden, not-men may use other visual features to distinguish themselves from men. Thus, Tahitian *mahus*, who no longer dress like women, mark themselves off from men by not shaving (Biddle, 1968).

SOCIAL BEHAVIOR

Displaying important aspects of women's behavior is a universal gender-mixing feature that can become its most visible index in diverse circumstances, particularly when style of dress does not distinguish not-men from men. This behavioral aspect can be featured if cross-dressing is prohibited, or if, as among the Chukchee, ordinary men also dress like women (Bogoras, 1907). Wikan (1977) describes a swaying walk, falsetto voice, strong perfume, and heavy makeup as xanith features. Yet berdaches could temporarily abandon behavior culturally defined as woman-like in order to beat husbands, attack personal or tribal enemies, or assault police (Callender & Kochems, 1983). Apart from such fairly dramatic behavior, gender-mixing males probably never completely assumed women's behavior and retained important features of men's. Thus, Chukchee not-men, who were shamans, kept their masculine names and also practiced ventriloquism, a technique culturally defined as characteristic of men and not used by women (Bogoras, 1907). In Moslem societies, gender-mixing males have the legal status of men (Chabot, 1950; Wikan, 1982). If a culture limits social interaction between men and women, its not-men are usually free to associate with members of both statuses and to move freely between them.

OCCUPATIONAL INVERSION

The occupational aspects of a gender-mixing status are particularly significant. Engaging in the forms of work associated with women was the most important kind of behavior defining a Native American male as a berdache (Callender & Kochems, 1983; Whitehead, 1981). The sexual division of labor had a comparable significance in some other cultures with gender-mixing statuses, including Tahiti (Levy, 1973) and Oman (Wikan, 1982). It probably becomes significant wherever occupation is, in Whitehead's terms, "elaborated" as a gender-marking feature. Conversely, refusal to follow an occupation defined as an essential gender index for men can assign one to a gender-mixing status. Thus, the Toradja of Celebes, who considered warrior service an essential attribute of men, automatically defined as a not-man any male who rejected or abandoned the warrior role (Adriani & Kruyt, 1951). While occupational inversion was a significant index of gender-mixing statuses, its specific forms varied.

Berdaches could potentially combine or alternate between the occupational roles of men and women, hunting as well as making artifacts valued in systems of exchange. Berdaches were sometimes shamans, yet shamanism was not usually confined to their status. Some gender-mixing statuses outside North America were similarly diffuse, while others were very specialized.

One example of specialization is the definition of gender-mixing males as shamans in several cultures. While shamans' interstitial status as persons who were neither men nor women facilitated their mediation between the human and divine worlds (Thayer, 1980), shamanism itself could also represent occupational inversion. It was a profession not-men shared with women among the Toradja of Celebes (Adriani & Kruyt, 1951) and the Ngadju of Borneo (van der Kroef, 1954). Occupational inversion seems implicit even among the Araucanians and other groups where shamanism was formerly the exclusive vocation of not-men. As the Araucanian gender-mixing status disappeared, women took over shamanism. The first women who engaged in it, perhaps themselves gender-mixing, affected the dress and behavior of men (Metraux, 1942). The profession was ultimately redefined as an occupation for women. A similar shift is occurring in south Celebes as women assume the ritual duties of the gender-mixing *bissu* (Chabot, 1950). In still another form, characterizing the Chukchee and Iban, gender-mixing males were invariably shamans, but men might also enter this profession even though they had less power (Bogoras, 1907; Roth, 1896). In these groups, occupational inversion for not-men consisted of housework.

Occupational inversion in other societies may also take the form of professional entertainment or prostitution. These roles probably shade off into each other (Sheperd, 1978) and vary from occasional individual activity to a characteristic of the entire gender-mixing status. Omani xaniths support themselves as household servants and prostitutes, with the former occupation limited to them and to slaves. The latter occupation defines their status, and engaging in prostitution constitutes entry into that status (Wikan, 1977). Prostitution is the main occupational and defining feature of washoga as well (Shepherd, 1978). In Celebes, as the ritual functions of bissu disappeared or were taken over by women, the not-men who formerly lived in the royal courts and enacted this role often became dancers and prostitutes (Chabot, 1950).

The occasional concentration of gender-mixing males in the households of chiefs or other rulers, or at temples, may represent another occupational aspect of their status. The Bugi and Makassarese cultures of southern Celebes provide the clearest examples, with the bissu living in royal courts and caring for the sacred objects symbolizing the power of the rulers.

SEXUALITY

A significant feature indexing gender-mixing statuses was the absence of sexual relations among status members. Socially defined by themselves and their cultures as not-men, not-men limited sexual acts to partners belonging to other gender statuses, men or women. It was intercourse with individuals outside their status, rather than homosexual acts per se, that most consistently defined the sexual aspects of the gender-mixing status.

Gender-mixing males usually have sexual intercourse with men. Within four cultures homosexual behavior is a requirement for membership in this status, met either through prostitution or marriage to men. The xanith status consists of not-men who accept payment as receptors in acts of sexual intercourse with men (Wikan, 1982). Males usually become xaniths about 12 or 13 by engaging in homosexual prostitution. Prostitution similarly defines the washoga status (Shepherd, 1978). The definitive sexual features of both statuses seem to be receiving of payment, i.e., prostitution as an occupation, rather than as sexual behavior. Wikan reports that male homosexual relationships based on love or friendship do not define either participant as a xanith. Both the xanith and washoga statuses also diverge from the others in being temporary rather than permanent. While movement out of gender-mixing statuses is possible (Callender & Kochems, 1983; Levy, 1973; Linton, 1933), it seems rare. However, washoga who accumulate enough wealth marry women and redefine themselves as men. Those who are unsuccessful become procurors for female prostitutes. A xanith, who is conceptually impotent, may redefine himself as a man by abandoning his prostitution, marrying, and proving his potency. Failing to leave his status he is apparently classified with older men as he ages. In both statuses, then, the main indexing feature is the occupation of homosexual prostitute; when this activity ceases, one abandons the status.

Chukchee and Iban not-men were required to engage in homosexual relations and to marry men. A gender-mixing Chukchee, after adopting the appearance and behavior of a woman, sought lovers among the young men of his community. He married one of them, forming a stable union that usually lasted until death. The major purpose of the marriage was to strengthen his shamanistic power. He simultaneously married his spirit-helper, becoming his wife as well as the wife of his human husband. By binding his spirit-helper much more closely to him, marriage gave him power transcending that of shamans who were defined as men or women (Bogoras, 1907). Gender-mixing Iban shamans, who similarly outranked other practitioners, entered their gender status as adults after spending their earlier years as men. Roth (1896) suggested that marriage to men confirmed their shift of gender status and facilitated their adoption of children. In both cultures marriage to men constituted a special form of homosexual relations.

Most cultures with gender-mixing statuses permitted rather than prescribed sexual intercourse between not-men and men. Homosexual intercourse was often a personal choice for berdaches (Callender & Kochems, 1983). Although the Tanala accepted sexual relations between men and not-men, including marriage, Linton (1933) refuted the assertion that homosexuality was a feature defining their gender-mixing status. Biddle (1968) held that it was not an essential requirement for membership in the mahu status; Levy (1973) reported that Tahitians disagreed about its necessity. The Samoan definition of their comparable *fa'afafine* status does not stress sexuality (Shore, 1981). Even if most not-men engaged in sex with men, not all did so. Some cultures may have promoted homosexual relations as validation of membership in a gender-mixing status, but the only aspect of sexual behavior that was consistently an indexing feature was the lack of sexual relations with others occupying these statuses.

Another aspect of gender-mixing statuses involves sexual relations between not-men and women. Several Native American cultures defined berdaches as bisexual; in others, individual berdaches could have sexual intercourse exclusively with women (Callender & Kochems, 1983). If elsewhere some of the recorded heterosexual experiences may have been only incidental for not-men (Biddle, 1968; Levy, 1973; Suggs, 1966), in other places the evidence is more decisive. Not-men could marry women in southern Celebes and the Marquesas Islands (Chabot, 1950; Suggs, 1966); Rencurel's (1900) Merina (Madagascar) informant engaged in intercourse only with women.

The four previously mentioned gender-mixing statuses that required sexual relations with men are particularly relevant here. Chukchee gender-mixing shamans, who had to marry men, could also have sexual relations with women, surreptitiously or openly (Bogoras, 1907). Their Iban counterparts were heterosexually married before becoming not-men. The xanith and washoga statuses allow their members to redefine themselves as men by becoming heterosexual. Thus, compulsory homosexuality did not rule out heterosexual relations among the Chukchee, was preceded by heterosexual marriage among the Iban, and was ideally followed by an exclusively heterosexual orientation in Oman and Mombasa.

It has been generally assumed that the specific role of not-men in sexual encounters with men was exclusively that of receptor (e.g., Trumbach, 1977). Owing to the problems of data gathering, information bearing on this point is very limited. An English missionary in Tahiti accidentally intruded upon a chief fellating another man, apparently a mahu (Levy, 1973). In describing a sexual episode, one of Levy's informants reported that a mahu, after fellating him, asked the informant to reciprocate. This request shows that reciprocation was conceptually possible. Finally, Chabot (1950) describes the mode of sex between men and not-men in southern Celebes as mutual masturbation, thus lacking the inserter-receptor distinction.

Even if not-men usually took the receptor role in sexual intercourse with men, they were not the only males in their societies to do so. Unfortunately, ethnographers have usually ignored casual homosexual relations among men. If a gender-mixing status existed in a culture, very little was reported about homosexual sex that did not involve not-men. Judging from the data available, this silence reflects lack of observation or reporting rather than the absence of homosexual activity. Hilger (1957), however, reports that homosexual intercourse among unmarried Araucanian men was common and openly discussed, but this claim might be discounted. She studied the Araucanian culture after its gender-mixing status had disappeared, and her informant on the topic was a non-Araucanian. Some information is available for other cultures with intact gender-mixing statuses. Sternberg (1925) described homosexuality as common among the Chukchee and Koryak, apart from sexual relations with not-men. Homosexual practice among Marquesans seems similar (Daniellson, 1956; Linton, 1939; Suggs, 1966). Shore (1981) notes casual homosexuality among Samoan men. This activity also occurs in Oman, but secretly (Wikan, 1982). Homosexuality often characterized Tanala professional male dancers, an occupation closed to not-men (Linton, 1933). The Native American data also provide evidence for sexual relations among men who were not berdaches. These data support Whitehead's (1981) conclusion that "if all a person really wanted to do was engage in homosexual activity, there were opportunities for doing so without all the ballyhoo of a special identity" (p. 97).

The nature of sexual activity associated with gender-mixing statuses leads to three conclusions. First, although the existence of such a status affords opportunities for sexual intercourse between males that was sanctioned and accepted, this fact did not channel all male homosexual activity into pairings of men and not-men. Homosexual relations also occurred between males who were defined as men. Second, the sexual activity of not-men was not homogeneous. Setting aside the few statuses that actually required intercourse with men, some not-men probably did not engage in sex at all, while most of them probably had sex with men. Others had sexual relations with women, either exclusively or in addition to their relations with men. Third, in spite of the sexual latitude offered by most gender-mixing statuses, their members did not have sexual relations with each other.

These conclusions indicate that equating not-men with homosexuals is misleading, not only in the case of berdaches but also for gender-mixing statuses in general. Even the four statuses discussed here, which required sexual intercourse with men, qualified this requirement by stressing a particular form of relationship, either prostitution or marriage, rather than sexual intercourse itself. The Chukchee status allowed not-men to have intercourse with women, even though they had to marry men. The Iban, xanith, and washoga statuses, if exclusively homosexual, did not last throughout life. Iban not-men entered this status as adults after a prior term of heterosexual marriage. Xanith and washoga ideally left their statuses by marrying women. Thus, even these mandatory and exclusively homosexual relationships counterbalance an earlier or later period of exclusively heterosexual relationships.

Moreover, men who moved into a gender-mixing status did not usually do so simply by engaging in sex with other men or by desiring such activity. The most common critical factor was the display of specific behaviors that a particular culture defined as inappropriate for men. Forms of sexual activity were rarely the criteria used for assigning males to the status of not-men, even though they might become significant once this status had been achieved.

THEORETICAL IMPLICATIONS

Sexual attraction and sexual relations are cultural constructions. As such, they are constituted in the cultural arrangement of gender statuses, categories, and features. The usefulness of this analysis and the appropriateness of the distinction between gender category and gender status may be elucidated by comparing not-men with homosexual men in American society, those ranking 5 or 6 on the Kinsey scale (Kinsey, 1948). This comparison highlights three significant contrasts between these groups.

First, while not-men do not engage in sexual relations with each other but only with members of other gender statuses, homosexual men usually choose other homosexuals as sexual partners. This behavior contrasts sharply with the practice of not-men, whose sexual partners always belong to other gender statuses. Thus, gay men do not represent a distinct gender status and are not culturally perceived as constituting one.

Second, the status of not-men contains a set of indexing features in which sexuality is significant only in that it is directed toward persons belonging to other gender statuses. American gender ideology includes a rather similar constellation of indexing features that categorize men as homosexual. If a man displays mannerisms, for example, that the gender ideology conceptualizes as inappropriate for men, it inevitably raises doubts about his heterosexuality. Because such behavior is secondary, the man is not decisively identified as homosexual (cf. Newton, 1972). Many homosexual men occasionally engage in social gender-mixing behavior. Female impersonation, cross-dressing, and camp humor exemplify its most obvious forms. The contextual display of "effeminate" behavior in some form is probably common (Gorman, 1980; Kochems, 1984; Newton, 1972). Nevertheless, these conscious gender-mixing gestures are not consistently used by homosexual men and do not index them as a status in the way that not-men are assigned a gender-mixing status.

The third and most important contrast between homosexual men and not-men is the absence of a gender-mixing status in American culture. Our gender system recognizes only the two gender statuses of men and women. Homosexual men, by choice of sexual object, are perceived as behaving too much like women to be real men. Rather than forming another gender status, American ideology perceives them as imperfect members of the men's status. While this ideology may define homosexual men as mixing gender features through their sexuality, it describes them as defective, malfunctioning, and impaired. Consequently, unlike not-men, who are socially legitimated by membership in a gender-mixing status, homosexual men have been traditionally viewed as deviants needing therapy to restore their sexual behavior to a form consonant with their gender status. In drawing these contrasts, however, we are not suggesting that a gender-mixing status would offer homosexual men the advantage of social acceptance and legitimation, any more than we accept the hypothesis that such statuses consist of homosexuals.

In spite of major differences in gender construction, the cultural features affecting American perceptions of gender resemble those in cultures with gender-mixing statuses. The difference lies in their relative significance. Whitehead (1981) argues that Native Americans gave most weight to occupation, followed by dress and demeanor, with choice of sexual object the least significant feature. American culture, on the contrary, singles out choice of sexual object as by far the most important feature. It would seem that, wherever gender-mixing statuses exist, choice of sexual object has less significance in gender construction than either occupation or dress and demeanor. Further, if perceptions of gender emphasize sexual object-choice as their primary feature, gender construction takes a form that rules out gender-mixing statuses.

In making choice of sexual object the primary feature for constructing gender status, American ideology explicitly links gender status to the genitalia and the "natural" functions of penis as inserter, vagina as receptor. The conjunction of penis and vagina becomes the only acceptable form of sexual intercourse (cf. Schneider, 1980). American gender ideology therefore defines only one form of sexual intercourse as natural, linking it closely to genital anatomy (Kochems, 1984). While gender status includes other features such as occupation, dress, and social behavior, choice of sexual object remains primary in defining gender status. A homosexual male, through his sexuality, confounds "nature" itself according to the American ideological definition of it. Like not-men, he remains in the male gender category, where anatomy overrides strictly cultural features. Unlike not-men, he also retains the gender status of man, even while his sexual behavior contradicts his maleness. A shift in his gender status would entail a comparable shift in gender category, which his anatomy prevents. American ideology resolves this contradiction by stigmatizing the homosexual male as deviant, a person acting in defiance of the cultural order embodied in such ideology.

SUMMARY

Gender construction, as analyzed here, consists of three aspects: categories, features, and statuses. Gender categories, closely tied to the biological elements of gender, are necessarily a binary division between males and females. Culturally defined traits form the gender statuses of men and women, with each trait defining men paired with a complementary trait defining women. These traits also make up the cultural aspect of gender categories and, while defining gender statuses, are simultaneously defined by them.

Thus, in spite of predictable cultural variability in the features indexing gender statuses, dress, social behavior, and occupation seem universally significant. Drawing its indexing features from the statuses of men and women, a gender-mixing status lacks features specific to itself except for the particular combination of features that compose it. Although a ritual feature may sometimes be exclusive to it, this feature usually combines men's and women's attributes. The construction of sexual relations outside a gender status or choice of sexual object is another universal indexing feature. While tolerance of intra-status sexual relations varies culturally, some restrictions seem always present. In this respect gender-mixing statuses combine attributes of men and women, not-men having sexual intercourse with both sexes, but not engaging in sex with each other. This analytic approach, particularly the distinctions drawn among gender category, gender status, and indexing features as aspects of a gender system, facilitates the description, analysis, and comparison of different systems of gender construction. This theoretical approach, a form of comparative anthropological analysis, allows objective analysis of the crucial, cross-cultural issues of sexuality and gender.

REFERENCES

Andriani, N., & Kruyt, A. C. (1951). *De Bar'e sprekende Toradjas van Midden-Celebes*. Amsterdam, Noord-Hollandsche Uitgeuers Maatschappij. (HRAF translation)

Biddle, G. (1968). *Tahitian journal*. Minneapolis: University of Minnesota Press.

Blackwood, E. (1984). Sexuality and gender in certain Native American tribes: The case of cross-gender females. *Signs: Journal of Women in Culture and Society, 10*, 27-42.

Bogoras, W. (1907). *The Chukchee*. New York: Memoirs of the American Museum of Natural History.

Bowers, A. (1965). Hidatsa social and ceremonial organization. *Bureau of American Ethnology Bulletin, 194*.

Callender, C., & Kochem, L. M. (1983). The North American berdache. *Current Anthropology, 24*.

Carrier, J. M. (1980). Homosexual behavior in cross-cultural perspective. In J. Marmor (Ed.), *Homosexual behavior: A modern reappraisal* (pp. 100-122). New York: Basic Books.

Chabot, H. T. V. (1950). *Stand en sexe in Zuid-Celebes*. Groningen-Jakarta: J. B. Wolters' Uitgeuersmaatschappi. (HRAF translation by R. Neusse)

Danielsson, B. (1956). *Love in the south seas*. New York: Reynal. (Translated by F. H. Lyon)

Devereux, G. (1937). Institutionalized homosexuality of the Mohave Indians. *Human Biology, 9*, 498-527.

Forgey, D. G. (1975). The institution of berdache among the northern American Plains Indians. *Journal of Sex Research, 11,* 1-15.

Gorman, M. (1980). *A new light on Zion: A study of three homosexual religious congregations in urban America.* Unpublished doctoral dissertation, Department of Anthropology, University of Chicago, Chicago, IL.

Hassrick, R. B. (1964). *The Sioux.* Norman, OK: University of Oklahoma Press.

Hilger, I. (1957). Araucanian child life and its cultural background. *Smithsonian Miscellaneous Collections, 133.*

Kehoe, A. G. (1983). Comment. *Current Anthropology, 24,* 460-461.

Kochems, L. M. (1983). *Massai women not as "not men"; Gender relations and gender construction in a nomadic pastoral society.* Unpublished master's thesis, Department of Anthropology, University of Chicago, Chicago, IL.

Kochems, L. M. (1984). *Gay subculture: Identity and assertive symbolic activity among gay men in America.* Dissertation proposal, Department of Anthropology, University of Chicago, Chicago, IL.

Kroef, J. M. van der. (1954). Transvestism and the religious hermaphrodite in Indonesia. *University of Manila Journal of East Asiatic Studies, 3,* 257-265.

Levy, R. I. (1973). *Tahitians: Mind and experience in the Society Islands.* Chicago: University of Chicago Press.

Linton, R. (1933). The Tanala, a hill tribe of Madagascar. *Field Museum of Natural History Anthropology Series, 22.*

Metraux, A. (1942). Le shamanisme Araucan. [Araucan Shaminism]. *Revista del Instituto Antropologica Universidad Nacional Tucuman, 2.*

Munroe, R., & Munroe, R. (1977). Male transvestism and subsistence economy. *Journal of Social Psychology, 103,* 307-308.

Nadel, S. F. (1947). *The Nuba.* London: Oxford University Press.

Newton, E. (1972). *Mother camp: Female impersonators in America.* Chicago: University of Chicago Press.

Powers, W. K. (1983). Comment. *Current Anthropology, 24,* 461-462.

Rencurel, M. (1900). Les Sarimbavy: Perversion sexuelle observe en Emyrne. *Annales d'hygiene et de médicine coloniales, 3,* 562-568.

Roth, H. L. (1896). *The natives of Sarawak and British North Borneo.* London: Truslove & Hanson.

Schneider, D. (1980). *American kinship: A cultural account.* Chicago: University of Chicago Press.

Shepherd, G. (1978). Transsexualism in Oman? *Man, 13,* 133-136.

Shore, B. (1981). Sexuality and gender in Samoa: Concepts and missed conceptions. In S. B. Ortner & H. Whitehead (Eds.), *Sexual meanings: The cultural construction of gender and identity.* London: Cambridge University Press.

Sternberg, L. (1925). *Divine election in primitive religion.* Goteborg: XXI Congrès International des Américanistes.

Suggs, R. C. (1966). *Marquesan sexual behavior.* New York: Harcourt, Brace & World.

Thayer, J. S. (1980). The berdache of the northern Plains: A socioreligious perspective. *Journal of Anthropological Research, 36,* 287-293.

Trumbach, R. (1977). London's sodomites: Homosexual behavior and Western culture in the 18th century. *Journal of Social History, 4,* 1-33.

Whitehead, H. (1981). The bow and the burden strap: A new look at institutionalized homosexuality in native North America. In S. B. Ortner & H. Whitehead (Eds.), *Sexual meanings: The cultural construction of gender and sexuality* (pp. 80-115). London: Cambridge University Press.

Why Was the Berdache Ridiculed?

David F. Greenberg, PhD

New York University

ABSTRACT. Several anthropological explanations of why North American Indian berdaches were ridiculed are considered and rejected in favor of the proposal that berdaches were laughed at largely in the context of traditional joking relationships. Consequently, reports that Indians ridiculed berdaches need not be interpreted as evidence that they held negative views of homosexuality.

Berdache is the name given to North American Indians, usually male but sometimes female, who abandoned the gender ordinarily associated with their anatomical sex, and laid claim to the gender associated with the opposite sex. Usually this change entailed adopting the clothing, occupational specializations, mannerisms and speech patterns of the opposite gender (Angelino & Shedd, 1955; Callender & Kochems, 1983; Forgery, 1975; Jacobs, 1968; Katz, 1976; Thwaites, 1899; Whitehead, 1981). Under white influence, however, some components of the transformation, such as cross-dressing, were sometimes suppressed (Lurie, 1953). Berdaches' choice of sexual partners was usually homosexual, and some berdaches married same-sex spouses, but this was not invariably the case.

Early writings (Angelino & Shedd, 1955) spoke of berdaches as adopting the gender associated with the opposite sex, but recent writings suggest a more complex reality. While berdaches may have claimed to be members of the opposite sex, and tried to gain acceptance for their claim, it appears not to have been always credited. At least in some tribes, possibly many, the berdache status may have been that of a third or intermediate gender, somewhere between male and female, and embodying some aspects and privileges of each (Callender & Kochems, 1983; Jacobs, 1983; Mandelbaum, 1940; Martin & Voorhies, 1975; Miller, 1982, Whitehead, 1981). In other groups, their claims do appear to have been fully accepted (Blackwood, 1984).

David Greenberg is Professor of Sociology at New York University, New York, NY 10003. His scholarly interests are in criminology, law, deviance and social control, comparative and historical sociology, and social statistics. He is grateful to Jessica Lefevre for bibliographical assistance, and to Jane Adams, Evelyn Blackwood, Karen Blu, Charles Callender, Sue-Ellen Jacobs, Lee Kochems, Stephen Murray, Connie Sutton, Robert Ulin, Walter L. Williams and Harriet Whitehead for helpful comments and suggestions.

The anthropological literature describes the social responses berdaches evoked within their own groups in apparently contradictory terms. On the one hand, berdaches were accepted or even revered; on the other, they were scorned and ridiculed. The present paper is an attempt to resolve this conflict.

RESPONSES TO BERDACHES

Missionaries, explorers and anthropologists say that some tribes highly respected the berdache. On his first voyage down the Mississippi in 1673-1677, Father Marquette found that the Illinois and Nadowesi berdaches

> . . . are summoned to the Councils, and nothing can be decided without their advice . . . through their profession of leading an Extraordinary life, they pass for Manitous—that is to say, for Spirits,— or persons of consequence. (Thwaites, 1899, p. 129).

Similarly, the Chippewas "looked upon them as Manitous, or at least as for great and incomparable geniuses" (Hoffman, 1891, p. 153). Davydov, a Russian explorer who visited Kodiak Island off the coast of Alaska in 1812, reported that among the Koniag Indians, male children raised from birth or early childhood to be female "are not looked down upon, but instead they are obeyed in a settlement and are not seldom wizards" (Hrdlicvka, 1944).

A number of tribes reserved special ritual functions for berdaches. Among the Oglala and Tetons, berdaches gave new names to tribal members who were undergoing a life crisis (Fire, 1972; Powers, 1977). The Crow berdache chopped down the first tree for the Sun Dance (Lowie, 1935). At the conclusion of a successful military campaign, Cheyenne berdaches organized and conducted the Scalp Dance. Navaho, Creek, and Yokut berdaches performed special functions at funerals (Jacobs, 1968). A Zuni berdache

> was called upon by her own clan and also by the clans of her foster mother and father when a long prayer had to be repeated or a grace was to be offered over a feast. In fact she was the chief personage on many occasions. (Stevenson, 1904, p. 310)

As the passage from Davydov quoted above suggests, the attribution of unusual spiritual powers to berdaches in some Indian groups enabled some of them to become shamans, thereby gaining the respect and material income of healers. Even when no distinctive occupational role is noted for berdaches, sources commonly refer to the great respect in which they were held (Bowers, 1965; Fages, 1970; Hill, 1935; Hoebel, 1978; Lafitau, 1976; Landes, 1970; Lurie, 1953). Other sources speak of berdaches as being accepted by their tribes without necessarily being held in unusually high esteem (Beals, 1933; Dorsey, 1894; James & Say, 1976; Kroeber, 1925; Olson, 1936; Stewart, 1942; Tanner, 1956). Indeed, berdaches were not barred from high honors. Stories exist of a Snake woman who ''by some fearless actions . . . has obtained the title of 'brave' and the privilege of admittance to the council of the chiefs'' (de Smet, 1976), and of a Gros Ventre woman who was made one of the leading Crow chiefs in recognition of her daring military exploits (Denig, 1976).

Alongside the sources that refer to berdaches as honored or accepted, there are others that describe negative tribal responses. The Papago ''scorned'' berdaches (Drucker, 1941); the Cocopa ''apparently disliked'' them (Gifford, 1933). The Choctaws held them ''in great contempt'' (Bossu, 1976), the Seven Nations ''in the most sovereign contempt'' (de Charlevoix, 1976). The Klamath subjected berdaches to ''scorn and taunting'' (Spier, 1930); the Sioux ''derided'' them (Hassrick, 1964). Pima berdaches were ridiculed, though not otherwise sanctioned (Hill, 1938), as were Mohave berdaches who claimed to possess the genitals of the opposite sex (Devereaux, 1937). The Apache treated berdaches respectfully when present, but ridiculed them behind their backs (Opler, 1965, 1969). The Zuni accepted their berdache, ''although there was some joking and laughing about his ability to attract the young men to his home'' (Stewart, 1960). In some groups, the partners of berdaches were also ridiculed or despised (Devereaux, 1937; Drucker, 1941; Linton, 1936; Mirsky, 1937).

While some reports of hostility may express the author's feelings rather than those of the Indians, many—particularly those that describe berdaches as being ridiculed—have the ring of authenticity. This range in variation of responses has never been adequately explained. For the most part, anthropologists merely describe the berdache phenomenon, or speculate about the reasons individuals become berdaches. The social responses berdaches evoked have received comparatively little attention. A growing interest in attitudes toward homosexuality in stratified societies, however, (Boswell, 1980; Davies, 1982; Goodich, 1979; Greenberg & Bystryn, 1982, 1984) suggests that these responses may be worth exploring in more egalitarian stateless societies as well.

EXPLAINING NEGATIVE RESPONSES TO BERDACHES

Werner (1979) has observed that, in a world-wide sample, acceptance of homosexuality is strongly correlated with acceptance of abortion and infanticide. He suggests that concern with population control governs attitudes toward all such practices. If this assertion is true, social responses to homosexuality should be hostile when there are strong social reasons for encouraging population growth. This relationship should hold true for all manifestations of homosexuality, not just those that involve gender transformation.

Werner's explanation should apply to the berdache, since most berdaches engaged in homosexuality. Unfortunately, his sample contains only seven North American Indian groups, too few to test his theory. Moreover, his sample cannot readily be extended because reliable information about the way most Indian groups responded to berdaches is not at hand. The majority of ethnographic reports on the berdaches are brief and superficial, often devoting no more than a sentence or two to the topic. As mentioned above, some of the reports may reflect their authors' prejudices rather than those of the Indians. Some Indian groups felt that the berdaches should be kept secret from whites, making it difficult for anthropologists to learn much about them.

A second possibility is that variability in responses to berdaches had its origins in differential acculturation to white attitudes. There is evidence that Indians were sometimes influenced by exposure to white people's repugnance or contempt for transvestism and homosexuality (Hill, 1935; Powers, 1983). Thus, Lurie (1953) found that among the Winnebago,

> Most informants felt that the berdache was at one time a highly honored and respected person, but that the Winnebago had become ashamed of the custom because the white people thought it was amusing or evil.

Yet it is doubtful whether all the reports of ridicule can be attributed to white influence. After all, in the nineteenth and early twentieth centuries the prevalent white attitude toward homosexuality was not mild amusement, but rather horror and disgust. It seems likely that in at least some groups, the practice of ridiculing berdaches was indigenous.

One possible explanation for ridiculing behavior can be derived from the relation of the berdache role to warfare. Chronic fighting with neighboring groups was an extremely widespread feature of American Indian life, though more so for some groups than for others. The berdache role, it has been argued, was chosen by men who were unable to hunt and fight, or feared death or injury, or had overprotective mothers (Devereaux, 1937; Hassrick, 1964; Hoebel, 1949, 1978). There appears to have been, however, no relationship between the presence of berdaches in a group and a cultural emphasis on fighting. Indeed, in some groups berdaches fought along with or accompanied warriors to battle, carrying food and retrieving the dead (Callender & Kochems, 1983; Goldberg, 1962; Katz, 1976). Further, the observation that male berdaches could not wage war leaves the female berdache totally unexplained. Yet, even if false, it is conceivable that the Indians themselves believed some version of this theory. Men who underwent the risk of injury and death might have envied and resented men whose gender role allowed them to avoid risk. Ridicule, in some cases, could have been a way of coping with this ambivalence.

This explanation implies that berdaches were not ridiculed because of their homosexuality, but because of their gender role. Such a distinction is meaningful, since not all berdaches were homosexual, and not all individuals who engaged in homosexuality were berdaches; berdaches' sexual partners were invariably persons of conventional gender (Angelino & Shedd, 1955; Callender & Kochems, 1983; Devereaux, 1937; Whitehead, 1981). Yet there are reasons for being skeptical of this reasoning. Among the Mohave, ridicule focused on the male berdache's claims to have a female anatomy rather than on their supposed cowardice. Mohave berdaches themselves teased other men for being cowardly (Devereaux, 1937), something they would not have done if they themselves were vulnerable to this accusation. Sometimes a berdache's partners were ridiculed, even though they did engage in combat (Devereaux, 1937; Drucker, 1941; Linton, 1936; Mirsky, 1937). Had homosexuality been responsible for the ridicule, the ridiculers should have been only men. In some groups, however, men accepted the berdaches while women scorned them (Spier, 1933). This explanation also leaves the ridicule aimed at female berdaches unexplained.

Ridicule and Joking Relationships

Landes' (1968) study of the Santee Dakota, a Sioux-speaking group, suggests an alternative explanation. She describes the process by which, over a period of several years, a young Santee man became a *winkte*, the Sioux term for berdache. As a boy, he had preferred beadwork and housework to boys' sports. With approval for his transformation coming through his dreams, he adopted female attire and forms of speech. Dreams were a basis for making important life choices in many American Indian groups.

The winkte's transvestism elicited no particular response until he began to flirt with and attempt to seduce many of the men in his village. At this point the people of the village held a formal ceremony in which they exiled the winkte for life. This was a very severe penalty, greater than that imposed for homicide.

Following his exile, the winkte took up residence in a neighboring village. Landes indicates that he was welcomed by the women, who were grateful for his contribution to women's work (male berdaches often excelled in performing traditionally female tasks), and by the men, who were happy to partake of his "hospitality" (not described further, but presumably the reference is to sexual hospitality). Despite this seemingly positive reception, the winkte was persistently subjected to flirtatious teasing (Landes, 1968).

Why would two Santee villages have responded so differently to the same behavior? Almost all the men in a Santee village were members of a single patrilineal clan. Kinship was classificatory, with remote ties counting almost as strongly as immediate ones. Marriage was exogamous, with residence preferentially patrilocal (Landes, 1968). Thus, the men of the winkte's natal village were members of his own patriclan, and consequently forbidden to him by rules of exogamy. The winkte then, was not exiled because of his homosexual proclivities, but because of his disregard for incest taboos. Had he attempted to seduce his classificatory sisters, he would also have been exiled, for this was the standard penalty in cases of heterosexual incest (Landes, 1968).

The men of the second village were classificatory cross-cousins. As such, they were acceptable marriage or sexual partners for the winkte: "Sexual liberties were allowed between a berdache and men of the strange village, who were all unrelated to him" (Landes, 1968). Yet if sexual liberties were allowed, why was the winkte ridiculed for taking advantage of them? The explanation may lie in joking relationships. Landes notes that

> Joking relatives—cross-cousins and siblings-in-law—were properly maligned in public. . . . Cross-cousins of both sexes and siblings-in-law of both sexes were supposed to joke publicly. As among the Ojibwa, this included flirting that was officially "innocent" but that actually ran often to sexual intercourse, and it included public taunting which also might ignore limits. (Landes, 1968, pp. 37-38)

The institutionalization of teasing and ridicule was far from unique to the Santee; on the contrary, such joking relationships were an indigenous culture-trait that was present throughout North American Indian groups (Aberle, 1961; Driver, 1969; Drucker, 1941; Hoebel, 1978; Landes, 1937; Spinder & Spinder, 1957; Stewart, 1942). These practices did not always involve cross-cousins, as they did among the Santee, the Ojibwa and the Cree; sometimes they involved uncles and aunts or siblings-in-law, or even persons who did not stand in a special kinship relationship to one another (private communications from Charles Callender & Lee Kochems, 1983; and from Walter L. Williams, 1983). The joking often involved sexual themes.

The few instances of strongly negative responses reported for North American Indian groups may have been a response, not to the status of the berdaches but to their violations or attempted violations of traditional rules of sexual exogamy. The ridicule to which berdaches were subjected in some groups may have amounted to nothing more than the treatment persons in joking relationships—ordinarily relatives, but sometimes others—routinely meted out to one another.[1] Indeed, in many instances it may have been a way for one person to signal sexual interest.[2]

A single example from the Santee makes an inadequate basis from which to generalize to all Indian groups. With the exception of Landes' study, however, the published ethnographic reports provide little information about the contexts in which berdaches were ridiculed, or about the social identities of the ridiculers and their kinship ties, if any, to the berdache.

Nevertheless, the Santee were not alone in subjecting homosexual relationships to the same rules of incest and exogamy that governed heterosexual relationships. Hill (1935) mentions that this was the case for the Navaho *nadle*, or berdache. A number of South American and Melanesian cultures also tolerated or even institutionalized homosexuality while restricting it to the usual rules of exogamy applicable to heterosexual relationships (Deacon, 1934; Godelier, 1976; Herdt, 1981; Hugh-Jones, 1979; Kelly, 1976; Levi-Strauss, 1943, 1969; Roheim, 1933; Schieffelin, 1976; Van Baal, 1966; Williams, 1936).

As for descriptions of the ridiculing of berdaches, none of the sources suggests that berdaches were subject to ridicule more than other joking partners. Devereaux (1937), who reports several episodes in which Mohave berdaches or their partners were teased, also notes that the Mohave attitude toward sex was "completely humoristic," so much so that it was difficult to obtain serious answers to interview questions (Devereaux, 1950). Moreover, Walter Williams (personal communication, 1983) has indicated that his observations of the Omaha, Sioux, Crow, Arapaho, North Cheyenne, Ute, and Maya Indians of the Yucatan largely confirm the suggestion made here.

The teasing berdaches received, therefore, may have centered on their homosexual preferences without having been caused by them. Berdaches might have been teased just as much had their sexual partners been of the opposite sex. Moreover, persons of respect and prestige, including chiefs, were not spared ridicule. Ridicule was a mild form of social control used to take pretentious persons down a peg or two (Burland, 1973; Hoebel, 1978). Consequently, there would have been no inconsistency between ridiculing berdaches (especially when they made false claims about their anatomy) and holding them in respect.

IMPLICATIONS FOR ANTHROPOLOGY

Considering the importance that anthropologists have traditionally given to the role of kinship and incest taboos in structuring the choice of marital and sexual partners, it is striking that those studying American Indians have not considered the implications of kinship categories for an understanding of social responses to berdaches. Possibly individual views of homosexuality and transvestism as abnormal—explicit in the writings of some anthropologists (e.g., Devereaux, 1950)—prevented them from seeing that homosexual relationships among the Indians were as normatively structured as heterosexual relationships. As a result, anthropologists who would not assert that heterosexual relationships were despised because heterosexual incest was considered unacceptable, may have made an analogous error concerning homosexual relationships which occur in the context of gender transformation. This error may have led to a fundamental misunderstanding of how American Indians responded to transvestism and homosexuality.

Given the argument in this paper, published cross-cultural codings for attitudes toward homosexuality (Broude & Green, 1976; Ford & Beach, 1951; Minturn, Grosse & Haider, 1969) must be seriously questioned. Trumbach (1977) has already challenged a number of the codings Ford and Beach adopted on the grounds that they are arbitrary and misrepresent their sources. Indeed, many codings were based on little more than an off-hand remark by a single informant of unknown reliability. Here we suggest an additional difficulty. The codings rely on verbal and behavioral responses for assessing attitudes. They assume ridicule reflects attitudes that are mildly negative, or less than fully accepting. Yet, if ridicule reflects nothing more than routinized joking between members of joking relationships, this supposition is in error. Consequently, analyses such as Werner's (1979), which are based on these codings, may be badly distorted.

NOTES

1. Evans (1978) has independently conjectured that the ridicule of berdaches grew out of joking relationships, but provides no evidence.

2. A contemporary example of the simultaneous teasing and flirtatious expression of sexual interest in a young man whose behavior was not unlike that of a berdache has been reported for the Hare Indians of Northwest Canada (Broch, 1977). Bogoras (1904, pp. 450-52) likewise reports that neighbors gossip and joke about the transvestite shamans of the Siberian Chukchee, though only in whispers, because they fear the shamans' supernatural powers. That these jokes originate in frustrated sexual attraction is suggested by Bogoras' remark that the transformed shaman "has all the young men he could wish striving to obtain his favor. From these he chooses his lover, and after a time takes a husband." These observations cannot easily be reconciled with rejection of tranvestism or homosexuality, even to a mild degree.

REFERENCES

Aberle, D. (1961). Navaho. In D. M. Schneider & K. Gouch (Eds.), *Matrilineal kinship* (pp. 96-201). Berkeley: University of California Press.

Angelino, H., & Shedd, C. L. (1955). A note on Berdache. *American Anthropologist, 57,* 121-125.

Beals, R. L. (1933). Ethnology of the Nisenan. *University of California Publications in American Archaeology and Ethnology, 31,* 410.

Blackwood, E. (1984). Sexuality and gender in certain Native American tribes: The case of cross-gender females. *Signs: Journal of Women in Culture and Society, 10,* 27-42.

Bossu, J. B. (1976). Most of them are addicted to sodomy. In J. Katz (Ed.), *Gay American history* (p. 291). New York: Crowell. (Originally published 1751-1762)

Boswell, J. (1980). *Christianity, social tolerance and homosexuality.* Chicago: University of Chicago Press.

Bowers, A. (1965). *Hidatsa social and ceremonial organization.* U.S. Bureau of American Ethnology, Bulletin No. 194. Washington, D.C.: Government Printing Office.

Broch, H. B. (1977). A note on Berdache among the Hare Indians of northwestern Canada. *Western Canadian Journal of Anthropology, 7,* 95-101.

Broude, G. J., & Greene, S. J. (1976). Cross-cultural codes on twenty sexual attitudes and practices. *Ethnology, 15,* 409-429.

Burland, C. (1973). Middle America. In P. Rawson (Ed.), *Primitive erotic art* (pp. 107-14). New York, G. P. Putnam's Sons.

Callender, C., & Kochems, L. (1983). The North American Berdache. *Current Anthropology, 24,* 443-456.

de Charlevoix, P. F. X. (1976). Effeminacy and lewdness. (Originally published 1721) In J. Katz (Ed.), *Gay American history* (p. 290). New York: Crowell.

Davies, C. (1982). Sexual taboos and social boundaries. *American Journal of Sociology, 87,* (pp. 1032-1063).

Deacon, A. B. (1934). *Malekula: A vanishing people in the New Hebrides.* London: Routledge & Kegan Paul.

Denig, E.T. (1976). *Biography of a woman chief.* (Originally published 1953). In J. Katz (Ed.), *Gay American history* (pp. 308-311). New York: Crowell.

Devereaux, G. (1937). Institutionalized homosexuality of the Mohave Indians. *Human Biology, 9,* 498-527.

Devereaux, G. (1950). Heterosexual behavior of the Mohave Indians. In G. Roheim (Ed.), *Psychoanalysis and the social sciences,* Vol. 2 (pp. 85-128). New York: International Universities Press.

Dorsey, J. O. (1894). *A study of Siouan cults.* In Eleventh annual report of the Bureau of Ethnology (pp. 361-553). Washington, D.C.: Government Printing Office.

Driver, H. E. (1969). *Indians of North America.* Chicago: University of Chicago Press.

Drucker, P. (1941). Cultural element distributions: XVII, Yuman-Piman. *Anthropological Records, 6,* 91-230.

Evans, A. (1978). *Witchcraft and the gay counterculture.* Boston: Fag Rag.

Fages, P. (1970). The Chumash Indians of Santa Barbara. In R. F. Heizer & M. A. Whipple (Eds.), *The California Indians: A source book* (p. 213). Berkeley: University of California Press.

Fire, J. with Erdoes, R. (1972). *Lame deer, seeker of visions.* New York: Simon & Schuster.

Ford, C. S., & Beach, F. A. (1951). *Patterns of sexual behavior.* New York: Harper.

Forgery, D. G. (1975). The institution of Berdache among the Northern American Plains Indians. *Journal of Sex Research, 11,* 1-15.

Gifford, E. W. (1933). The Cocopa. *University of California Publications in American Archaeology and Ethnology, 31,* 257-333.

Godelier, M. (1976). Le sexe comme fondement ultime de l'ordre social et cosmique chez les Baruya de Nouvelle Guinée. [Sex as the ultimate foundation of the social and cosmic order of the New Guinea Baruya]. In A. Verdiglione (Ed.), *Sexualité et Pouvoir* (pp. 268-306). Paris: Traces Puyot.

Goldberg, R. (1962). War and its relationship with sexual tensions and identification conflict. Senior Honors Thesis, Radcliff College.

Goodich, M. (1979). *The unmentionable vice: Homosexuality in the later Medieval period.* Santa Barbara, CA: ABC-Clio.

Greenberg, D. F., & Bystryn, M. H. (1982). Christian intolerance of homosexuality. *American Journal of Sociology, 88,* 515-548.

Greenberg, D. F., & Bystryn, M. H. (1984). Capitalism, bureaucracy and male homosexuality. *Contemporary Crises, 8,* 33-56.

Hassrick, R. (1964). *The Sioux: Life and customs of a warrior society.* Norman, OK: University of Oklahoma.

Herdt, G. (1981). *Guardians of the flutes.* New York: McGraw-Hill.

Hill, W. W. (1935). The status of the hermaphrodite and transvestite in Navaho culture. *American Anthropologist, 37,* 273-279.

Hill, W. W. (1949). Note on the Pima Berdache. *American Anthropologist, 40*, 338-340.

Hoebel, E. A. (1949). *Man in the primitive world.* New York: McGraw-Hill.

Hoebel, E. A. (1978). *The Cheyenne: Indians of the Great Plains.* New York: Holt, Rinehart & Winston.

Hoffman, W. J. (1891). *The Mide'wiwin or "Grand Medicine Society" of the Ojibwa.* Seventh Annual Report of Bureau of American Ethnology (pp. 143-300). Washington, D.C.: Government Printing Office.

Hrdlicvka, A. (1944). *The anthropology of Kodiak Island.* Philadelphia: Wistar Institute.

Hugh-Jones, S. (1979). *The palm and the Pleiades.* New York: Cambridge University.

Jacobs, S. E. (1968). Berdache: A brief review of the literature. *Colorado Anthropologist, 1*, 25-40.

Jacobs, S. E. (1983). Commentary on Callender and Kochems. *Current Anthropology, 24*, 459-460.

James, E., & Say, T. (1976). Sodomy is not uncommonly committed. (Originally published 1822.) In J. Katz (Ed.), *Gay American history*, p. 299. New York: Crowell.

Katz, J. (Ed.) (1976). *Gay American history.* New York: Crowell.

Kelly, R. C. (1976). Witchcraft and sexual relations: An exploration in the social and semantic implications of the structure of belief. In P. Brown & G. Buchbinder (Eds.), *Man and woman in the New Guinea highlands.* Washington, D.C.: American Anthropological Association.

Kroeber, A. L. (1925). *Handbook of the Indians of California.* U.S. Bureau of American Ethnology, Bulletin No. Washington, D.C.: Government Printing Office.

Lafitau, J. J. (1976). Men who dress as women. (Originally published in 1821.) In J. Katz (Ed.), *Gay American history* (W. Johanssohn, Trans.). (pp. 288-289). New York: Crowell.

Landes, R. (1937). The Ojibwa of Canada. In M. Mead (Ed.), *Cooperation and competition among primitive peoples.* New York: McGraw-Hill.

Landes, R. (1968). *The Mystic Lake Sioux: Sociology of the Mdewakantonwan Santee.* Madison, WI: University of Wisconsin Press.

Landes, R. (1970). *The prairie Potawotami: Tradition and ritual in the twentieth century.* Madison, WI: University of Wisconsin Press.

Levi-Strauss, C. (1943). Social uses of kinship terms among Brazilian Indians. *American Anthropologist, 45*, 395-401.

Levi-Strauss, C. (1969). *The elementary forms of kinship.* Boston: Beacon Press.

Linton, R. (1936). *The study of man.* New York: Appleton.

Lowie, R. H. (1935). *The Crow Indians.* New York: Farrar & Rinehart.

Lurie, N. O. (1953). The Winnebago Berdache. *American Anthropologist, 55*, 708-712.

Mandelbaum, D. G. (1940). The Plains Cree. *Anthropological Papers of the American Museum of Natural History, 37*, 155-316.

Martin, M. K., & Voorhies, B. (1975). *Female of the species.* New York: Columbia University Press.

Miller, J. (1982). People, Berdaches, and left-handed bears: Human variation in native America. *Journal of Anthropological Research, 38*, 274-287.

Minturn, L. Grosse, M., & Haider, S. (1969). Cultural patterning of sexual beliefs and behavior. *Ethnology, 8*, 301-318.

Mirsky, J. (1937). The Dakota. In M. Mead (Ed.), *Cooperation and competition among primitive peoples* (pp. 000-000). New York: McGraw-Hill.

Olson, R. L. (1936) The Quinault Indians. *University of Washington Publications in Anthropology, 6*, 1-90.

Opler, M. E. (1965). *An Apache life-way.* (Original work published 1941). New York: Cooper Square.

Opler, M. E. (1969). *Apache odyssey: A journey between two worlds.* New York: Holt, Rinehart & Winston.

Powers, W. K. (1977). *Oglala religion.* Lincoln, NE: University of Nebraska Press.

Powers, W. K. (1983). Commentary on Callender and Kochems. *Current Anthropology, 24*, 461-462.

Roheim, G. (1933). Women and their life in central Australia. *Journal of Royal Anthropological Institute of Great Britain and Ireland, 63*, (pp. 207-265).

Schieffelin, E. S. (1976). *The sorrow of the lonely and the burning of the dancers.* New York: St. Martin's Press.

de Smet, P. J. (1976). A woman . . . who once dreamed she was a man. (Original work published 1905). In J. Katz (Ed.), *Gay American history* (pp. 302-303). New York: Crowell.

Spier, L. (1930). *Klamath ethnography.* Berkeley: University of California Press.

Spier, L. (1933). *Yuman tribes of the Gila River*. Chicago: University of Chicago Press.

Spindler, G. D., & Spindler, L. S. (1957). American Indian personal types and their sociocultural roots. *Annals of the American Academy of Political Science, 311*, 83-292.

Stevenson, M. C. (1904). *The Zuni Indians: Their mythology, esoteric societies, and ceremonies*. Twenty-Third Annual Report, U.S. Bureau of American Ethnology, 1901-1902. Washington, D.C.: Government Printing Office.

Stewart, O. C. (1942). Culture element distribution: XVIII, Ute-Southern Paiute. *Anthropological Records, 6*, 231-354.

Stewart, O. C. (1960). Homosexuality among American Indians and other native peoples, Part 2. *Mattachine Review, 6*(2), 13-19.

Tanner, J. (1956). *A Narrative of the captivity and adventure of John Tanner*. (Original work published 1830). (E. James, Ed.) Minneapolis: Ross & Haines.

Thwaites, R. G. (1900). *The Jesuit relations and allied documents: Vol. 59. Travels and explorations of the Jesuit missionaries in New France, Lower Canada, Illinois, Ottowas, 1673-1677*. Cleveland: Burrows Brothers.

Trumbach, R. (1977). London's sodomites: Homosexual behavior and western culture in the eighteenth century. *Journal of Social History, 11*, 1-33.

Van Baal, J. (1966). *Dema*. The Hague: Martinus Nifhoff.

Werner, D. (1979). A cross-cultural perspective on theory and research on male homosexuality. *Journal of Homosexuality, 4*, 345-362.

Whitehead, H. (1981). The bow and the burden strap: A new look at institutionalized homosexuality in Native North America. In S. B. Ortner & H. Whitehead (Eds.), *Sexual meanings: The cultural construction of gender and sexuality* (pp. 80-115). Cambridge: Cambridge University Press.

Williams, F. E. (1936). *Papuans of the trans-fly*. Oxford: Clarendon Press.

Persistence and Change
in the Berdache Tradition
Among Contemporary Lakota Indians

Walter L. Williams, PhD
University of Southern California

ABSTRACT. This article explores the gender non-conformity role of *berdache*, which ethnographers have often assumed has died out among contemporary American Indians. Ethnohistorical sources indicate intense suppression of berdaches by missionaries and government officials. The authors fieldwork in 1982 on Lakota reservations in South Dakota reveals that individuals recognized as berdaches continue to hold a social and ceremonial role. A gender-mixing status seldom talked about with outsiders (including heterosexual ethnographers) was observed. This role involves more emphasis on sexual contact with men that has been noted in recent anthropological writings.

The *berdache* tradition in American Indian culture has been discussed since the earliest Spanish and French explorers confronted aboriginal societies. Frontiersmen and early ethnographers also described it, and a few even interviewed berdaches as late as the 1930s (Stevenson 1901-2; Hill, 1935). Nevertheless, most of the first-hand writings on the subject were based upon statements by non-berdache Indians or by whites who may have had only fleeting contact with a berdache. Some of these white observers approached the subject in a neutral manner, but the majority (including some anthropologists) expressed condemnatory attitudes reflective of western prejudices. Most reports devoted only a paragraph or two to the berdaches, preferring to focus on less "disagreeable" topics.

Modern scholars analyzing the topic on a multi-tribal level have had to rely on these limited sources, as a basis for theorizing about the social

The author is Associate Professor of Anthropology and the Study of Women and Men in Society at the University of Southern California, Los Angeles, CA 90089-0661. He received his PhD from the University of North Carolina at Chapel Hill in 1974, and has done fieldwork among the Eastern Cherokees, Lakotas, Crows, Omahas, and Yucatan Mayas. Thanks are expressed to those who helped gain contact with traditionalist Lakotas and served as valuable resource advisors: Luis Kemnitzer, Elizabeth Grobsmith, Calvin Fast Wolf, Herbert Hoover, James Young, Al White Eyes, Dale Mason, Twila Giegle, Calvin Jumping Bull, and other Lakota people who wish to remain anonymous.

function of the berdache tradition (Angelino & Shedd, 1955; Blackwood, 1984; Callender & Kochems, 1983; Forgey, 1975; Jacobs, 1968; Katz, 1976; Thayer, 1980; Whitehead, 1981). The berdaches have been presented only abstractly, rather than in a personalized way as real people, due to the deficiencies of the available data. Berdaches have not been allowed to speak for themselves. Furthermore, most anthropologists assume that the berdache tradition has died out among contemporary American Indians. As with all traditional aspects of aboriginal societies the berdache tradition has changed, but it still persists among some tribes. Changes in the tradition are the result of cultural adaptations that Indian people have made to life in a homophobic colonial environment.

One group in which the berdache tradition survives is the traditionalist Lakotas, or Sioux, in the northern Plains. In their language the word for berdache is *winkte*, and refers only to biological males (Hassrick, 1964; Powers, 1977). According to Forgey (1975), a male on the Lower Brule reservation continued dressing in women's clothing in the 1970s, and was fully accepted as a winkte and as a respected member of the community. In 1971, the revered Lakota medicine man, Lame Deer, also reported the continued existence of winkte. In that year he held a conversation with a berdache, of whom he said, "I wasn't even sure of whether I was talking to a man or to a woman. . . . To us a man is what nature, or his dreams, make him. We accept him for what he wants to be. That's up to him. . . . There are good men among the winktes and they have been given certain powers" (Fire & Erdoes, 1972, p. 149).

Equipped with nothing more than these brief statements, I searched for information about berdaches among contemporary Lakotas. During the summer of 1982, I did fieldwork in South Dakota on the Pine Ridge and Rosebud reservations, with a brief trip to the Cheyenne River reservation. Lakota people generously took me into their households and allowed me to learn of their sacred traditions and ceremonies. Lakota berdaches spoke frankly to me of their lives and place in their tribal society.

The best way to understand winkte is to let the Lakota people speak for themselves. The people quoted here are full-blood Lakotas who have lived most of their lives on one of the Lakota reservations. They think of themselves as "traditionalists," meaning that they respect the institutionalized ways of the old people, participate in the aboriginal religious ceremonies, and reject Christianity and the competitive Protestant ethic.

Interview 1: The informant was a sixty-year-old man who identifies as a traditionalist, takes a leadership role in community ceremonies as a drummer and chanter, and is regarded as an authority on Lakota culture. He described the winktes as follows:

At one time the winktes were regarded as sacred people, but that has declined and today it is like "gay," like you have in California. People will tease each other about being winkte, but you would never tease a winkte himself. The attitude of respect changed around World War II or a little after, because of social pressures, as Indians who had been educated in white schools lost respect for the traditions. But even today elderly winktes are respected as holy persons, especially by the elderly and traditional people. They are feared because of their spiritual power. They could put a curse on people who don't respect them.

Becoming a winkte comes from different things. Winktes sometimes come from families with lots of sisters and brothers. It could be how they are brought up, I don't know. Sometimes a person will change, and no longer be a winkte. So if they stay that way it is more of their own choice. It is easy to pick out a winkte. They don't marry women, but they act and talk like a woman. But they're "half and half," and will dress mostly like men. Winktes had to assume their roles because if they didn't, something bad would happen to them or their familiy or their tribe. But there could also be other reasons for winkte, I'm not sure.

In ceremonials, winktes would dance like a woman and wear an article or two of women's clothing, but otherwise dress as a man. This still happens today. Fifteen or 20 years ago there were still quite a number of elderly winktes on the reservation, but most of them have died since then. I saw them at the ceremonies. People take for granted that they aren't going to change him. That's his life and they accept him. . . . But the white missionaries condemned winktes, and would tell families if something bad happened it was because of the winktes. They would not even accept them into the cemetery when a winkte died, saying "their souls are lost." They ostracized winktes.

Some younger people today are called winkte, but I don't think they are really winkte because they don't have spirituality. They are just "gay"; there is a difference. Maybe they got that way from drinking or smoking. And most of them don't even know about the winkte tradition. If they did they wouldn't drink or live with each other. None of the winktes I knew were married to men. They lived alone and men would visit them.

. . . A very few winktes married women and had children, but still fulfilled the winkte role. But most were not permitted by the spirits to be married. It varies from one person to another. Winkte means "different." It is neither man nor woman, but is a third group different from men and women. That is why winktes are regarded as sacred. Only Wakan Tanka, the great spirit, can explain it, so we accept it. Winktes are gifted persons.

Interview 2: The informant was a twenty-five-year-old man who was raised by his grandfather, a prominent traditionalist medicine man. At age 12 he began to take on a medicine role, under his grandfather's direction, and learned many of the old traditions. Today people come to him for curing and to help in preparing for ceremonies. He is also a road man for the Native American Church, conducting peyote meetings.

> Winktes know medicine, but they are not medicine men. They have good powers, especially for love medicine, for curing, and for childbearing. They can tell the future.
> Some say winktes were born that way and you cannot change them. They had a dream, seeing women's quillwork and tools. Winktes do top quality beadwork and crafts, women's work. Most winktes did not go to war, but my grandfather told me stories about one who did. He did the cooking and took care of the camp and cured the wounds of the warriors. Winktes give secret names to people to protect them through life. Some really have strong powers, but others just wanted to be like women. They call each other "sister." Winktes had high status, and some men married a winkte as a second or third wife. If not married, the winkte had his own tipi and his men friends could visit for sex. A married man would visit a winkte for sex during the time when his wife was pregnant, or in taboo days. But this varied from band to band. My grandfather told stories that in sex the winkte usually took the passive role, but sometimes he would exchange and take the active role with his men friends.
> Traditionally, winktes were both joked about and respected at the same time. But when people forgot the traditional ways and the traditional medicine, by going to missionaries and boarding schools, then they began to look down on winktes and lose respect. The missionaries and government officials said winktes were no good, and they tried to get winktes to change their ways. I heard sad stories of winktes committing suicide, hanging themselves rather than change. The 1920s and 1930s were the turning point in the winkte's decline, and after that those who remained would put on men's clothing.
> Today people would look down on winktes and might shun them. But a few years ago one man wore eye shadow and a woman's blouse, and many accepted him but he was shunned by others. Two men might have sex today, but they'd do it in secret and if discovered would be shunned. . . . If I had lived in traditional times, I might have had a winkte for a wife, but not today. The old respect is gone.

Interview 3: The informant was a twenty-eight-year-old woman who was raised in a traditionalist household. Although she now holds a wage job in a nearby town she continues to participate in the tribal ceremonies. She recently had gone through scarification in a Sun Dance and proudly displayed her scars.

> I grew up on the reservation, and still respect the old traditions. My uncle is now a winkte, and so was my grandfather. He died in 1980, in his 70s. He was married to my grandmother, and even had children, but was basically homosexual though he was secretive about his male lovers. He was effeminate, quiet, easy-going, very philosophical, and very respected on the reservation. He gave people sacred names. When someone died, it was the winkte who was the first one people came to, to help out with the funeral and the ceremonies. People who don't respect their Indian traditions criticize gays, but it was part of Indian culture. It makes me mad when I hear someone insult winktes. A lot of the younger gays, though, don't fulfill their spiritual role as winktes, and that's sad too.

Interview 4: A twenty-four year-old man does not identify as winkte, though other people think of him as winkte because of his feminine nature. He is a very gentle person who is well respected for his work with children.

> The last true traditional winkte on this reservation died in the 1960's. I remember seeing him at ceremonials. You never talked disrespectfully about a winkte because it is sacred. Every true winkte has sacred powers, some more, some less. They doctored illnesses, and were wakan [sacred]. If a person took ill, a winkte could give medicine that would make a miraculous cure. One doctored my grandfather and healed his broken leg in one day. This winkte wore a woman's breastplate, shawl, and underwear, but always wore men's pants. He could do anything and everything better than a woman. He was very neat and clean, good at crocheting and cooking. Winktes were always male, never a female, but they always danced with the women, dancing at the head of the circle leading the women. They talked in woman's dialect, but were different from both men and women.
>
> I heard a story that if a man wanted a winkte to name his child, then he would have sex with the winkte. If a winkte names a child, then that child will take on some winkte ways. That would be good because if there was a winkte in a family, that family would feel very fortunate. Due to white influence the younger generation sometimes ridiculed winktes, but the elders respected them almost like an immortal. Today, when Indians say winkte, they mean ''effeminate'' or ''like a woman.'' There are some gays on the reserva-

tion now, but "gay" and winkte are different; winkte is a gay with ceremonial sacred powers.

People have always called me winkte, in a joking or negative way, because of my effeminate mannerisms. I don't think I am spiritual enough. If I did it I would be very serious about it. But I don't want to be considered gay either, because that brings more kidding. I would be frightened to leave the reservation and my family, so I don't think I would fit into the gay lifestyle in the city.

Interview 5: A thirty-two-year-old man who identifies as winkte, dresses in men's clothes, but wears his hair very long like a woman. He is extremely feminine in voice and manner, and does not try to hide this but is very proud of it. He takes the traditional religion most seriously.

A winkte is two spirits, man and woman, combined into one spirit. That is me, and I get my holiness from the Sacred Pipe. From that holiness the Sioux people show respect. In the last few years, respect for winkte has increased somewhat, more than it had been, as more people return to respect for the traditions. Some mixed-blood Indians condemn "queers" but the traditional people stick up for them. Formerly, higher class winktes had up to twelve husbands. Chief Crazy Horse had one or two winktes for wives, as well as his female wives, but this has been kept quiet because Indians don't want whites to criticize. It's not so much that whites influenced Indian culture, because they didn't really care very much about anything other than getting the Indians' land and wealth, but Indians just keep things like this unknown to white who don't understand our sacred ways.

As a winkte, I accept my feminine nature as part of my being. I dress as a man, but I feel feminine and enjoy doing women's things. I would be terribly scared to be considered as a man. It is obvious from infancy that a boy is going to be a winkte. He is a beautiful baby and the sound of his voice is effeminate; it is inborn. The mother realizes this soon, and allows the boy to do feminine things. They all end up being sexually attracted to men.

I began to be sexually active when I was eight years old, and had an affair with a forty-year-old man. Since he was good to me and for me, it was considered by my family to be o.k. and my own private business—no one else's. I still, at age 32, live with my parents, and my men friends visit me at home. Straight Indian guys will go sexually with a gay here, in a way that whites don't. A man will go out with winktes and with women, but he is not considered to be a winkte. "Homosexuals" are two he-men who live together as a couple. That is not done here; it is an effeminate and a he-man. Married men are the best. I only want to play the passive role with a he-man, though sometimes the man wants to change sex roles. I want to lie with all the men. I used to keep a list of how many men I had been with. It would be unholy for me to have sex with a woman, or with another winkte. That would be wrong, and would violate the role set for me by the Sacred Pipe. The man could be gay, but he must be masculine. . . . A man and a winkte could go through a wedding ceremony, and it would be accepted by traditional people just as a marriage between men and women. It is by the Sacred Pipe. People know that on the reservation the spirit of Big Bull is watching them, so they cannot criticize winkte. But if they were away in the city, away from the kin groups, then they might be anti-gay. That is a different thing.

One person I know goes in and out of a winkte role, but that is very unusual. Usually winktes hold on to their role always, for its spiritual power. Sacred Pipe people, the traditionalists, would not object if a winkte dresses in woman's clothing in ceremonies. They would only see it as winkte getting more spiritual power. A couple of years ago I saw an eighty-year-old winkte dance in a ceremony with a woman's shawl and hairnet over his long braids, but otherwise he dressed as a man. That's the way he always dressed.

People are afraid to criticize winkte, because they fear the winkte spiritual power. To become a winkte, you have a medicine man put you on the hill for a vision quest. You can see a vision of a White Buffalo Bull Calf if you truly are a winkte by nature, or you might see another vision if Wakan Tanka wants you to.

Interview 6: The informant is a forty-nine year-old male who identifies as winkte. He dresses in pants, but they are women's style. His entire dress and manner suggest androgyny, with a mixture of both male and female aspects. He has always filled a winkte role and been accepted as such by his family and the reservation at large. He takes a leading role in the tribal ceremonies.

Winkte are wakan, which means that they have power as special people. Medicine men go to winkte for spiritual advice. Winktes can also be medicine men, but they're usually not because they already have the power. An example of this power is the sacred naming ceremony. It takes a winkte a full year to prepare for this. He starts with a fast and a vision quest, with sacrifices, to be fully sincere. He works with the family for the whole year, making preparations to the family and the child, and closely guiding the child for the year. A winkte can take on no more than about four children a year. Later, it is the winkte's responsibility to help look after that child.

The winkte makes a medicine bag for the child, with a piece of the winkte's skin and hair, and also a holy stone, which the child will carry for protection during the rest of his life. Traditionally it was the first born and the last born that got a winkte name, but nowadays it is very rare.

People know that a person will become a winkte very early in his life. About age twelve, parents will take him to a ceremony to communicate with past winktes who had power, to verify if it is just a phase or a permanent thing for his lifetime. If the proper vision takes place, and communication with past winkte is established, then everyone accepts him as a winkte. I am now nearly fifty years old, and I have always filled a winkte role.

I was just born this way, ever since I can remember. When I was eight I saw a vision, of a person with long grey hair and with many ornaments on, standing by my bed. I asked if he was female or male, and he said "both." He said he would walk with me for the rest of my life. His spirit would always be with me. I told my Grandfather, who said not to be afraid of spirits, because they have good powers. A year later, the vision appeared again, and told me he would give me great powers. He said his body was man's, but his spirit was woman's. He told me the Great Spirit made people like me to be of help to other people.

I told my Grandfather the name of the spirit, and Grandfather said it was a highly respected winkte who lived long ago. He explained winkte to me and said, "It won't be easy growing up, because you will be different from others. But the spirit will help you, if you pray and do the sweat." The spirit has continued to contact me throughout my life. If I practice the winkte role seriously, then people will respect me. If someone ever makes fun of me, something bad will happen to them. Once a half-breed woman said I was a disgrace to the Indian race. I told her that a century ago, I would have been considered that much more special. She died shortly after, and I think it was because she had insulted winkte.

My spirit takes care of me. I love children, and I used to worry that I would be alone without children. The Spirit said he would provide some. Later, some kids of drunks who did not care for them, were brought to me by neighbors. The kids began spending more and more time here, so finally the parents asked me to adopt them. In all, I have raised seven orphan children.

I worked as a nurse, and a cook in an old age home. I cook for funerals and wakes too. People bring their children to me for special winkte names, and give me gifts. If I show my generosity, then others help me in return. Once I asked the spirit if my living with a man and loving him was bad. The spirit answered that it was not bad because I had a right to release my feelings and express love for another, that I was good because I was generous and provided a good home for my children. I want to be remembered most for the two values that my people hold dearest: generosity and spirituality. If you say anything about me, say those two things.

CONCLUSIONS

From an ethnohistoric perspective, several themes emerge from the berdache tradition among Lakotas. Despite intense pressure from white missionaries and government officials, native culture has not succumbed to attempts at cultural genocide. Winktes had to change and become secretive, but they have not vanished. They retain the respect of traditional Lakota people, though respect has declined among acculturated Indians. Interestingly, cross-dressing is not seen as that important to a continuation of berdachism. But same-sex erotic behavior does continue to have a strong association with winkte status, more so than the recent literature would suggest. This behavior, however, is seen as distinct from the Western concepts of "gay" or "homosexual," because of the strong berdache association with femininity and spirituality.

Even the descriptive variations found in these interviews are evidence of the Lakota viewpoint that individuals decide spiritual truth for themselves. Nevertheless, the general characteristics of the winktes are graphically rendered: their spiritual power, respected status, homoeroticism, the mixture of women's and men's work, their repression in the last half century, and their survival. By creative, individualized adaptation, the berdache, like American Indian culture generally, has survived.

REFERENCES

Angelino, H. & Shedd, C. (1955). A note on berdache. *American Anthropologist, 57,* 121-25.

Blackwood, E. (1984). Sexuality and gender in certain native American tribes: The case of cross-gender females. *Signs: Journal of Women in Culture and Society, 10,* 27-42.

Callender, C. & Kochems, L. (1983). The North American berdache. *Current Anthropology, 24,* 443-470.

Fire, J. & Erodoes, R. (1972). *Lame deer, seeker of visions.* New York: Simon and Schuster.

Forgey, D. (1975). The institution of berdache among the North American Plains Indians. *Journal of Sex Research, 11,* 1-15.

Hassrick, R. (1964). *The Sioux: Life and customs of a warrior society.* Norman: University of Oklahoma Press.

Hill, W. W. (1935). The status of the hermaphrodite and transvestite in Navaho culture. *American Anthropologist, 37,* 27-68.

Jacobs, S. (1968). Berdache: A brief review of the literature. *Colorado Anthropologist, 1,* 25-40.

Katz, J. (1976). *Gay American history.* New York: Thomas Crowell.

Powers, W. (1977). *Oglala religion.* Lincoln: University of Nebraska Press.

Stevenson, M. C. (1901-2). The Zuni Indians. *Bureau of American Ethnology Annual Report, 23*, 38ff.

Thayer, J. (1980). The berdache of the Northern Plains: A socioreligious perspective. *Journal of Anthropological Research, 36*, 287-293.

Whitehead, H. (1981). The bow and the burden strap: A new look at institutionalized homosexuality in Native North America. In S. Ortner & H. Whitehead (Eds.), *Sexual meanings* (pp. 80-115). Cambridge: Cambridge University Press.

BOOK REVIEW

RITUALIZED HOMOSEXUALITY IN MELANESIA. Gilbert H. Herdt, Editor. *Berkeley, University of California Press, 1984, 409 pp.*

In many Melanesian societies, real men do it with others of their sex, first as boy initiate "insertees," then as fierce young warrior "insertors." Manhood thus secured and demonstrated in native ideology, they proceed to take wives and father children, move into leadership positions in their communities, and assume the prideful aggressive style so common to men throughout the Melanesian area. No evidence can be found of "effeminacy" or of enduring homosexual preferences, even among those whose pederastic tutelage has occupied their entire youth. Melanesian ethnographic cases provide material to blow away many a Western stereotype about the nature and ontogenesis of homosexuality. With the edited volume, *Ritualized Homosexuality in Melanesia,* anthropologist Gilbert Herdt, who personally studied a "ritualized homosexuality" society in New Guinea, brings out his third book centered on this important intellectual mission. Before asking how well this mission is accomplished, we will take an overview of the book's contents.

For the scholar seeking materials on nonwestern homosexual practices or for the Melanesian specialist, the collection performs some welcome ethnographic services. In his introduction, Herdt surveys the sources on ritualized homosexuality as exhaustively as any author to date and for the most part does so with sensitivity and interpretive balance. Additionally, in an unusual stroke, a number of the authors of early accounts of Melanesian ritualized homosexuality or related institutions have been asked to distill and rethink their past work in light of its current topicality. Thus, amazingly, Jan Van Baal has condensed many of the highlights of his 988-page opus on Marind-Anim culture into a 38-page essay. Michael Allen combines his own research with early ethnographic sources on the New Hebrides to give an interesting comparative political portrait of New Hebridean homosexuality themes. Laurent Serpenti amplifies his 1965 account of the ritual cycle of the Kimam of Frederik Hendrik Island with new ethnographic material quite probably brought to mind by more recent portraits of New Guinea concepts about the circulation of life-force and the role of sexual practices therein. Finally Kenneth E. Read, the "father," in a sense, of ethnographic concern over antagonism between the sexes in the New Guinea Highlands (and Melanesia more broadly) provides perhaps the most astute, and certainly the calmest overview of the question of Melanesian masculinity in the entire collection.

The other contributors are not so "ancestral" to the main topic, but all are experienced New Guinea hands (New Guinea is the greater part of Melanesia) who are adding to, rethinking, and, in some cases, injecting extensive theoretical speculation into their materials. Herdt expands upon his by-now-familiar "Sambia" pederasts, considering for the first time the relationship of their sexual transactions to their tribal exchange system. He seems to be attuned to the ideas suggested by Shirley Lindenbaum in her largely theoretical contribution: a contrast between Lowland New Guinea and Highland New Guinea cultures in which the former are cast as "ritualized homosexuality" cultures and the latter as "posthomosexual." Arve Sorum publishes for the first time material on the Bedamini initiatory practices; his essay, simple and accessible, echoes many of the themes brought out by Raymond Kelly's work on the Etoro who are the immediate neighbors of the Bedamini. Brian Schwimmer adds new material on the Ai'i of Oro Province in a collage of speculative thought that takes as its starting point the male dancing partnerships common in New Guinea societies.

The contributors have before them a homosexual situation significantly different in meaning and psychodynamics from the most highly theorized form of Western homosexuality, that of the perferential homosexual with evidence of psychological identification with the opposite sex. On the issue of psychodynamics, Herdt makes it clear that these ritualized homosexuality cultures are not organized by preferential homosexuals. To quote him:

> In spite of universal involvement in homosexual activities, no data indicate that these males become habitually motivated to same-sex contact later in life, or that the incidence of aberrant lifelong homosexuality . . . is greater in [ritualized homosexuality] groups than elsewhere in the world. (p. 65)

The majority of Herdt's Sambia men, the only Papuan New Guineans closely interviewed on this question, state a preference for genital heterosexual sex (pp. 188, 190). In every other case on which there is reasonably extensive ethnography, there is similar evidence of adult male enthusiasm for heterosexual activity, official cultural views of women's harmful powers notwithstanding.

Yet this evidence fails to prevent Herdt and several of his contributors from attributing to Melanesians a deeply insecure masculinity and proceeding from there to revive many of the theoretical circularities of the old "culture and personality" approach. In this approach, the overriding assumption is the psychiatric one: that homosexuality is a psychodynamic aberration based upon imperfect sexual or gender development; wherever we find it it somehow, at some level, must carry this meaning. Thus Michael Allen interlards his political argument with a view of homosexual rites as rituals of woman-envy that are needed to effect the difficult transformation to manhood of boys feminized by too much mother-son joint sleeping arrangements (pp. 119-121). Van Baal, displaying at points a rather unscholarly repugnance for his "tribe," finds the Mirind-Anim practices riddled with evidence of castration anxiety, woman-fear, and masculine overcompensation (pp. 152, 162-164). And, despite the fact that the larger picture his data evoke keeps threatening to undermine his argument, Brian Schwimmer satisfies an unexplained craving for the Irving Bieber model of homosexuality by projecting "close binding intimate mother" figures onto the peripheral symbolic details of the cultures he examines. Shirley Lindenbaum too attributes "gender ambiguity" to her "homosexual" cultures. The structure of her argument is such as to make the non-homosexual cultures developmentally more advanced. Finally, the editor, Gilbert Herdt, unwilling or unable to settle on any consistent theoretical approach, simply throws up his hands and pronounces Melanesian homosexuality to be the "synergistic effect" of all the causes that have ever been suggested (p. 72)—which of course includes the ones just cited! It would appear that rather than successfully "challenging" our western psychiatric notions of homosexuality, the Melanesians are being tarred by the same brush.

Of a piece with this inability to escape the terms of the western depth psychological discourse, is the construction—mainly on the part of Herdt and Lindenbaum—of a ritualized homosexuality "type" of Melanesian society which stands in contrast to those Mesanesian societies that lack the custom, the "posthomosexuals" in Lindenbaum's phrase. Although there is a contrast between the various man-making initiatory rituals of Melanesia (at least on the New Guinea mainland), it is only partly, and poorly, explored in this volume. This contrast exists between groups that emphasize the transmission of semen as a ritual means for growing boys into men and those that, with the same end in mind, purge the boys of blood (conceptualized as female blood). The semen-transmittors occupy that broad belt of the southern Lowlands that Herdt identifies as the "ritualized homosexuality" area, while throughout the northern area blood-purging is the emphasized technique. (Groups in border areas, like Herdt's Sambia, often utilize both practices.) Ritualized homosexuality occurs as a mode of semen-transmission. Herdt makes much of this fact in his essay on the Sambia, but he does not adequately call to our attention the fact that throughout the semen-transmission culture area, homosexuality is not the only mode of semen-transmission. Simply smearing the boys' bodies with semen is reported to be the technique of choice among certain groups, the Onabasulu of the Papuan Plateau, and the Pataye group of southern Angans (Kelly, 1980; Mimica, 1981). Ingestion of inseminated substances is the mode of transmission among the Bimin-Kuskusmin, a between-area group combining both themes (Poole, 1981, 1982). Interestingly, Herdt discusses none of these cases in his survey (although he cites the reference on the Onabasulu). Their lack of homosexuality seems to exclude them from the historical complex of which they are an obvious part.

In a counterpart move, Lindenbaum, working out a model in which Lowland New Guinea cultures are "homosexual" types while Highland New Guineans "cherish heterosexuality," passes over in silence the northern New Guinea Lowlanders, none of whom practice ritualized homosexuality. (The north is blood-purging territory.) This omission partly vitiates her innovative, if slap-dash, attempt to connect ritual sexual practices to forms of wealth and woman-exchange. As she and Herdt rightly sense, a connection exists but, in my opinion, it will not be forged correctly as long as the hypothesis of a ritualized homosexuality type of society persists. Ironically, the anxious over-centering of our theorists on homosexuality itself is the principal theoretical flaw of this volume on homosexuality.

Of the contributors who enter into the debate over Melanesian sexual psychology, only Kenneth Read keeps a cool head. He finds no particular paradox in the conjunction of homoerotic/misogynistic elements with an ethic of battle-ready comradely manhood. A homoerotic/misogynistic atmosphere, though no official homosexual practice, is to be found in the "man-making" rituals of the blood-purging groups, including Read's Gahuku-Gama. The same atmosphere (and sometimes behavior) is, for that matter, common to western male-exclusive institutions. Demurring from deeper psychological interpretation on the grounds that he has no data on this issue (in fact, none of the contributors offers any depth psychological data), Read seems to be gently hinting that, once all the psychiatric heavy-breathing is put aside, what we are seeing in Melanesia may be simply men-in-groups. The cultures that officially practice homosexuality are not different in psychological tone from those that do not; indeed, the whole matter of why one does and why another does not may be unresolvable on the psychological level.

Ritualized Homosexuality in Menalesia is a useful and interesting book. Its interest lies as much in the theoretical paradoxes it poses as in the abundant information it contains.

Harriet Whitehead, PhD
Brown University

Harriet Whitehead received her PhD in Anthropology from The University of Chicago, and is co-editor, with Sherry Ortner, of the collection, *Sexual Meanings* (1981). She is currently a Research Associate at the Pembroke Center for Teaching and Research on Women at Brown University.

REFERENCES

Kelly, R. (1980). *Etoro social structure*. Ann Arbor: University of Michigan Press.

Mimica, J. (1981). *Omalyce: An ethnography of the Ikwaye view of the cosmos*. Unpublished doctoral dissertation, ANU.

Poole, F. J. P. (1981). Transforming "natural" woman: Female ritual leaders and gender ideology among Bimin-Kuskusmin. in S. B. Ortner & H. Whitehead (Eds.), *Sexual meanings: the cultural construction of gender and sexuality*. NY: Cambridge University Press.

Poole, F. J. P. (1982). The ritual forging of identity: Aspects of person and self in Bimin-Kuskusmin male initiation. In G. Herdt (Ed.), *Rituals of manhood: Male initiation in Papua New Guinea*. Berkeley: University of California Press.

ABSTRACTS
OF CURRENT PUBLICATIONS

Ana Villavicencio-Stoller, Abstracts Editor

Miller, H. II. (1984). An argument for the application of equal protection heightened scrutiny to classifications based on homosexuality. *Southern California Law Review, 57*(5), 797-836.

The Court has recognized that certain groups are in need of judical protection. This article argues that, "the courts should apply equal protection and heightened scrutiny to classifications based on homosexuality on the premise that it is wrong for the government to discriminate against gays solely because they are gay." The article discusses in detail why homosexuals should be granted this "heightened scrutiny," because they are the subject of official discrimination. The argument for heightened scrutiny is that it is "a status, and not a chosen activity." This makes homosexuality a characteristic that an individual has no control over. Therefore, no one individual can control the sexual orientation of another. Homosexuals are the victims of incorrect and erroneous stereotypes which also lead to discrimination. It is significant to note that homosexuality is a subject of controversy that is not apt to change easily, but "for any relief to be effective, courts must have a means to strike down the prejudice and the stereotypes embodied in laws that discriminate against gays, as well as the laws themselves."

Van Wyk, P. H., & Geist, C. S. (1984). Psychosexual development of heterosexual, bisexual and homosexual behavior. *Archives of Sexual Behavior, 13*(6), 505-544.

Attempts have been made to find the relationship between overtly expressed homosexual and heterosexual behaviors, as indicated by the Kinsey scale (K scale), and social learning theory, which emphasizes strength of association and learning experiences. This study attempts to establish a relationship between elevated K scores and the influence of early sexual experience and of gender-related familial variables on the development of these behaviors. The study included 5550 female and 5919 male subjects, took place at the Kinsey Institute for Research on Sex, Gender, and Reproduction at Indiana University. The sample included only Caucasian, non-delinquent subjects. The sources for evaluation were subject interviews. Subjects' K scale ratings were based on adult overt sociosexual experience.

Female interviewees with high K scores, indicating a high degree of homosexuality, usually had established their sexual preference by age 17. Their homosexual preference was established in a graded sequence: (1) by age 10, they had few girl companions; (2) few male companions at 16; (3) had learned to masturbate by being masturbated by a female; (4) had intense prepubertal contact with men; (5) were aroused by the thought or sight of a female (but not male) by age 18; (6) by age 18 had homosexual contact; and (7) had a higher K at age 17 and higher first year homosexual behavior frequency.

Male interviewees with high K scores had established their homosexual preference usually by age 17. Their sexual preference demonstrated a parallel sequence: (1) they had more female companions by age 10; (2) reported a poor teenage relationship with their fathers; (3) had fewer male companions at ages 10 and 16; (4) avoided participation in sports; (5) learned of homosexuality by experience; (6) learned to masturbate by being masturbated by a male; (7) had intense prepubertal sexual contact with men; (8) by age 18, had neither heterosexual contact or an orgasm; (9) were aroused by the sight or thought of a male (not female) by age 18; (10) had homosexual contact by age 18; (11) showed a high K score at ages 16 and 17; and (12) showed a higher, first-year frequency of homosexual behavior.

In summary, the conclusions were that adult sexual orientation and expression is greatly influenced by early, intense sexual experiences and the presence or absence of any feelings of arousal, pleasure, or distress associated with these experiences. Factors that are related to biological sex follow in strength of association and are succeeded by those associated with familial influences. It appears that later sexual preference is highly influenced by learning through experience, which explains why more males than females overtly express homosexual preference. Males are described as being the more "adventurous" in sexual pursuits. It was noted that the earlier a sexual preference has been established, the more resistant to change it becomes. It takes a relatively short period of time for these preferences to solidify, since the highest K scores occur within one year of frequent, intense sexual activity.

Whitam, F. L., & Zent, M. (1984). A cross-cultural assessment of early cross-gender behavior and familial factors in male homosexuality. *Archives of Sexual Behavior, 13*(5), 427-437.

The nature and origins of homosexual behavior is the subject of this cross-cultural study. An attempt was made to delineate any signs of cross-gender behavior in early childhood and/or the influence of familial factors on male homosexuality. The sources for evaluation were based on interviews and questionnaires of non-clinical homosexual and heterosexual males in four different societies: The United States, Guatemala, Brazil, and The Philippines.

It was found that for all four societies, there was a consistency in the pattern fo cross-gender behavior. Namely, boys who displayed effeminate behavior in youth also tended to cross-dress and play with girls' toys more often than heterosexual boys and in adulthood expressed a homosexual identity.

The expected effect of familial influences, however, did not correspond with the study's findings. The conclusions showed that consistent, early cross-gender behavior was noted among males of the four countries studied and was linked to male homosexuality. Also, familial factors that were believed to be a causative agent to the development of a homosexual identity were found, rather, to be a direct result of or a reaction to emerging homosexuality. Instead of the "distant father" relationship being the cause of a son's homosexuality, it is possible that the emergence of homosexuality in the son would cause the father to become distanced.

Schwenger, P. (1984). *Phallic critiques*. London: Routledge and Kegan Paul.

The themes of "masculine" writing styles is examined in 20th century literature. Explored are novels by Ernest Hemingway, Normal Mailer, Alberto Moravia, and Yukio Mishima. In his introduction, Schwenger notes, "in each of these men, self-consciousness undermines their masculine assertion. Beneath the blatant machismo one finds considerable ambivalence towards the traditional masculine role." This "ambivalence" is examined across cultural boundaries and through the "international nature of masculine styles."

Index

abortion 181
adolescence
  female institutionalized friendships during
    97-116
  ritualized homosexuality during 25-29,
    55-68
adultery, under Islamic law 12
Africa, *see also* specific countries and ethnic
  groups
  age-structured homosexuality in 21
  lesbianism in 10-11,12
Afro-Brazilian spirit possession cults
  137-153,156,157
  analytical interpretation 146-152
  categories 138-139
  cult houses 139-140
  cult leadership 139-140,142,143,144,
    146-150,151
  female spirit possession 144-145
  gender roles 141-142
  homosexual membership 142-152
  organization 139-140
  rituals 140
  sexual activity restrictions 143-144
  transsexual trance 144-145
  women in 150-151,152n.
Almeida, Piers de 158
Ambiente, *see* Mexico,
  homosexual public interactions in
American Indians, *see also* specific tribes
  berdaches 165-189,191-200
    cross-dressing by 169,179,183,192,193,
      195,197,199
    definition 179
    descriptions 179-181,192-199
    females as 179,182,183
    gender-mixing status 166-178
    homosexual activity by 181-182,183,184,
      185,186
    "homosexual niche" theory of 4
    occupational inversion of 170-171
    responses to 180-185
    ritual functions of 180
    social behavior of 169-170
    as third gender 179
  female cross-gender role 13
  incest taboos 184,185-186
  lesbianism among 9
androgyne 50

anthropological theory
  of homosexuality 2-4
  of lesbianism 7-15
Apache, berdache role among 181
Araucanian culture, gender-mixing role
  among 169,171,174
Arjuna 40-41
asceticism
  creative 39-41
  Hindu concept of 48
  of holy men 149
Australian aborigines
  adolescent sex play among 11
  age-structured homosexuality among 29-30
  lesbianism among 11-12,30
  "sexual abnormalities" of 3
Azande
  age-structured homosexuality among 23-24
  lesbianism among 8,10-11

bachelorhood 20-21
Bahuchara Mata 35,39,40,48
bars, homosexual/lesbian 83,84,88
Batuque 139, *see also* spirit possession cults
berdache 165-189,191-200
  cross-dressing by 169,179,183,192,193,
    195,197,199
  definition 179
  descriptions of
    by American Indians 192-199
    historical 179-181,191-192
  females as 179,182,183
  gender-mixing status 166-178
  homosexual activity by 181-182,183,184,
    185,186
  "homosexual niche" theory of 4
  occupational inversion of 170-171
  responses to 180-185
    joking relationship 183-185
    respect 180-181
    ridicule 182-185,186
  ritual functions 180
  social behavior of 169-170
  as third gender 179
Belém, spirit possession cults in 137-153
bicha 137
  definition 141
  gender role 141-142
  in spirit possession cults 142-152